Excel 2007 offers some new conditional formatting rules that allow you to add icons to your dashboards. With icons, you can represent and distinguish values from one another by using different shapes and colors. Here's a quick glance at the Icon Sets that come with Excel 2007.

Icon Set Name	Icons	Icon Set Name	Icons
3 Arrows (Colored)		4 Arrows (Colored)	
3 Arrows (Gray)		4 Arrows (Gray)	
3 Flags		Red to Black	
3 Traffic Lights (Rimmed)		4 Traffic Lights	
3 Traffic Lights (Unrimmed)		4 Ratings	
3 Symbols (Circled)		5 Arrows (Colored)	
3 Symbols (Uncircled)		5 Arrows (Gray)	
3 Signs		5 Ratings	
		5 Quarters	

If you're working in an environment where not everyone has Excel 2007, definitely avoid using Excel 2007's Icon Set conditional formatting. Why? Icon Sets aren't backwards compatible, so anyone who doesn't have Excel 2007 can't use them.

Excel® 2007 Dashboards & Reports For Dummies®

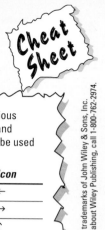

Cheat Sheet

A creative alternative to using the Icon Sets offered with conditional formatting is to use the various symbol fonts that come with Office. The symbol fonts are Wingdings, Wingdings2, Wingdings3, and Webdings. Each character/font combination shown in the table below displays an icon that can be used to represent a value in your dashboard.

Character	Font	Icon	Character	Font	Icon
3	Webdings	◄	f	Wingdings 3	←
4	Webdings	►	g	Wingdings 3	→
5	Webdings	▲	h	Wingdings 3	↑
6	Webdings	▼	i	Wingdings 3	↓
l	Wingdings	●	j	Wingdings 3	↖
n	Wingdings	■	k	Wingdings 3	↗
t	Wingdings	♦	l	Wingdings 3	↙
P	Wingdings	⚑	m	Wingdings 3	↘
C	Wingdings	☜	p	Wingdings 3	▲
D	Wingdings	☝	q	Wingdings 3	▼
J	Wingdings	☺	t	Wingdings 3	◄
K	Wingdings	☺	u	Wingdings 3	►
L	Wingdings	☹	r	Wingdings 3	△
O	Wingdings 2	✗	s	Wingdings 3	▽
P	Wingdings 2	✓	v	Wingdings 3	◁
Q	Wingdings 2	☒	w	Wingdings 3	▷
R	Wingdings 2	☑			

It's always nice to see the approach others have taken to design their reporting mechanisms. Here's a list of sites (in no particular order) dedicated to business intelligence and the presentation of data through dashboards. I often visit these sites to get ideas and fresh new perspectives on dashboards and reports.

✔ **www.dashboardspy.com**: The Dashboard Spy posts examples of business intelligence dashboards, pointing out examples of good and bad dashboard design. This is a virtual warehouse of dashboarding ideas.

✔ **www.perceptualedge.com**: Visualization expert Stephen Few provides some fascinating insights on data visualization and dashboarding. A generous amount of articles and examples can be found at his site and his blog.

✔ **www.juiceanalytics.com/writing**: Zach and Chris Gemignani of Juice Analytics use their site as a platform to critique charts and offer interesting ideas around reporting data.

✔ **http://blog.instantcognition. com/category/visualization**: Instant Cognition is a blog where you'll find loads of articles on the latest visualization and Web analytics trends. You're sure to get plenty of ideas from the wide array of topics presented at this blog.

✔ **www.edwardtufte.com/bboard**: Professor Edward Tufte is an icon in the field of information design and data visualization. He shares his thoughts around visual communication in a series of articles at his site. Although many of these ideas are academic in nature, they'll get you thinking in new ways about how to best present data.

For Dummies: Bestselling Book Series for Beginners

Excel® 2007 Dashboards & Reports

FOR DUMMIES®

by Michael Alexander

WILEY

Wiley Publishing, Inc.

Excel® 2007 Dashboards & Reports For Dummies®

Published by
Wiley Publishing, Inc.
111 River Street
Hoboken, NJ 07030-5774

www.wiley.com

Copyright © 2008 by Wiley Publishing, Inc., Indianapolis, Indiana

Published by Wiley Publishing, Inc., Indianapolis, Indiana

Published simultaneously in Canada

For general information on our other products and services, please contact our Customer Care Department within the U.S. at 800-762-2974, outside the U.S. at 317-572-3993, or fax 317-572-4002.

For technical support, please visit www.wiley.com/techsupport.

Wiley also publishes its books in a variety of electronic formats. Some content that appears in print may not be available in electronic books.

Library of Congress Control Number: 2008921207

ISBN: 978-0-470-22814-2

Manufactured in the United States of America

10 9 8 7 6 5 4 3 2 1

WILEY

About the Author

Michael Alexander is a Microsoft Certified Application Developer (MCAD) with over 14 years experience consulting and developing office solutions. He is the author/co-author of several books on business analysis using Microsoft Excel and Access. Michael is one of 96 Microsoft Excel MVPs worldwide who has been recognized for his contributions to the Excel community. He is also the principal player behind *DataPigTechnologies.com,* a site that offers video tutorials to beginning and intermediate Excel and Access users. He currently lives in Frisco, Texas where he works as a Senior Program Manager for a top technology firm. Michael can be contacted at `mike@datapig technologies.com`.

Dedication

For my family.

Author's Acknowledgments

My deepest thanks to Greg Croy, Christopher Morris, Loren Abdulezer and all the professionals at Wiley who have helped bring this book to fruition. And a special thank you to my beautiful wife Mary who will open this book long enough to read the dedication and acknowledgments.

Publisher's Acknowledgments

We're proud of this book; please send us your comments through our online registration form located at www.dummies.com/register/.

Some of the people who helped bring this book to market include the following:

Acquisitions, Editorial, and Media Development

Senior Project Editor: Christopher Morris

Executive Editor: Gregory S. Croy

Copy Editor: Jennifer Riggs

Technical Editor: Loren Abdulezer

Editorial Manager: Kevin Kirschner

Assistant Producer: Kit Malone

Media Development Coordinator: Jenny Swisher

Editorial Assistant: Amanda Foxworth

Sr. Editorial Assistant: Cherie Case

Cartoons: Rich Tennant (www.the5thwave.com)

Composition Services

Project Coordinator: Katie Key

Layout and Graphics: Stacie Brooks, Reuben W. Davis, Alissa D. Ellet, Joyce Haughey, Christine Williams

Proofreader: Joni Heredia

Indexer: Potomac Indexing, LLC

Publishing and Editorial for Technology Dummies

> **Richard Swadley,** Vice President and Executive Group Publisher
>
> **Andy Cummings,** Vice President and Publisher
>
> **Mary Bednarek,** Executive Acquisitions Director
>
> **Mary C. Corder,** Editorial Director

Publishing for Consumer Dummies

> **Diane Graves Steele,** Vice President and Publisher
>
> **Joyce Pepple,** Acquisitions Director

Composition Services

> **Gerry Fahey,** Vice President of Production Services
>
> **Debbie Stailey,** Director of Composition Services

Contents at a Glance

Table of Contents

Introduction

The term *business intelligence (BI),* coined by Howard Dresner of the Gartner Group, describes the set of concepts and methods to improve business decision-making by using fact-based support systems. Practically speaking, BI is what you get when you analyze raw data and turn that analysis into knowledge. BI can help an organization identify cost-cutting opportunities, uncover new business opportunities, recognize changing business environments, identify data anomalies, and create widely accessible reports, among other things.

Over the last few years, the BI concept has overtaken corporate executives who are eager to turn impossible amounts of data into knowledge. As a result of this trend, whole industries have been created. Software vendors that focus on BI and dashboarding are coming out of the woodwork. New consulting firms touting their BI knowledge are popping up virtually every week. And even the traditional enterprise solution providers, like Business Objects and SAP, are offering new BI capabilities.

This need for BI has manifested itself in many forms. Most recently, it's come in the form of dashboard fever. *Dashboards* are reporting mechanisms that deliver business intelligence in a graphical form.

Maybe *you've* been hit with dashboard fever. Or maybe your manager is hitting you with dashboard fever. Nevertheless, you're probably holding this book because you're being asked to create BI solutions (that is, dashboards) in Excel.

Although many IT (information technology) managers would scoff at the thought of using Excel as a BI tool, Excel is inherently part of the enterprise BI tool portfolio. Whether IT managers are keen to acknowledge it, most of the data analysis and reporting done in business today is done by using spreadsheets. Here are several significant reasons to use Excel as the platform for your dashboards and reports:

> ✔ **Tool familiarity:** If you work in corporate America, you're conversant in the language of Excel. You can send even the most seasoned of senior vice presidents an Excel-based reporting tool and trust he'll know what to do with it. With an Excel reporting process, your users spend less time figuring how to use the tool and more time looking at the data.

- ✔ **Built-in flexibility:** With most enterprise dashboarding solutions, the capability to perform analyses outside the predefined views is either disabled or unavailable. How many times have you dumped enterprise-level data into Excel so you can analyze it yourself? I know I have. You can bet that if you give users an inflexible reporting mechanism, they'll do what it takes to create their own usable reports. In Excel, features, such as pivot tables, autofilters, and Form controls allow you to create mechanisms that don't lock your audience into one view. And because you can have multiple worksheets in one workbook, you can give them space to do their own side analysis as needed.

- ✔ **Rapid development:** Building your own reporting capabilities in Excel can liberate you from the IT department's resources and time limitations. With Excel, not only can you develop reporting mechanisms faster, but you have the flexibility to adapt more quickly to changing requirements.

- ✔ **Powerful data connectivity and automation capabilities:** Excel isn't the toy application some IT managers make it out to be. With its own native programming language and its robust object model, Excel can be used to automate processes and even connect to various data sources. With a few advanced techniques, you can make Excel a hands-off reporting mechanism that practically runs on its own.

- ✔ **Little to no incremental costs:** Not all of us can work for multi-billion dollar companies that can afford enterprise-level reporting solutions. In most companies, funding for new computers and servers is limited, let alone funding for expensive BI reporting packages. For those companies, leveraging Microsoft Office is frankly the most cost-effective way to deliver key business reporting tools without compromising too deeply on usability and functionality.

All that being said, so many reporting functions and tools are in Excel that it's difficult to know where to start. Enter your humble author, spirited into your hands via this book. Here, I show you how you can turn Excel into your own personal BI tool. With a few fundamentals and some of the new BI functionality Microsoft has included in this latest version of Excel, you can go from reporting data with simple tables to creating a meaningful reporting component that's sure to wow management.

About This Book

The goal of this book is to show you how to leverage Excel functionality to build and manage better reporting mechanisms. Each chapter in this book provides a comprehensive review of the technical and analytical concepts that help you create better reporting components — components that can be used for both dashboards and reports.

It's important to note that this book isn't a guide to visualizations or dash-boarding best practices. Those are subjects worthy of their own book. This book focuses on understanding the technical aspects of using Excel's various tools and functionality and applying them to reporting.

The chapters in this book are designed to be standalone chapters that you can selectively refer to as needed. As you move through this book, you can create increasingly sophisticated dashboard and report components. After reading this book, you can

- ✔ Analyze large amounts of data and report that data in a meaningful way.
- ✔ Get a better understanding of data by viewing it from different perspectives.
- ✔ Quickly slice data into various views on the fly.
- ✔ Automate redundant reporting and analyses.
- ✔ Create interactive reporting processes.

Foolish Assumptions

I make three assumptions about you as the reader, which are:

- ✔ You've already bought and installed Excel 2007.
- ✔ You have some familiarity with the basic concepts of data analysis, such as working with tables, aggregating data, and performing calculations.
- ✔ You have a strong grasp of basic Excel concepts, such as managing table structures, creating formulas, referencing cells, filtering, and sorting.

How This Book 1s Organized

The chapters in this book are organized into six parts. Each of these parts includes chapters that build on the previous chapters' instructions. The idea is that as you go through each part, you can build dashboards of increasing complexity until you're an Excel reporting guru.

Part I: Making the Move to Dashboards

Part I is all about helping you think about your data in terms of creating effective dashboards and reports. Chapter 1 introduces you to the topic of dashboards and reports, giving you some of the fundamentals and basic ground rules for creating effective dashboards and reports. Chapter 2 shows you a few concepts around data structure and layout. In this chapter, I demonstrate the impact of a poorly-planned data set and show you the best practices for setting up the source data for your dashboards and reports.

Part II: Building Basic Dashboard Components

In Part II, you take an in-depth look at some of the basic dashboard components you can create using Excel 2007. This part begins with Chapter 3 where I introduce you to pivot tables and discuses how a pivot table can play an integral role in Excel-based dashboards. Chapter 4 provides a primer on building charts in Excel 2007, giving beginners a solid understanding of how Excel charts work. Chapter 5 introduces you to the new and improved conditional formatting functionality found in Excel 2007. In this chapter, I present several ideas for using the new conditional formatting tools in dashboards and reports. In Chapter 6, you explore the various techniques that can be used to create dynamic labels, allowing for the creation of a whole new layer of visualization.

Part III: Building Advanced Dashboard Components

In Part III, you go beyond the basics to take a look at some of the advanced components you can create with Excel 2007. This part consists of three chapters, starting with Chapter 7, in which I demonstrate how to represent time trending, seasonal trending, moving averages, and other types of trending in dashboards. You're also introduced to Sparklines in this chapter. In Chapter 8, you explore the many methods used to *bucket* data, or put data into groups for reporting. Chapter 9 demonstrates some of charting techniques that help you display and measure values versus goals.

Part IV: Advanced Reporting Techniques

Part IV focuses on techniques that help you automate your reporting processes and give your users an interactive user interface. Chapter 10 provides a clear understanding of how macros can be leveraged to supercharge and automate your reporting systems. Chapter 11 illustrates how you can provide your clients with a simple interface, allowing them to easily navigate through and interact with their reporting systems.

Part V: Working with the Outside World

The theme in Part V is importing and exporting information to and from Excel. Chapter 12 explores some of the ways to incorporate data that doesn't originate in Excel. In this chapter, I show you how to import data from external sources as well as how to create systems that allow for dynamic refreshing of external data sources. Chapter 13 wraps up this look on Excel dashboards and reports by showing you the various ways to distribute and present your work.

Part VI: The Part of Tens

Part VI is the classic Part of Tens section found in almost all *For Dummies* series titles. The chapters found here each present ten or more pearls of wisdom, delivered in bite-sized pieces. In Chapter 14, I share with you ten or so chart-building best practices, helping you design more effective charts. In Chapter 15, I provide a checklist of questions you should ask yourself before sharing your Excel dashboards and reports.

Sample Files for This Book

This book comes with samples files that can be downloaded from the Wiley Web site at the following URL:

```
www.dummies.com/go/dashboards
```

Icons Used In This Book

Throughout this book, you may notice little icons in the left margin that act as road signs to help you quickly pull out the information that's most important to you. Here's what they look like and what they represent.

Information tagged with a Remember icon identifies general information and core concepts that you may already know but should certainly understand and review.

Tip icons include short suggestions and tidbits of useful information.

Look for Warning icons to identify potential pitfalls, including easily-confused or difficult-to-understand terms and concepts.

Technical Stuff icons highlight technical details that you can skip unless you want to bring out the tech geek in you.

Where to Go from Here

If you want to get an understanding of best practices and techniques to get started with a dashboarding project, start with Chapters 1 and 2.

If you're looking for a quick tutorial on reporting data with pivot tables, Chapter 3 is what you need.

If you're relatively new to Excel and you're looking to get a sense of the basic reporting tools available in Excel, Chapters 4, 5 and 6 will get you started.

If you're a bit more experienced and you'd like to discover some advanced techniques for reporting data and automating you dashboards, you can explore Chapters 7 through 11.

Working in an environment where you have to share your reporting with the outside world? Chapters 12 and 13 will show you how to use external data and some of the ways you can distribute your dashboards.

You can also just open the book to any chapter you want and dive right into the art and science of building reporting mechanisms with Excel.

Part I

Making the Move to Dashboards

In this part . . .

In this section, you discover how to think about your data in terms of creating effective dashboards and reports. Chapter 1 introduces you to the topic of dashboards and reports, giving you some of the fundamentals and basic ground rules for creating effective dashboards and reports. Chapter 2 shows you a few concepts around data structure and layout. In this part, you discover the impact of a poorly-planned data set and the best practices for setting up the source data for your dashboards and reports.

Chapter 1

Getting in the Dashboard State of Mind

In This Chapter

▶ Comparing dashboards to reports

▶ Getting started on the right foot

▶ Dashboarding best practices

*I*n his song, "New York State of Mind," Billy Joel laments the differences between California and New York. In this homage to the Big Apple, he implies a mood and a feeling that comes with thinking about New York. I admit it's a stretch, but I'll to extend this analogy to Excel — don't laugh.

In Excel, the differences between building a dashboard and creating standard table-driven analyses are as great as the differences between California and New York. To approach a dashboarding project, you truly have to get into the dashboard state of mind. As you'll come to realize in the next few chapters, dashboarding requires far more preparation than standard Excel analyses. It calls for closer communication with business leaders, stricter data modeling techniques, and the following of certain best practices. It's beneficial to have a base familiarity with fundamental dashboarding concepts before venturing off into the mechanics of building a dashboard.

In this chapter, you get a solid understanding of these basic dashboard concepts and design principles as well as what it takes to prepare for a dashboarding project.

Defining Dashboards and Reports

It isn't difficult to use *report* and *dashboard* interchangeably. In fact, the line between reports and dashboards frequently gets muddied. I've seen countless reports that have been referred to as dashboards just because they included a few charts. Likewise, I've seen many examples of what could be considered dashboards but have been called reports.

Now this may all seem like semantics to you, but it's helpful to clear the air a bit and understand the core attributes of what are considered to be reports and dashboards.

Defining reports

Reports are probably the most common application of business intelligence. A *report* can be described as a document that contains data used for reading or viewing. It can be as simple as a data table or as complex as a subtotaled view with interactive drilling, similar to Excel's Subtotal functionality.

The key attribute of a report is that it doesn't lead a reader to a predefined conclusion. Although a report can include analysis, aggregations, and even charts, reports often allow for the end user to apply his own judgment and analysis to the data.

To clarify this concept, Figure 1-1 shows an example of a report. This report shows the National Park overnight visitor statistics by period. Although this data can be useful, it's clear this report isn't steering the reader in any predefined judgment or analysis; it's simply presenting the aggregated data.

Figure 1-1: Reports present data for viewing but don't lead readers to conclusions.

	A	B	C	D	E	F	G
1	**National Park Overnight Visitor Stats**						
2	Period	Backcountry Campers	RV Campers	Tent Campers	Concessioner Logding	Concessioner Campgrounds	Total
3	Jan-05	2,397,098	4,446,370	3,934,114	3,235,039	838,932	14,851,553
4	Feb-05	2,395,236	4,378,491	4,221,920	3,386,345	814,734	15,196,726
5	Mar-05	2,329,845	4,663,020	4,153,999	3,312,100	650,088	15,109,052
6	Apr-05	2,424,227	4,596,036	3,601,198	3,317,010	644,543	14,583,014
7	May-05	2,579,716	4,232,793	3,747,293	3,486,041	725,979	14,771,822
8	Jun-05	1,978,867	3,943,183	3,586,062	3,527,045	733,121	13,768,278
9	Jul-05	1,680,414	3,759,294	3,460,005	3,538,176	743,256	13,181,145
10	Sep-05	1,644,691	3,788,528	3,955,795	3,726,504	786,102	13,901,620
11	Oct-05	1,574,706	4,043,206	3,921,104	3,787,463	852,820	14,179,299
12	Nov-05	1,617,706	3,937,271	3,929,665	3,880,622	865,694	14,230,958

Defining dashboards

A *dashboard* is a visual interface that provides at-a-glance views into key measures relevant to a particular objective or business process. Dashboards have three main attributes:

- ✔ Dashboards are typically graphical in nature, providing visualizations that help focus attention on key trends, comparisons, and exceptions.

- ✔ Dashboards often display only data that are relevant to the goal of the dashboard.

- ✔ Because dashboards are designed with a specific purpose or goal, they inherently contain predefined conclusions that relieve the end user from performing his own analysis.

Figure 1-2 illustrates a dashboard that uses the same data shown in Figure 1-1. This dashboard displays key information about the National Park overnight visitor stats. As you can see, this presentation has all the main attributes that define a dashboard. First, it's a visual display that allows you to quickly recognize the overall trending of the overnight visitor stats. Second, you can see that not all the detailed data is shown here; only the key pieces of information that's relevant to support the goal of this dashboard. Finally, by virtue of its objective, this dashboard effectively presents you with analysis and conclusions about the trending of overnight visitors.

Figure 1-2:
Dashboards provide at-a-glance views into key measures relevant to a particular objective or business process.

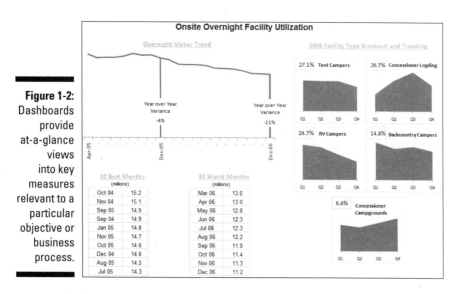

Preparing for Greatness

Imagine your manager asks you to create a dashboard that tells him everything he should know about monthly service subscriptions. Do you jump to action and slap together whatever comes to mind? Do you take a guess at what he wants to see and hope it's useful? These questions sound ridiculous but such situations happen more that you think. I'm constantly called to action to create the next great reporting tool but am rarely provided the time to gather the true requirements for it. Between limited information and unrealistic deadlines, the end product often ends up being unused or having little value.

This brings me to one of the key steps in preparing for dashboarding — collecting user requirements.

In the non-IT world of the Excel analyst, user requirements are practically useless because of sudden changes in project scope, constantly changing priorities, and shifting deadlines. The gathering of user requirements is viewed to be a lot of work and a waste of valuable time in the ever-changing business environment. But as I mention at the start of this chapter, it's time to get into the dashboard state of mind.

Consider how many times a manager has asked you for an analysis and then said "No, I meant this." Or, "Now that I see it, I realize I need this." As frustrating as that can be for a single analysis, imagine running into this during the creation of a complex dashboard with several data integration processes. The question is, would you rather spend your time on the front end gathering user requirements or spend time painstakingly redesigning the dashboard you'll surely come to hate?

The process of gathering user requirements doesn't have to be an overly complicated or formal one. Here are some simple things you can do to ensure you have a solid idea of the purpose of the dashboard.

Establish the audience and purpose for the dashboard

Chances are your manager has been asked to create the reporting mechanism, and he has passed the task to you. Don't be afraid to clarify the source of the initial request and talk to them about what they're really asking for. Discuss the purpose of the dashboard and the triggers that caused them to ask for a dashboard in the first place. You may find, after discussing the matter, that a simple Excel report meets their needs, foregoing the need for a full-on dashboard.

If a dashboard is indeed warranted, talk about who the end users are. Take some time to meet with some of the end users and talk about how they'd use the dashboard. Will the dashboard be used as a performance tool for regional managers? Will the dashboard be used to share data with external customers? Talking through these fundamentals with the right people helps align your thoughts and avoids the creation of a dashboard that doesn't fulfill the necessary requirements.

Delineate the measures for the dashboard

Most dashboards are designed around a set of measures, or *key performance indicators (KPIs).* A KPI is an indicator of the performance of a task deemed to be essential to daily operations or processes. The idea is that a KPI reveals performance that is outside the normal range for a particular measure, so it therefore often signals the need for attention and intervention. Although the measures you place into your dashboards may not officially be called KPIs, they undoubtedly serve the same purpose — to draw attention to problem areas.

The topic of creating effective KPIs for your organization is a subject worthy of its own book and is out of the scope of this endeavor. For a detailed guide on KPI development strategies, pick up David Parmenter's *Key Performance Indicators: Developing, Implementing, and Using Winning KPIs* (Wiley). This book provides an excellent step-by-step approach to developing and implementing KPIs.

The measures used on a dashboard should absolutely support the initial purpose of that dashboard. For example, if you're creating a dashboard focused on supply chain processes, it may not make sense to have human resources headcount data incorporated. It's generally a good practice to avoid inclusion of nice-to-know data into your dashboards simply to fill white space or because the data is available. If the data doesn't support the core purpose of the dashboard, leave it out.

Here's another tip: When gathering the measures required for the dashboard, I find that it often helps to write a sentence to describe the measure needed. For example, instead of simply adding the word *Revenue* into my user requirements, I write what I call a *component question,* such as, "What is the overall revenue trend for the last two years?" I call it a *component question* because I intend to create a single component, such as a chart or a table, to answer the question. For instance, if the component question is, "What is the overall revenue trend for the last two years?," you can imagine a chart component answering that question by showing the two-year revenue trend.

I sometimes take this a step further and actually incorporate the component questions into a mock layout of the dashboard to get a high-level sense of the data the dashboard will require. Figure 1-3 illustrates an example.

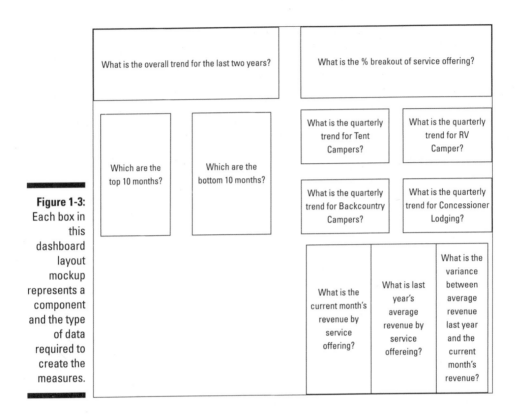

Figure 1-3:
Each box in
this
dashboard
layout
mockup
represents a
component
and the type
of data
required to
create the
measures.

Each box in this dashboard layout mockup represents a component on the dashboard and its approximate position. The questions within each box provide a sense of the types of data required to create the measures for the dashboard.

Catalog the required data sources

When you have the list of measures that need to be included on the dashboard, it's important to take a tally of the available systems to determine if the data required to produce those measures are available. Ask yourself the following questions:

- ✔ Do you have access to the data sources necessary?
- ✔ How often are those data sources refreshed?
- ✔ Who owns and maintains those data sources?
- ✔ What are the processes to get the data from those resources?
- ✔ Does the data even exist?

These are all questions you need answered when negotiating development time, refresh intervals, and phasing.

Conventional wisdom says that the measures on your dashboard shouldn't be governed by the availability of data. Instead, you should let dashboard KPIs and measures govern the data sources in your organization. Although I agree with the spirit of that statement, I've been involved in too many dashboard projects that have fallen apart because of lack of data. Real-world experience has taught me the difference between the ideal and the ordeal.

If your organizational strategy requires that you collect and measure data that is nonexistent or not available, press pause on the dashboard project and turn your attention to creating a data collection mechanism that will get the data you need.

Define the dimensions and filters for the dashboard

In the context of reporting, a *dimension* is a data category used to organize business data. Examples of dimensions are Region, Market, Branch, Manager, or Employee. When you define a dimension in the user requirements stage of development, you're determining how the measures should be grouped or distributed. For example, if it's determined that your dashboard should report data by employee, you need to ensure that your data collection and aggregation processes include employee detail. As you can imagine, adding a new dimension after the dashboard is built can get complicated, especially when your processes require many aggregations across multiple data sources. The bottom line is that locking down the dimensions for a dashboard early in the process definitely saves you headaches.

Along those same lines, you want to get a clear sense of the types of filters that are required. In the context of dashboards, *filters* are mechanisms that allow you to narrow the scope of the data to a single dimension. For example, you can filter on Year, Employee, or Region. Again, if you don't account for a particular filter while building your dashboarding process, you'll likely be forced into an unpleasant redesign of both your data collection processes and your dashboard.

If you're confused by the difference between dimensions and fields, think about a simple Excel table. A dimension is like a column of data (such as a column containing employee names) in an Excel table. A filter, then, is the mechanism that allows you to narrow your table to show only the data for a particular employee. For example, if you apply Excel's AutoFilter to the employee column, you are building a filter mechanism into your table.

Determine the need for drill-down features

Many dashboards provide *drill-down features* that allow users to "drill" into the details of a specific measure. You want to get a clear understanding of the types of drill-downs your users have in mind.

To most users, *drill-down feature* means the ability to get a raw data table supporting the measures shown on the dashboard. Although getting raw data isn't always practical or possible, discussing these requests will at a minimum allow you to talk to your users about additional reporting, links to other data sources, and other solutions that may help them get the data they need.

Establish the refresh schedule

A *refresh schedule* refers to the schedule by which a dashboard is updated to show the latest information available. Because you're the one responsible for building and maintaining the dashboard, you should have a say in the refresh schedules. Your manager may not know what it takes to refresh the dashboard in question.

While you're determining the refresh schedule, keep in mind the refresh rates of the different data sources whose measures you need to get. You can't refresh your dashboard any faster than your data sources. Also, negotiate enough development time to build macros that aid in automation of redundant and time-consuming refresh tasks.

A Quick Look at Dashboard Design Principles

When collecting user requirements for your dashboarding project, there's a heavy focus on the data aspects of the dashboard: The types of data needed, the dimensions of data required, the data sources to be used, and so on. This is a good thing — without solid data processes, your dashboards won't be effective or maintainable. That being said, here's another aspect to your dashboarding project that calls for the same fervor in preparation: the *design aspect*.

Excel users live in a world of numbers and tables, not visualization and design. Your typical Excel analyst has no background in visual design and is often left to rely on his own visual instincts to design his dashboards. As a result, most Excel-based dashboards have little thought given to effective visual design, often resulting in overly cluttered and ineffective user interfaces.

The good news is that dashboarding has been around for such a long time, there's a vast knowledge base of prescribed visualization and dashboard design principles. Many of these principles seem like common sense; even so, these are concepts that Excel users don't often find themselves thinking about. Because this chapter is about getting into the dashboard state of mind, I break that trend and review a few dashboard design principles that improve the design aspect of your Excel dashboards.

 Many of the concepts in this section come from the work of *Stephen Few*, visualization expert and author of several books and articles on dashboard design principles. As this book is primarily focused on the technical aspects of building reporting components in Excel, this section offers a high-level look at dashboard design. If you find that you're captivated by the subject, feel free to visit Stephen Few's Web site at www.perceptualedge.com.

Rule number 1: Keep it simple

Dashboard design expert, Stephen Few, has the mantra, "Simplify, Simplify, Simplify." The basic idea is that dashboards cluttered with too many measures or too much eye candy can dilute the significant information you're trying to present. How many times has someone told you that your reports look "busy"? In essence, this complaint means that too much is going on in the page or screen, making it hard to see the actual data.

Here are a few actions you can take to ensure simpler and more effective dashboard designs.

Don't turn your dashboard into a data repository

Admit it. You include as much information onto a report as possible, primarily to avoid being asked for additional information. We all do it. But in the dashboard state of mind, you have to fight the urge to force every piece of data available onto your dashboards.

Overwhelming users with too much data can cause them to lose sight of the primary goal of the dashboard and focus on inconsequential data. The measures used on a dashboard should support the initial purpose of that dashboard. Avoid the urge to fill white space for the sake of symmetry and appearances. Don't include nice-to-know data just because the data is available. If the data doesn't support the core purpose of the dashboard, leave it out.

Avoid the fancy formatting

The key to communicating effectively with your dashboards is to present your data as simply as possible. There's no need to wrap it in eye candy to make it more interesting. It's okay to have a dashboard with little to no color or formatting. You'll find that the lack of fancy formatting only serves to call attention to the actual data. Focus on the data and not the shiny happy graphics. Here are a few guidelines:

- ✔ **Avoid using colors or background fills to partition your dashboards.** Colors in general should be used sparingly, reserved for providing information about key data points. For example, assigning the colors red, yellow, and green to measures traditionally indicates performance level. Adding these colors to other sections of your dashboard only serves to distract your audience.

- ✔ **De-emphasize borders, backgrounds, and other elements that define dashboard areas.** Try to use the natural white space between your components to partition your dashboard. If borders are necessary, format them to hues lighter than the ones you've used for your data. Light grays are typically ideal for borders. The idea is to indicate sections without distracting from the information displayed.

- ✔ **Avoid applying fancy effects, such as gradients, pattern fills, shadows, glows, soft edges, and other formatting.** Excel 2007 makes it easy to apply effects that make everything look shiny, glittery, and generally happy. Although these formatting features make for great marketing tools, they don't do your reporting mechanisms any favors.

- ✔ **Don't try to enhance your dashboards with clip art or pictures.** Not only do they do nothing to further data presentation, they often just look tacky.

Limit each dashboard to one printable page

Dashboards in general should provide at-a-glance views into key measures relevant to particular objectives or business processes. This implies that all the data is immediately viewable on the one page. Although including all your data on one page isn't always the easiest thing to do, there's much benefit to being able to see everything on one page or screen. You can compare sections more easily, you can process cause and effect relationships more effectively, and you rely less on short term memory. When a user has to scroll left, right, or down, these benefits are diminished. Furthermore, users tend to believe that when information is placed out of normal view (areas that require scrolling), it's somehow less important.

But what if you can't fit all the data on one sheet? First, review the measures on your dashboard and determine if they really need to be there. Next, format your dashboard to use less space (format fonts, reduce white space, and adjust column and row widths). Finally, try adding interactivity to your dashboard, allowing users to dynamically change views to show only those measures that are relevant to them.

Use layout and placement to draw focus

As I discuss earlier in this chapter, only measures that support the dashboard's utility and purpose should be included in the dashboard. However, it should be said that just because all measures on your dashboard are significant, they may not always have the same level of importance. In other words, you'll frequently want one component of your dashboard to stand out from the others.

Instead of using bright colors or exaggerated sizing differences, you can leverage location and placement to draw focus to the most important components on your dashboard.

Various studies have shown that readers have a natural tendency to focus on particular regions of a document. For example, researchers at the Poynter Institute's Eyetracker III project have found that readers view various regions on a screen in a certain order, paying particular attention to specific regions on the screen. They use the diagram in Figure 1-4 to illustrate what they call *priority zones*. Regions with the number 1 in the diagram seem to have high prominence, attracting the most attention for longer periods of time. Meanwhile, priority 3 regions seem to have low prominence.

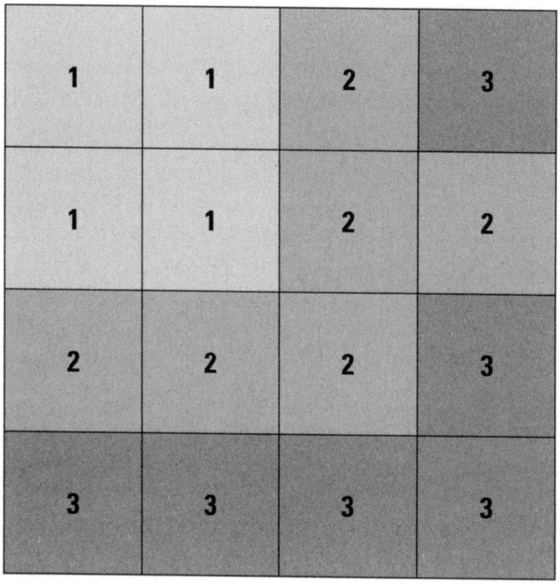

Figure 1-4:
Studies show that users pay particular attention to the upper-left and middle-left of a document.

1	1	2	3
1	1	2	2
2	2	2	3
3	3	3	3

You can leverage these priority zones to promote or demote certain components based on significance. If one of the charts on your dashboard warrants special focus, you can simply place that chart in a region of prominence.

Note that surrounding colors, borders, fonts, and other formatting can affect the viewing patterns of your readers, de-emphasizing a previously high prominence region.

Format numbers effectively

There will undoubtedly be lots of numbers in your dashboards. Some of them will be in charts, and others will be in tables. Remember that every piece of information on your dashboard should have a reason for being there. It's important that you format your numbers effectively to allow your users to understand the information they represent without confusion or hindrance. Here are some guidelines to keep in mind when formatting the numbers in your dashboards and reports:

- ✔ **Always use commas to make numbers easier to read.** For example, instead of 2345, show 2,345.

- ✔ **Only use decimal places if that level of precision is required.** For instance, there's rarely benefit for showing the decimal places in a dollar amount, such as $123.45. Likewise in percentages, use only the minimum number of decimals required to represent the data effectively. For example instead of 43.21%, you may be able to get away with 43%.

- ✔ **Only use the dollar symbol when you need to clarify that you're referring to monetary values.** If you have a chart or table that contains all revenue values, and there's a label clearly stating this, you can save rooms and pixels by leaving out the dollar symbol.

- ✔ **Format very large numbers to the thousands or millions place.** For instance, instead of displaying 16,906,714, you can format the number to read 17M.

You can easily format large numbers in Excel by using the Format Cells dialog box, shown in Figure 1-5. Here, you can specify a custom number format by selecting Custom in the Category list and entering the desired number format code in the Type input box. In Figure 1-5, the format code 0, , "M" ensures the numbers are formatted to millions with an M appendage.

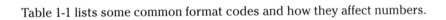

Figure 1-5: Select Custom in the Category list and enter a number format code in the Type input box.

Table 1-1 lists some common format codes and how they affect numbers.

Table 1-1	Number Format Codes
Number Format Code	*How 16,906,714 Would be Displayed*
0,	16907
0,0,	16,907
0.00,	16,906.71
0,"K"	16907K
0,0,"K"	16,907K
0.00,"K"	16,906.71K
$0,0,"K"	$16,907K
0,,	17
0,,"M"	17M
0.0,,"M"	16.9M
0.00,,"M"	16.91M
$0.0,,"M"	$16.9M

Use titles and labels effectively

It's common sense, but many people often fail to label items on dashboards effectively. If your manager looks at your dashboard and asks you, "What is this telling me?," you likely have labeling issues. Here are a few guidelines for effective labeling in your dashboards and reports:

- **Always include a timestamp on your reporting mechanisms.** This minimizes confusion when distributing the same dashboard or report in monthly or weekly installments.

- **Always include some text indicating when the data for the measures was retrieved.** In many cases, timing of the data is a critical piece of information when analyzing a measure.

- **Use descriptive titles for each component in your dashboard.** This allows users to clearly identify what they're looking at. Be sure to avoid cryptic titles with lots of acronyms and symbols.

- **Although it may seem counterintuitive, it's generally good practice to de-emphasize labels by formatting them to hues lighter than the ones used for your data.** Lightly colored labels give your users the information they need without distracting them from the information displayed. Ideal colors to use for labels are colors that are commonly found in nature: soft grays, browns, blues, and greens.

Chapter 2

Building a Super Model

In This Chapter

▶ Understanding the best data modeling practices

▶ Leveraging Excel functions to deliver data

▶ Creating smart tables that expand with data

*O*ne of Excel's most attractive features is its flexibility. You can create an intricate system of interlocking calculations, linked cells, and formatted summaries that work together to create a final analysis. However, years of experience has brought me face-to-face with an ugly truth. Although Excel is like the cool gym teacher that lets you do anything you want, a lack of structure in your data models can lead to some serious headaches in the long run.

What's a data model? A *data model* provides the foundation upon which your reporting mechanism is built. When you build a spreadsheet that imports, aggregates, and shapes data, you're essentially building a data model that feeds your dashboards and reports.

Creating a poorly-designed data model can mean hours of manual labor maintaining and refreshing your reporting mechanisms. On the other hand, creating an effective model allows you to easily repeat monthly reporting processes without damaging your reports or your sanity.

The goal of this chapter is to show you the concepts and techniques that help you build effective data models. In this chapter, you discover that creating a successful reporting mechanism requires more than slapping data onto a spreadsheet. Although you'll see how to build cool dashboard components in later chapters, those components won't do you any good if you can't effectively manage your data models. On that note, let's get started.

Data Modeling Best Practices

Building an effective model isn't as complicated as you may think. It's primarily a matter of thinking about your reporting processes differently. Most people spend very little time thinking about the supporting data model behind a reporting process. If they think about it at all, they usually start by imagining a mockup of the finished dashboard and work backward from there.

Instead of seeing just the finished dashboard in your head, try to think of the end-to-end process. Where will you get the data? How should the data be structured? What analysis will need to be performed? How will the data be fed to the dashboard? How will the dashboard be refreshed?

Obviously the answers to these questions are highly situation-specific. However, some data modeling best practices will guide you to a new way of thinking about your reporting process. These are discussed in the next few sections.

Separating data, analysis, and presentation

One of the most important concepts in a data model is the separation of data, analysis, and presentation. The fundamental idea is that you don't want your data to become too tied into any one particular way of presenting that data.

To get your mind around this concept, think about an invoice. When you receive an invoice, you don't assume the financial data on that invoice is the true source of your data. It's merely a presentation of data that's actually stored in some database. That data can be analyzed and presented to you in many other manners: in charts, in tables, or even on Web sites. This sounds obvious, but Excel users often fuse data, analysis, and presentation together.

For instance, I've seen Excel workbooks that contain 12 tabs, each representing a month. On each tab, data for that month is listed along with formulas, pivot tables, and summaries. Now what happens when you're asked to provide summary by quarter? Do you add more formulas and tabs to consolidate the data on each of the month tabs? The fundamental problem in this scenario is that the tabs actually represent data values that are fused into the presentation of your analysis.

For an example more in-line with reporting, take a look at Figure 2-1. Hard-coded tables, such as this, are common. This table is an amalgamation of data, analysis, and presentation. Not only does this table tie you to a specific analysis, but there's little to no transparency into what the analysis exactly consists of. Also, what happens when you need to report by quarters or when another dimension of analysis is needed? Do you import a table that consists of more columns and rows? How does that affect your model?

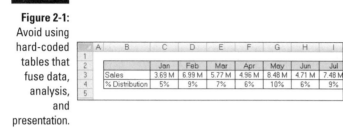

The alternative is to create three layers in your data model: a data layer, an analysis layer, and a presentation layer. You can think of these layers as three different spreadsheets in an Excel workbook. One sheet to hold the raw data that feeds your report, one sheet to serve as a staging area where the data is analyzed and shaped, and one to serve as the presentation layer. Figure 2-2 illustrates the three layers of an effective data model.

As you can see in Figure 2-2, the raw dataset is located on its own sheet. Although the dataset has some level of aggregation applied to keep it manageably small, no further analysis is done on the data sheet.

The analysis layer consists primarily of formulas that analyze and pull data from the data layer into formatted tables (commonly referred to as *staging tables*). These staging tables ultimately feed the reporting components in your presentation layer. In short, the sheet that contains the analysis layer becomes the staging area where data is summarized and shaped to feed the reporting components. Notice in the analysis tab in Figure 2-2, the formula bar illustrates that the table consists of formulas that reference the data tab.

There are a couple of benefits to this setup. First, the entire reporting model can easily be refreshed by simply replacing the raw data with an updated dataset. The formulas in the analysis tab continue to work with the latest data. Second, any additional analysis can easily be created by using different combinations of formulas on the analysis tab. If you need data that doesn't exist in the data sheet, you can easily append a column to the end of the raw dataset without disturbing the analysis or presentation sheets.

Note that you don't necessarily have to place your data, analysis, and presentation layers on different spreadsheets. In small data models, you may find it easier to place your data in one area of a spreadsheet while building your staging tables in another area of the same spreadsheet.

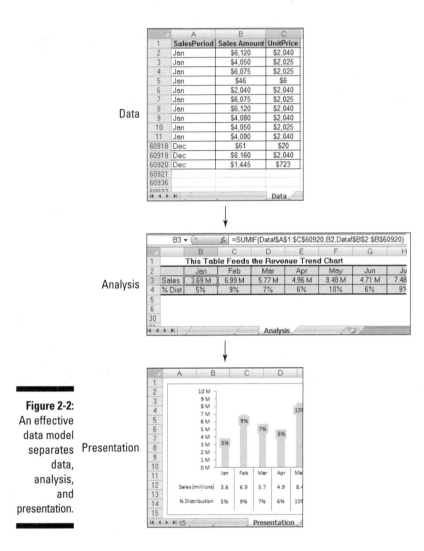

Figure 2-2:
An effective
data model
separates
data,
analysis,
and
presentation.

Along those same lines, remember that you're not limited to just three spread-sheets either. That is to say you can have several sheets that provide the raw data, several sheets that analyze, and several that serve as the presentation layer.

Wherever you choose to place the different layers, keep in mind that the idea remains the same. The analysis layer should primarily consist of formulas that pull data from the data sheets into staging tables used to feed your pre-sentation. Later in this chapter, you explore some of the formulas that can be used in your analysis sheets.

Starting with appropriately structured data

Not all datasets are created equal. Although some datasets work in a standard Excel environment, they may not work for data modeling purposes. Before building your data model, ensure your source data is appropriately structured for dashboarding purposes.

At the risk of oversimplification, I assert that datasets typically used in Excel come in three fundamental forms:

 ✔ **The spreadsheet report**

 ✔ **The flat data file**

 ✔ **The tabular dataset**

The punch line is that only flat data files and tabular datasets make for effective data models. I review and discuss each of these different forms in the next few sections.

Spreadsheet reports make for ineffective data models

Spreadsheet reports display highly-formatted, summarized data and are often designed as presentation tools for management or executive users. A typical spreadsheet report makes judicious use of empty space for formatting, repeats data for aesthetic purposes, and presents only high level analysis. Figure 2-3 illustrates what I mean by *spreadsheet report*.

Figure 2-3: A spreadsheet report.

	A	B	C	D	E	F	G
1							
2		Europe				North America	
3	**France**				**Canada**		
4	Segment	Sales Amount	Unit Price		Segment	Sales Amount	Unit Price
5	Accessories	$48,942	$7,045		Accessories	$119,303	$22,381
6	Bikes	$3,597,879	$991,098		Bikes	$11,714,700	$3,908,691
7	Clothing	$129,508	$23,912		Clothing	$383,022	$72,524
8	Components	$871,125	$293,854		Components	$2,246,255	$865,410
9							
10	**Germany**				**Northeast**		
11	Segment	Sales Amount	Unit Price		Segment	Sales Amount	Unit Price
12	Accessories	$35,681	$5,798		Accessories	$51,246	$9,666
13	Bikes	$1,602,487	$545,175		Bikes	$5,690,285	$1,992,517
14	Clothing	$75,593	$12,474		Clothing	$163,442	$30,969
15	Components	$337,787	$138,513		Components	$1,051,702	$442,598
16							
17	**United Kingdom**				**Northwest**		
18	Segment	Sales Amount	Unit Price		Segment	Sales Amount	Unit Price
19	Accessories	$43,180	$7,419		Accessories	$53,308	$11,417
20	Bikes	$3,435,134	$1,094,354		Bikes	$10,484,495	$3,182,041
21	Clothing	$120,225	$21,981		Clothing	$201,052	$40,055
22	Components	$712,588	$253,458		Components	$1,784,207	$695,876

Although a spreadsheet report may look nice, it doesn't make for an effective data model. Why? The primary reason is that these reports offer you no separation of data, analysis, and presentation. You're essentially locked into one analysis.

Although you could make charts from the report shown in Figure 2-3, it'd be impractical to apply any analysis outside what's already there. For instance, how would you calculate and present the average of all bike sales? How would you calculate a list of the top ten best performing markets?

With this setup, you're forced into very manual processes that are difficult to maintain month after month. Any analysis outside the high-level ones already in the report is basic at best — even with fancy formulas. Furthermore, what happens when you're required to show bike sales by month? When your data model requires analysis with data that isn't in the spreadsheet report, you're forced to search for another dataset.

Flat data files lend themselves nicely to data models

The next type of file format is flat file. *Flat files* are data repositories organized by row and column. Each row corresponds to a set of data elements, or a *record*. Each column is a *field*. A field corresponds to a unique data element in record. Figure 2-4 contains the same data as the report in Figure 2-3 but is in flat data file format.

Figure 2-4:
A flat
data file.

	A	B	C	D	E	F	G	H
				Jan Sales	Feb Sales	Mar Sales	Apr Sales	May Sal
1	Region	Market	Business Segment	Amount	Amount	Amount	Amount	Amou
2	Europe	France	Accessories	2,628	8,015	3,895	1,803	6,1
3	Europe	France	Bikes	26,588	524,445	136,773	37,959	519,8
4	Europe	France	Clothing	6,075	17,172	6,043	5,152	11,7
5	Europe	France	Components	20,485	179,279	54,262	8,992	103,3
6	Europe	Germany	Accessories	2,769	6,638	2,615	2,862	4,4
7	Europe	Germany	Bikes	136,161	196,125	94,840	161,260	140,9
8	Europe	Germany	Clothing	7,150	12,374	7,159	5,765	8,6
9	Europe	Germany	Components	46,885	56,611	29,216	25,407	35,4
10	Europe	United Kingdom	Accessories	4,205	2,579	5,745	3,732	2,2
11	Europe	United Kingdom	Bikes	111,830	175,522	364,844	86,695	170,3
12	Europe	United Kingdom	Clothing	7,888	6,763	12,884	6,546	4,3
13	Europe	United Kingdom	Components	31,331	39,005	124,030	19,291	22,3
14	North America	Canada	Accessories	3,500	12,350	9,768	3,162	10,0
15	North America	Canada	Bikes	327,476	425,669	501,427	305,118	348,9

Notice that every data field has a column, and every column corresponds to one data element. Furthermore, there's no extra spacing, and each row (or record) corresponds to a unique set of information. But the key attribute that makes this a flat file is that no single field uniquely identifies a record. In fact, you'd have to specify four separate fields (Region, Market, Business Segment, and a month's sales amount) before you could uniquely identify the record.

Flat files lend themselves nicely to data modeling in Excel because they can be detailed enough to hold the data you need and still be conducive to a wide array of analysis with simple formulas — SUM, AVERAGE, VLOOKUP, and SUMIF, just to name a few. Later in this chapter, you explore formulas that come in handy in a reporting data model.

Tabular datasets are perfect for pivot table driven data models

Many effective data models are driven primarily by pivot tables. Pivot tables (which I cover in Chapter 3) are Excel's premier analysis tools. For those of you who have used pivot tables before, you know they offer an excellent way to summarize and shape data for use by reporting components, such as charts and tables.

Tabular datasets are ideal for pivot table driven data models. Figure 2-5 illustrates a tabular dataset. Note that the primary difference between a tabular dataset, as shown in Figure 2-5, and a flat data file is that the column labels don't double as actual data. For instance, in Figure 2-4, the month identifiers are integrated into the column labels. In Figure 2-5, the Sales Period column contains the month identifier. This subtle difference in structure is what makes tabular datasets optimal data sources for pivot tables. This structure ensures that key pivot table functions, such as sorting and grouping, work the way they should.

	A	B	C	D	E	F
1	Region	Market	Business Segment	Sales Period	Sales Amount	Unit Price
2	Europe	France	Accessories	Jan	1,706	385
3	Europe	France	Accessories	Feb	3,767	700
4	Europe	France	Accessories	Mar	1,219	251
5	Europe	France	Accessories	Apr	3,091	557
6	Europe	France	Accessories	May	7,057	942
7	Europe	France	Accessories	Jul	5,930	770
8	Europe	France	Accessories	Aug	9,628	1,281
9	Europe	France	Accessories	Sep	4,279	500
10	Europe	France	Accessories	Oct	2,504	528
11	Europe	France	Accessories	Nov	7,493	848
12	Europe	France	Accessories	Dec	2,268	283
13	Europe	France	Bikes	Jan	64,895	24,101
14	Europe	France	Bikes	Feb	510,102	166,174
15	Europe	France	Bikes	Mar	128,806	45,711
16	Europe	France	Bikes	Apr	81,301	26,314

Figure 2-5:
A tabular
dataset.

The attributes of a tabular dataset are as follows:

- The first row of the dataset contains field labels that describe the information in each column.

- The column labels don't pull double-duty as data items that can be used as filters or query criterion (such as months, dates, years, regions, markets, and so on).

- There are no blank rows or columns — every column has a heading, and a value is in every row.

- Each column represents a unique category of data.

- Each row represents individual items in each column.

Avoiding turning your data model into a database

In Chapter 1, you might have read that measures used on a dashboard should absolutely support the initial purpose of that dashboard. The same concept applies to the backend data model. You should only import data that's necessary to fulfill the purpose of your dashboard or report.

In an effort to have as much data as possible at their fingertips, many Excel users bring into their spreadsheets every piece of data they can get their hands on. You can spot these people by the 40 megabyte files they send through e-mail. You've seen these spreadsheets — two tabs that contain presentation and then six hidden tabs that contain thousands of lines of data (most of which isn't used). They essentially build a database in their spreadsheet.

What's wrong with utilizing as much data as possible? Well, here are a few issues:

✔ **Aggregating data within Excel increases the number of formulas.** If you're bringing in all raw data, you have to aggregate that data in Excel. This inevitably causes you to exponentially increase the number of formulas you have to employ and maintain. Remember that your data model is a vehicle for presenting analyses, not processing raw data. The data that works best in reporting mechanisms is what's already been aggregated and summarized into useful views that can be navigated and fed to dashboard components. Importing data that's already been aggregated as much as possible is far better. For example, if you need to report on Revenue by Region and Month, there's no need to import sales transactions into your data model. Instead, use an aggregated table consisting of Region, Month, and Sum of Revenue.

✔ **Your data model will be distributed with your dashboard.** In other words, because your dashboard is fed by your data model, you need to maintain the model behind the scenes (likely in hidden tabs) when distributing the dashboard. Besides the fact that it causes the file size to be unwieldy, including too much data in your data model can actually degrade the performance of your dashboard. Why? When you open an Excel file, the entire file is loaded into memory (or *RAM*) to ensure quick data processing and access. The drawback to this behavior is that Excel requires a great deal of RAM to process even the smallest change in your spreadsheet. You may have noticed that when you try to perform an action on a large formula-intensive dataset, Excel is slow to respond, giving you a Calculating indicator in the status bar. The larger your dataset is, the less efficient the data crunching in Excel is.

✔ **Large datasets can cause difficulty in scalability.** Imagine that you're working in a small company and you're using monthly transactions in your data model. Each month holds 80,000 lines of data. As time goes on, you build a robust process complete with all the formulas, pivot tables, and macros you need to analyze the data that's stored in your neatly maintained tab. Now what happens after one year? Do you start a new tab? How do you analyze two datasets on two different tabs as one entity? Are your formulas still good? Do you have to write new macros?

These are all issues that can be avoided by importing only aggregated and summarized data that's useful to the core purpose of your reporting needs.

Using tabs to document and organize your data model

Wanting to keep your data model limited to one worksheet tab is natural. In my mind, keeping track of one tab is much simpler than using different tabs. However, limiting your data model to one tab has its drawbacks, including the following:

✔ **Using one tab typically places limits on your analysis.** Because only so many datasets can fit on a tab, using one tab limits the number of analyses that can be represented in your data model. This in turn limits the analysis your dashboard can offer. Consider adding tabs to your data model to provide additional data and analysis that may not fit on just one tab.

✔ **Too much on one tab makes for a confusing data model.** When working with large datasets, you need plenty of staging tables to aggregate and shape the raw data so that it can be fed to your reporting components. If you use only one tab, you're forced to position these staging tables below or to the right of your datasets. Although this may provide all the elements needed to feed your presentation layer, a good deal of scrolling is necessary to view all the elements positioned in a wide range of areas. This makes the data model difficult to understand and maintain. Use separate tabs to hold your analysis and staging tables, particularly in data models that contain large datasets occupying a lot of real estate.

✔ **Using one tab limits the amount of documentation you can include.** You'll find that your data models easily become a complex system of intertwining links among components, input ranges, output ranges, and formulas. Sure, it all makes sense while you're building your data model, but try coming back to it after a few months. You'll find you've forgotten what each data range does and how each range interacts with the final presentation layer. To avoid this problem, consider adding a model map tab to your data model. The model map tab essentially summarizes the key ranges in the data model and allows you to document how each range interacts with the reporting components in the final presentation layer. As you can see in Figure 2-6, the model map is nothing fancy; just a table that lists some key information about each range in the model.

Figure 2-6:
A model map allows you to document how each range interacts with your data model.

Tab	Range	Purpose	Linked Component/s
Analysis 1	A2:A11	Provides the data source for the trend graph component	United States trend 1
Analysis 2	A3:A11	Data source for the List Box Component	List Box 1
Analysis 2	C1	Output range for the selected item in the List Box component.	Conditional Trend Icon
Analysis 2	D1:R1	Vlookup formulas that reference cell C1. This range also serves as the source data for the Combination Chart component.	Combination Chart 1
Data	C4:R48	Main Dataset for this data model	

You can include any information you think appropriate in your model map. The idea is to give yourself a handy reference that guides you through the elements in your data model.

Testing your data model before building reporting components on top of it

This best practice is simple. Make sure your data model does what it's supposed to do before building dashboard components on top of it. In that vein, here are a few things to watch for:

- ✔ **Test your formulas to ensure they're working properly:** Make sure your formulas don't produce errors and that each formula outputs expected results.

- ✔ **Double-check your main dataset to ensure it's complete:** Check that your data table has not truncated when transferring to Excel. Also, be sure that each column of data is present with appropriate data labels.

- ✔ **Make sure all numeric formatting is appropriate:** Be sure that the formatting of your data is appropriate for the field. For example, check to see that dates are formatted as dates, currency values are formatted properly, and that the correct number of decimal places are displayed where needed.

The obvious goal here is to eliminate easily avoidable errors that may cause complications later.

Speaking of documenting your data model . . . .

Another way to document the logic in your data model is to use comments and labels liberally. It's amazing how a few explanatory comments and labels can help clarify your spreadsheets. The general idea here is that the logic in your model should be clear to you even after you've been away from your data model for a long period of time.

Also, consider using colors to identify the ranges in your data model. Using colors in your data model enables you to quickly look at a range of cells and get a basic indication of what that range does. The general concept behind

this best practice is that each color represents a range type. For example, you could use yellow to represent staging tables used to feed the charts and the tables in your presentation layer. You could use gray to represent formulas that aren't to be altered or touched, or purple to represent reference tables used for lookups and drop-down lists.

You can use any color you want; it's up to you to give these colors meaning. The important thing is that you have a visual distinction between the various ranges being used in your data model.

Excel Functions That Really Deliver

As you discover in this chapter, the optimal data model for any reporting mechanism is one where data, analysis, and presentation is separated into three layers. Although all three layers are important, the analysis layer is where the real art comes into play. The fundamental task of the analysis layer is to pull information from the data layer and then create staging tables that feed your charts, tables, and other reporting components. To do this effectively, you need to employ formulas that serve as data delivery mechanisms — formulas that deliver data to a destination range.

You see, the information you need lives in your data layer (typically a table containing aggregated data). *Data delivery formulas* are designed to get that data and deliver it to the analysis layer so it can be analyzed and shaped. The cool thing is that after you've set up you data delivery formulas, your analysis layer automatically updates each time your data layer is refreshed.

Confused? Don't worry — in this section, I show you a few Excel functions that work particularly well in data delivery formulas. As you go through the examples here, you'll start to see how these concepts come together.

The VLOOKUP function

The VLOOKUP function is the king of all lookup functions in Excel. I'd be willing to bet you've at least heard of VLOOKUP, if not used it a few times yourself.

The purpose of VLOOKUP is to find a specific value from a column of data where the leftmost row value matches a given criterion.

VLOOKUP basics

Take a look a Figure 2-7 to get the general idea. The table on the left shows sales by month and product number. The table on the right translates those product numbers to actual product names. The VLOOKUP function can help in associating the appropriate name to each respective product number.

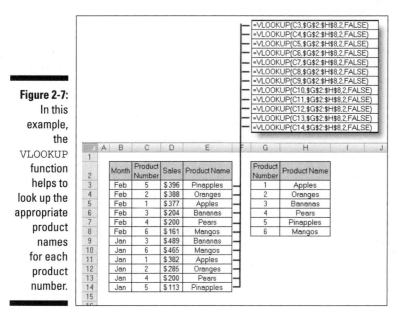

Figure 2-7: In this example, the VLOOKUP function helps to look up the appropriate product names for each product number.

To understand how VLOOKUP formulas work, take a moment to review the basic syntax. A VLOOKUP formula requires four arguments:

```
VLOOKUP(Lookup_value, Table_array, Col_index_num,
        Range_lookup)
```

Lookup_value: The Lookup_value argument identifies the value being looked up. This is the value that needs to be matched to the lookup table. In the example in Figure 2-7, the Lookup_value is the product number. Therefore the first argument for all the formulas shown in Figure 2-7 reference column C (the column that contains the product number).

Table_array: The Table_array argument specifies the range that contains the lookup values. In Figure 2-7, that range is G2:H8. Here are a couple points to keep in mind with this argument. First, for a VLOOKUP to work, the leftmost column of the table must be the matching value. For instance, if you're trying to match product numbers, the leftmost column of the lookup table must contain product numbers. Second, notice that the reference used for this argument is an absolute reference. This means the column and row references are prefixed with dollar ($) signs — as in $G$2:$H$8. This ensures that the references don't shift while you copy the formulas down or across.

Col_index_num: The *Col_index_num* argument identifies the column number in the lookup table that contains the value to be returned. In the example in Figure 2-7, the second column contains the product name (the value being looked up), so the formula uses the number 2. If the product name column was the fourth column in the lookup table, the number 4 would be used.

Range_lookup: The *Range_lookup* argument specifies whether you're looking for an exact match or an approximate match. If an exact match is needed, you'd enter FALSE for this argument. If the closest match will do, you'd enter TRUE or leave the argument blank.

Applying VLOOKUP formulas in a data model

As you can imagine, there are countless ways to apply a VLOOKUP formula in your data model. No reason to start bland though. Let me show you one of the more intriguing ways is to implement VLOOKUPs.

With a few VLOOKUP formulas and a simple drop-down list, you can create a data model that not only delivers data to the appropriate staging table but allows you to dynamically change data views based on a selection you make. Figure 2-8 illustrates the setup.

To see this effect in action, get the Chapter 2 Sample File.xlsx workbook from this book's companion Web site. Open that workbook to see a VLOOKUP1 tab.

Figure 2-8:
Using the
VLOOKUP
function to
extract and
shape data.

```
=VLOOKUP(C3,$C$9:$F$5000,2,FALSE)
=VLOOKUP(C3,$C$9:$F$5000,3,FALSE)
=VLOOKUP(C3,$C$9:$F$5000,4,FALSE)
=F2/F3
=F2/F4
```

	A	B	C	D	E	F
1						
2			AccountName		YTD Rev	2,230,673
3	Enter Customer Name Here>>		Chevron		YTD Rev Plan	6,491,094
4					YTD Rev Last Year	7,181,869
5					Rev vs Plan	34%
6					Rev vs Last Year	31%
7						
8						
9	**Hub**	**Acct Id**	**AccountName**	**YTD Rev**	**YTD Rev Plan**	**YTD Rev Last Year**
10	Australia	1	Wal-Mart Stores	125,911,787	343,723,442	353,071,100
11	Canada	2	Exxon Mobil	3,446,386	11,113,858	12,312,078
12	Central	3	General Motors	1,090,629	2,981,840	3,420,955
13	France	4	Chevron	2,230,673	6,491,094	7,181,869
14	Germany	5	ConocoPhillips	774,796	2,402,490	2,164,995
15	Northeast	6	General Electric	3,212,397	9,994,928	9,399,860
16	Northwest	7	Ford Motor	716,829	1,851,000	2,667,172
17	Southeast	8	Citigroup	503,816	885,366	950,911

The data layer in the model shown in Figure 2-8 resides in the range A9:F209. The analysis layer is held in range E2:F6. The data layer consists of all formulas that extract and shape the data as needed. As you can see, the VLOOKUP formulas use the Customer Name value in cell C3 to look up the appropriate data from the data layer. So, if you entered **General Motors** in cell C3, the VLOOKUP formulas would extract the data for General Motors.

You may have noticed that the VLOOKUP formulas in Figure 2-8 specify a Table_array argument of $C$9:$F$5000. This means that the lookup table they're pointing to stretches from C9 to F5000. That seems strange because the table ends at F209. Why would you force your VLOOKUP formulas to look at a range far past the end of the data table?

Well, remember the idea behind separating the data layer and the analysis layer is so that your analysis layer can be automatically updated when your data is refreshed. When you get new data next month, you should be able to simply replace the data layer in model without having to rework your analysis layer. Allowing for more rows than necessary in your VLOOKUP formulas ensures that if your data layer grows, records won't fall outside the lookup range of the formulas.

Later in this chapter, I show you how to automatically keep up with growing data tables by using smart tables.

Using data validation drop-down lists in your data model

In the example illustrated in Figure 2-8, the data model allows you to select customer names from a drop-down list when you click cell C3. The customer name serves as the lookup value for the VLOOKUP formulas. Changing the customer name extracts a new set of data from the data layer. This allows you to quickly switch from one customer to another without having to remember and type the customer name.

Now, as cool as this seems, the reasons for this setup aren't all cosmetic. There are practical reasons for adding drop-down lists to your data models.

Many of your models consist of multiple analytical layers where each shows a different set of analyses. Although each analysis layer is different, they often need to revolve around a shared dimension, such as the same customer name, the same market, or the same region. For instance, when you have a data model that reports on Financials, Labor Statistics, and Operational Volumes, you want to make certain that when the model is reporting financials for the South region, the Labor statistics are for the South region as well.

An effective way to ensure this happens is to force your formulas to use the same dimension references. If cell C3 is where you switch customers, every analysis that is customer-dependent should reference cell C3. Drop-down lists allow you to have a predefined list of valid variables located in a single cell. With a drop-down list, you can easily switch dimensions while building and testing multiple analysis layers.

Adding a drop-down list is a relatively easy thing to do with Excel's Data Validation functionality. To add a drop-down list:

1. **Select the Data tab on the Ribbon.**

2. **Click the Data Validation button.**

3. **Select the Settings tab in the newly-activated Data Validation dialog box (see Figure 2-9).**

4. **In the Allow drop-down list, choose List.**

5. **In the Source input box, reference the range of cell that contain your predefined selection list.**

6. **Click OK.**

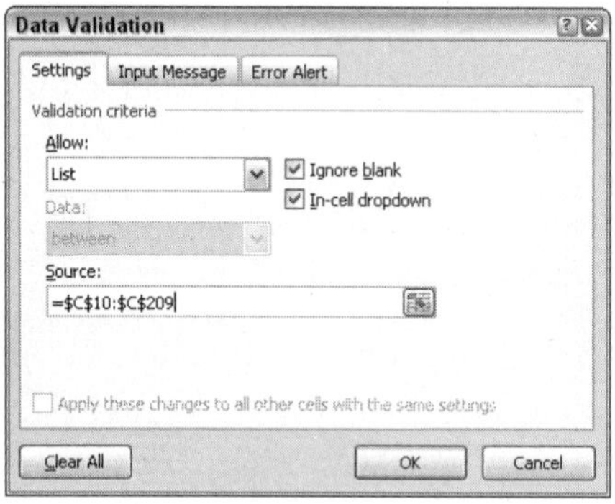

Figure 2-9: You can use data validation to create a predefined list of valid variables for your data model.

The HLOOKUP function

The HLOOKUP function is the less popular cousin of the VLOOKUP function. The *H* in HLOOKUP stands for *horizontal*. Because Excel data is typically vertically-oriented, most situations require a vertical lookup (or VLOOKUP). However, some data structures are horizontally-oriented, requiring a horizontal lookup; thus the HLOOKUP function comes in handy. The HLOOKUP searches a lookup table to find a single value from a row of data where the column label matches a given criterion.

HLOOKUP basics

Figure 2-10 demonstrates a typical scenario where HLOOKUP formulas are used. The table in C3 requires quarter-end numbers (March and June) for 2004. The HLOOKUP formulas use the column labels to find the correct month columns and then locates the 2004 data by moving down the appropriate number of rows. In this case, 2004 data is in row 4, so the number 4 is used in the formulas.

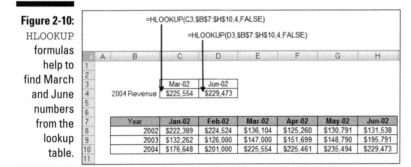

Figure 2-10: HLOOKUP formulas help to find March and June numbers from the lookup table.

To get your mind around how this works, take a look at the basic syntax of the HLOOKUP function.

```
HLOOKUP(Lookup_value, Table_array, Row_index_num,
        Range_lookup)
```

Lookup_value: The *Lookup_value* argument identifies the value being looked up. In most cases, these values are column names. In the example in Figure 2-10, the column labels are being referenced for the *Lookup_value*. This points the HLOOKUP function to the appropriate column in the lookup table.

Table_array: The *Table_array* argument identifies the range that contains the lookup table. In Figure 2-10, that range is B7:H10. Like the VLOOKUP examples earlier in this chapter, notice that the references used for this argument are absolute. This means the column and row references are prefixed with dollar ($) signs — as in $B$7:$H$10. This ensures that the reference doesn't shift while you copy the formula down or across.

Row_index_num: The *Row_index_num* argument identifies the row number that contains the value you're looking for. In the example in Figure 2-10, the 2004 data is located in row 4 of the lookup table. Therefore, the formulas use the number 4.

Range_lookup: The *Range_lookup* argument specifies whether you're looking for an exact match or an approximate match. If an exact match is needed, you'd enter FALSE for this argument. If the closest match will do, you'd enter TRUE or leave the argument blank.

Applying HLOOKUP formulas in a data model

HLOOKUPs are especially handy for shaping data into structures appropriate for charting or other types of reporting. A simple example is demonstrated in Figure 2-11. With HLOOKUPs, the data shown in the raw data table at the bottom of the figure is reoriented in a staging table at the top. When the raw data is changed or refreshed, the staging table captures the changes.

Figure 2-11: In this example, HLOOKUP formulas pull and reshape data without disturbing the raw data table.

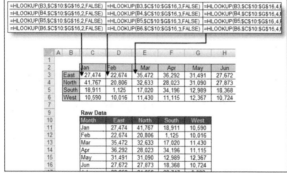

The SUMPRODUCT function

The SUMPRODUCT function is actually listed under the math and trigonometry category of Excel functions. Because the primary purpose of SUMPRODUCT is to calculate the sum product, most people don't know you can actually use it to look up values. In fact, you can use this versatile function quite effectively in most data models.

SUMPRODUCT basics

The SUMPRODUCT function is designed to multiply values from two or more ranges of data and then add the results together to return the sum of the products. Take a look at Figure 2-12 to see a typical scenario where the SUMPRODUCT is useful.

In Figure 2-12, you see a common analysis where you need the total sales for the years 2006 and 2007. As you can see, to get the total sales for each year, you first have to multiply Price by the number of Units to get the total for each Region. Then you have to sum those results to get the total sales for each year.

Year	Region	Price	Units	
2007	North	$40	751	$30,040
2007	South	$35	483	$16,905
2007	East	$32	789	$25,248
2007	West	$41	932	$38,212
2006	North	$40	877	$35,080
2006	South	$35	162	$5,670
2006	East	$32	258	$8,256
2006	West	$41	517	$21,197

2007 total	$110,405
2006 total	$70,203
Variance	$40,202

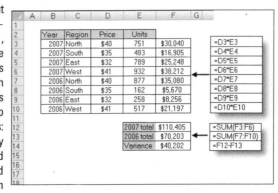

Figure 2-12: Without the SUMPRODUCT, getting the total sales for each year involves a two-step process: first multiply price and units and then sum the results.

With the SUMPRODUCT function, you can perform the two-step analysis with just one formula. Figure 2-13 shows the same analysis with SUMPRODUCT formulas. Instead of using 11 formulas, you can accomplish the same analysis with just 3!

Year	Region	Price	Units
2007	North	$40	751
2007	South	$35	483
2007	East	$32	789
2007	West	$41	932
2006	North	$40	877
2006	South	$35	162
2006	East	$32	258
2006	West	$41	517

2007 total	$110,405
2006 total	$70,203
Variance	$40,202

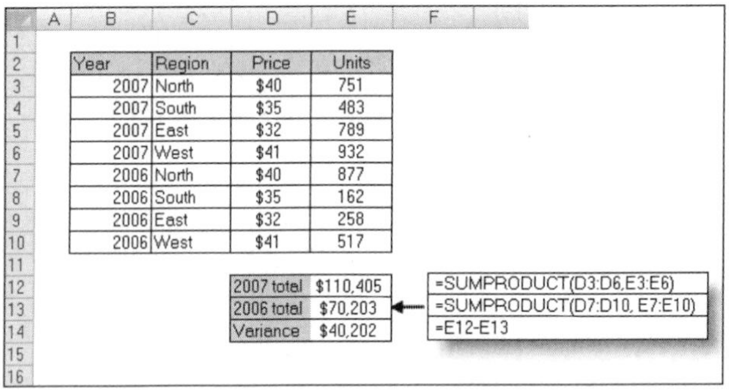

Figure 2-13: The SUMPRODUCT function allows you to perform the same analysis with just 3 formulas instead of 11.

The syntax of the SUMPRODUCT function is fairly simple:

```
SUMPRODUCT(Array1, Array2, . . .)
```

Array: *Array* represents a range of data. You can use anywhere from 2 to 255 arrays in a SUMPRODUCT formula. The arrays get multiplied together and then added. The only hard and fast rule you have to remember is that all the arrays must have the same number of values. That is to say, you can't use the SUMPRODUCT if range X has 10 values and Range Y has 11 values. Otherwise, you get the #VALUE! error.

A twist on the SUMPRODUCT function

The interesting thing about the SUMPRODUCT function is that it can be used to filter out values. Take a look at Figure 2-14 to see what I mean.

The formula in cell E12 is pulling the sum of total units for just the North region. Meanwhile, cell E13 is pulling the units logged for the North region in the year 2006.

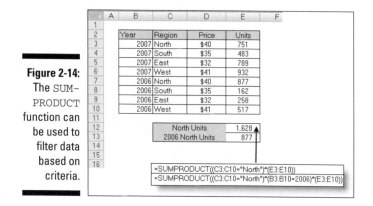

Figure 2-14: The SUM-PRODUCT function can be used to filter data based on criteria.

To understand how this works, take a look at the formula in cell E12 shown in Figure 2-14. That formula reads SUMPRODUCT((C3:C10="North")*(E3:E10)).

In Excel, TRUE evaluates to 1 and FALSE evaluates to 0. Every value in Column C that equals "North" evaluates to TRUE or 1. Where the value is not "North", it evaluates to FALSE or 0.The part of the formula that reads (C3:C10="North") enumerates through each value in the range C3:C10, assigning a 1 or 0 to each value. Then internally, the SUMPRODUCT formula translates to

```
(1*E3)+(0*E4)+(0*E5)+(0*E6)+(1*E7)+(0*E8)+(0*E9)+(0*E10).
```

This gives you the answer of 1628 because

```
(1*751)+(0*483)+(0*789)+(0*932)+(1*877)+(0*162)+(0*258)+(0
        *517)
```

equals 1628.

Applying SUMPRODUCT formulas in a data model

As always in Excel, you don't have to hard-code the criteria in your formulas. Instead of explicitly using "North" in the SUMPRODUCT formula, you could reference a cell that contains the filter value. You can imagine that cell A3 contains the word ""North"", in which case you can use (C3:C10=A3) instead of (C3:C10="North"). This way, you can dynamically change your filter criteria, and your formula keeps up.

Figure 2-15 demonstrates how you can use this concept to pull data into a staging table based on multiple criteria. Note that each of the SUMPRODUCT formulas shown here reference cells B3 and C3 to filter on Account and Product Line. Again, you can add data validation drop-down lists to cells B3 and C3, allowing you to easily change criteria.

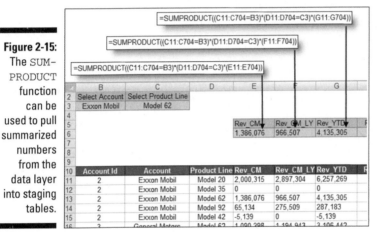

Figure 2-15: The SUM‑PRODUCT function can be used to pull summarized numbers from the data layer into staging tables.

The CHOOSE function

The CHOOSE function returns a value from a specified list of values based on a specified position number. For instance, if you enter the formulas CHOOSE (3,"Red", "Yellow", "Green", "Blue") into a cell, Excel returns Green because Green is the third item in the list of values. The formula CHOOSE(1,"Red", "Yellow", "Green", "Blue") would return Red. Although this may not look useful on the surface, the CHOOSE function can dramatically enhance your data models.

CHOOSE basics

Figure 2-16 illustrates how CHOOSE formulas can help pinpoint and extract numbers from a range cells. Note that instead of using hard-coded values, like Red, Green, and so on, you can use cell references to list the choices.

Take a moment to review the basic syntax of the CHOOSE function:

```
CHOOSE(Index_num, Value1, Value2, . . .)
```

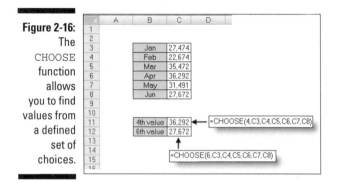

Figure 2-16:
The
CHOOSE
function
allows
you to find
values from
a defined
set of
choices.

Index_num: The *Index_num* argument specifies the position number of the chosen value in the list of values. If the third value in the list is needed, the *Index_num* is 3. The *Index_num* argument must be an integer between one and the maximum number of values in the defined list of values. That is to say, if there are ten choices defined in the CHOOSE formula, the *Index_num* argument can't be more than ten.

Value: Each *Value* argument represents a choice in the defined list of choices for that CHOOSE formula. The *Value* arguments can be hard-coded values, cell references, defined names, formulas, or functions. In Excel 2007, you can have up to 255 choices listed in your CHOOSE formulas. In Excel 2003, you're limited to 29 *Value* arguments.

Applying CHOOSE formulas in a data model

The CHOOSE function is especially valuable in data models where there are multiple layers of data that need to be brought together. Figure 2-17 illustrates an example where CHOOSE formulas help pull data together.

In this example, you have two data tables: one for Revenues and one for Net Income. Each contains numbers for separate regions. The idea is to create a staging table that pulls data from both tables so that the data corresponds to a selected region.

To understand what's going on, focus on the formula in cell F3, shown in Figure 2-17. The formula is CHOOSE($C$2,F7,F8,F9,F10). The *Index_num* argument is actually a cell reference that looks at the value in cell C2, which happens to be the number 2. As you can see, cell C2 is actually a VLOOKUP formula that pulls the appropriate index number for the selected region. The list of defined choices in the CHOOSE formula is essentially the cell references that make up the revenue values for each region: F7, F8, F9, and F10. So the formula in cell F3 translates to CHOOSE(2, 27474, 41767, 18911, 10590). The answer is 41,767.

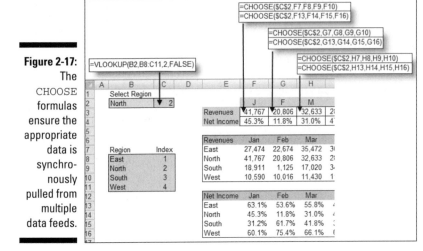

Figure 2-17:
The
CHOOSE
formulas
ensure the
appropriate
data is
synchro-
nously
pulled from
multiple
data feeds.

Using Smart Tables That Expand with Data

One of the challenges you can encounter when building data models is a data table that expands over time. That is to say, the table grows in the number of records it holds due to new data being added. To get a basic understanding of this challenge, take a look at Figure 2-18. In this figure, you see a simple table that serves as the source for the chart. Notice that the table lists data for January through June.

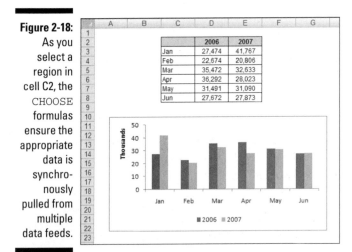

Figure 2-18:
As you
select a
region in
cell C2, the
CHOOSE
formulas
ensure the
appropriate
data is
synchro-
nously
pulled from
multiple
data feeds.

Imagine that next month, this table expands to include July data. You'll have to manually update your chart to include July data. Now imagine you had this same issue across your data model, with multiple data tables that link to multiple staging tables and dashboard components. You can imagine it'd be an extremely painful task to keep up with changes each month.

To solve this issue, you can use Excel's Table feature (you can tell they spent all night coming up with that name). The *Table feature* allows you to convert a range of data into a defined table that's treated independently of other rows and columns on the worksheet. After a range is converted to a table, Excel views the individual cells in the table as a single object that has functionality that a normal data range doesn't have.

For instance, Excel tables offer the following features:

✔ They're automatically enabled with auto filter drop-down headers so that you can filter and sort easily.

✔ They come with the ability to quickly add a Total row with various aggregate functions.

✔ You can apply special formatting to Excel tables independent of the rest of the spreadsheet.

✔ (Most importantly for data modeling purposes), they automatically expand to allow for new data.

The Table feature did exist in Excel 2003 under a different name: the List feature (found in Excel's Data menu). The benefit of this fact is that Excel tables are fully compatible with Excel 2003!

Converting a range to an Excel table

To convert a range of data to an Excel table, follow these steps:

1. **Highlight the range of cells that contain the data you want included in your Excel table.**

2. **On the Insert tab of the Ribbon, click the Table button.**

   This opens the Create Table dialog box, as shown in Figure 2-19.

3. **In the Create Table dialog box, verify the range for the table and specify whether the first row of the selected range is a header row.**

4. **Click OK to apply the changes.**

After the conversion takes place, notice a few small changes. Excel put auto filter drop-downs on your header rows, the rows in your table now have alternate shading, and any header that didn't have a value has been named by Excel.

You can use Excel tables as the source for charts, pivot tables, list boxes, or anything else for which you'd normally use a data range. In Figure 2-20, a chart has been linked to the Excel table.

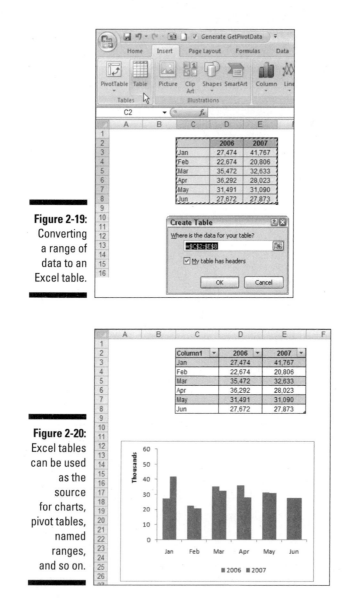

Figure 2-19:
Converting a range of data to an Excel table.

Figure 2-20:
Excel tables can be used as the source for charts, pivot tables, named ranges, and so on.

Here's the impressive bit. When data is added to the table, Excel automatically expands the range of the table and incorporates the new range into any linked object. That's just a fancy way of saying that any chart or pivot table tied to an Excel table automatically captures new data without manual intervention.

For example, if I add July and August data to the end of the Excel table, the chart automatically updates to capture the new data. In Figure 2-21, I added July with no data and August with data to show you that the chart captures any new records and automatically plots the data given.

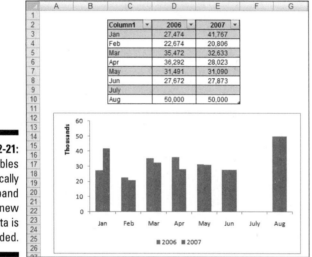

Figure 2-21: Excel tables automatically expand when new data is added.

Take a moment to think about what Excel tables mean to a data model. They mean pivot tables that never have to be reconfigured, charts that automatically capture new data, and ranges that automatically keep up with changes.

Converting an Excel table back to a range

If you want to convert an Excel table back to a normal range, you can follow these steps:

1. **Place your cursor in any cell inside the Excel table and select the Table Tools Design sub tab in the Ribbon.**

   2. **Click the Convert to Range button, as shown in Figure 2-22.**

   3. **When asked if you're sure (via a message box), click the Yes button.**

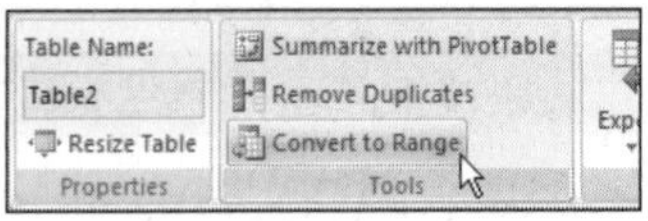

Figure 2-22:
To remove
Excel table
functionality,
convert the
table back
to a range.

Part II
Building Basic Dashboard Components

The 5th Wave   By Rich Tennant

"My girlfriend ran a spreadsheet of my life, and generated this chart. My best hope is that she'll change her major from 'Computer Sciences' to 'Rehabilitative Services.'"

In this part . . .

*I*n this section, you take an in-depth look at some of the basic dashboard components you can create using Excel 2007. You start with Chapter 3, where I introduce you to pivot tables and discuss how a pivot table can play an integral role in Excel-based dashboards. Chapter 4 provides a primer on building charts in Excel 2007, giving beginners a solid understanding of how Excel charts work. Chapter 5 introduces you to the new and improved conditional formatting functionality found in Excel 2007. In that chapter, I present several ideas for using the new conditional formatting tools in dashboards and reports. In Chapter 6, I explore the various techniques that can be used to create dynamic labels, allowing for the creation of a whole new layer of visualization.

Chapter 3

The Pivotal Pivot Table

1 know what you're thinking. Am I supposed to be jumping right in with pivot tables? My answer is an emphatic yes!

In Chapter 2, you were introduced to the concept of reporting models that separate the data, analysis, and presentation layers. As you will discover in this chapter, pivot tables lend themselves nicely to this concept. With pivot tables, you can build reporting models that not only can be easy to set up, but can be refreshed with a simple press of a button. This allows you to spend less time maintaining your dashboards and reports and more time doing other useful things. No utility in the whole of Excel allows you to achieve this efficient data model better than a pivot table.

For those who are new to pivot tables, relax a bit. After going through this introduction, you'll be pleasantly surprised at how easy it is to create and use pivot tables. Later, you'll find some time-saving techniques to help create some useful pivot-driven views for your dashboards and reports.

An Introduction to the Pivot Table

A *pivot table* is a robust tool that allows you to create an interactive view of your dataset, commonly referred to as a *pivot table report*. With a pivot table report, you can quickly and easily categorize your data into groups, summarize large amounts of data into meaningful analyses, and interactively perform a wide variety of calculations.

Pivot tables get their name from their ability to drag and drop fields within the pivot table report to dynamically change (or *pivot*) perspective and give you an entirely new analysis using the same data source.

Think of a pivot table as an object you can point at your dataset. When you look at your dataset through a pivot table, you can see your data from different perspectives. The dataset itself doesn't change, and it's not connected to the pivot table. The pivot table is simply a tool you are using to dynamically change analyses, apply varying calculations, and interactively drill down to the detail records.

The reason a pivot table is so well suited for dashboarding and reporting is that you can refresh the analyses shown through your pivot table by simply updating the dataset it is pointed to. This allows you to set up your analysis and presentation layers only one time; then, to refresh your reporting mechanism, all you have to do is press a button.

Let's start this exploration of pivot tables with a lesson on the anatomy of a pivot table.

The Four Areas of a Pivot Table

A pivot table is composed of four areas. The data you place in these areas defines both the utility and appearance of the pivot table. Take a moment to understand the function of each of these four areas.

Values area

The *values area,* as shown in Figure 3-1, is the large rectangular area below and to the right of the column and row headings. In this example, the values area contains a sum of the values in the Sales Amount field.

Region	(All)			

Sales Amount	Segment			
Market	Accessories	Bikes	Clothing	Components
Australia	23,974	1,351,873	43,232	203,791
Canada	119,303	11,714,700	383,022	2,246,255
Central	46,551	6,782,978	155,874	947,448
France	48,942	3,597,879	129,508	871,125
Germany	35,681	1,602,487	75,593	337,787
Northeast	51,246	5,690,285	163,442	1,051,702
Northwest	53,308	10,484,495	201,052	1,784,207
Southeast	45,736	6,737,556	165,689	959,337
Southwest	110,080	15,430,281	364,099	2,693,568
United Kingdom	43,180	3,435,134	120,225	712,588

Values area

Figure 3-1: The values area of a pivot table calculates and counts data.

The values area is the area that calculates and counts data. The data fields that you drag and drop here are typically those that you want to measure — fields, such as Sum of Revenue, Count of Units, or Average of Price.

Row area

The *row area* is shown in Figure 3-2. Placing a data field into the row area displays the unique values from that field down the rows of the left side of the pivot table. The row area typically has at least one field, although it's possible to have no fields.

Region	(All)			

Sales Amount	Segment			
Market	Accessories	Bikes	Clothing	Components
Australia	23,974	1,351,873	43,232	203,791
Canada	119,303	11,714,700	383,022	2,246,255
Central	46,551	6,782,978	155,874	947,448
France	48,942	3,597,879	129,508	871,125
Germany	35,681	1,602,487	75,593	337,787
Northeast	51,246	5,690,285	163,442	1,051,702
Northwest	53,308	10,484,495	201,052	1,784,207
Southeast	45,736	6,737,556	165,689	959,337
Southwest	110,080	15,430,281	364,099	2,693,568
United Kingdom	43,180	3,435,134	120,225	712,588

Row area

Figure 3-2: The row area of a pivot table gives you a row-oriented perspective.

The types of data fields that you would drop here include those that you want to group and categorize, such as, Products, Names, and Locations.

Column area

The *column area* is composed of headings that stretch across the top of columns in the pivot table.

As you can see in Figure 3-3, the column area stretches across the top of the columns. In this example, it contains the unique list of business segments.

Placing a data field into the column area displays the unique values from that field in a column-oriented perspective. The column area is ideal for creating a data matrix or showing trends over time.

Column area

Region	(All) ⬇

Sales Amount	Segment ⬇			
Market ⬇	Accessories	Bikes	Clothing	Components
Australia	23,974	1,351,873	43,232	203,791
Canada	119,303	11,714,700	383,022	2,246,255
Central	46,551	6,782,978	155,874	947,448
France	48,942	3,597,879	129,508	871,125
Germany	35,681	1,602,487	75,593	337,787
Northeast	51,246	5,690,285	163,442	1,051,702
Northwest	53,308	10,484,495	201,052	1,784,207
Southeast	45,736	6,737,556	165,689	959,337
Southwest	110,080	15,430,281	364,099	2,693,568
United Kingdom	43,180	3,435,134	120,225	712,588

Figure 3-3: The column area of a pivot table gives you a column-oriented perspective.

Filter area

The *filter area* is an optional set of one or more drop-downs at the top of the pivot table. In Figure 3-4, the filter area contains the Region field, and the pivot table is set to show all regions.

Placing data fields into the filter area allows you to filter the entire pivot table based on your selections. The types of data fields that you'd drop here include those that you want to isolate and focus on; for example, Region, Line of Business, and Employees.

Filter area

Region	(All) ▾		

Sales Amount	Segment ▾		
Market ▾	Accessories	Bikes	Clothing	Components
Australia	23,974	1,351,873	43,232	203,791
Canada	119,303	11,714,700	383,022	2,246,255
Central	46,551	6,782,978	155,874	947,448
France	48,942	3,597,879	129,508	871,125
Germany	35,681	1,602,487	75,593	337,787
Northeast	51,246	5,690,285	163,442	1,051,702
Northwest	53,308	10,484,495	201,052	1,784,207
Southeast	45,736	6,737,556	165,689	959,337
Southwest	110,080	15,430,281	364,099	2,693,568
United Kingdom	43,180	3,435,134	120,225	712,588

Figure 3-4:
The Filter Area allows you to easily apply filters to your pivot table report.

Creating Your First Pivot Table

If you've followed along so far, you now have a good understanding of the basic structure of a pivot table, so let's quit all the talking and use the following steps to walk through the creation of your first pivot table:

You can find the sample file for this chapter on this book's companion Web site.

1. **Click any single cell inside your *data source* (the table you'll use to feed the pivot table).**

2. **Select the Insert tab in the Ribbon. Here, find the PivotTable icon, as shown in Figure 3-5. Choose PivotTable from the drop-down list beneath the icon.**

   This activates the Create PivotTable dialog box, as shown in Figure 3-6. As you can see, this dialog box asks you to specify the location of your source data and the place you want to put the pivot table.

   Notice that in the Create PivotTable dialog box, Excel makes an attempt to fill in the range of your data for you. In most cases, Excel gets this right. However, always make sure the correct range is selected.

Figure 3-5:
Start a pivot table via the Insert tab.

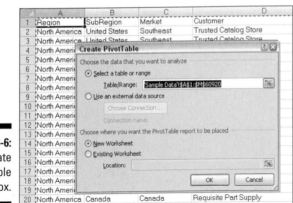

You will also note in Figure 3-6 that the default location for a new pivot table is New Worksheet. This means your pivot table will be placed in a new worksheet within the current workbook. You can change this by selecting the Existing Worksheet option and specifying the worksheet you want the pivot table to be placed.

 3. Click OK.

At this point, you have an empty pivot table report on a new worksheet. Next to the empty pivot table, you see the PivotTable Field List dialog box, shown in Figure 3-7.

The idea here is to add the fields you need into the pivot table by using the four *drop zones* found in the PivotTable Field List — Report Filter, Column Labels, Row Labels, and Values. Pleasantly enough, these drop zones correspond to the four areas of the pivot table you review at the beginning of this chapter.

If clicking the pivot table doesn't activate the PivotTable Field List dialog box, you can manually activate it by right-clicking anywhere inside the pivot table and selecting Show Field List.

Now before you go wild and start dropping fields into the various drop zones, it's important that you ask yourself two questions; "What am I measuring?" and "How do I want to see it?." The answer to these questions gives you some guidance when determining which fields go where.

For your first pivot table report, you want to measure the dollar sales by market. This automatically tells you that you will need to work with the Sales Amount field and the Market field.

How do you want to see that? You want markets to go down the left side of the report and sales amount to be calculated next to each market. Remembering the four areas of the pivot table, you'll need to add the Market field to the Row Labels drop zone, and the Sales Amount field to the Values drop zone.

4. **Find the Market field in field selector and place a check next to it, as demonstrated in Figure 3-8.**

   Now that you have regions in your pivot table, it's time to add the dollar sales.

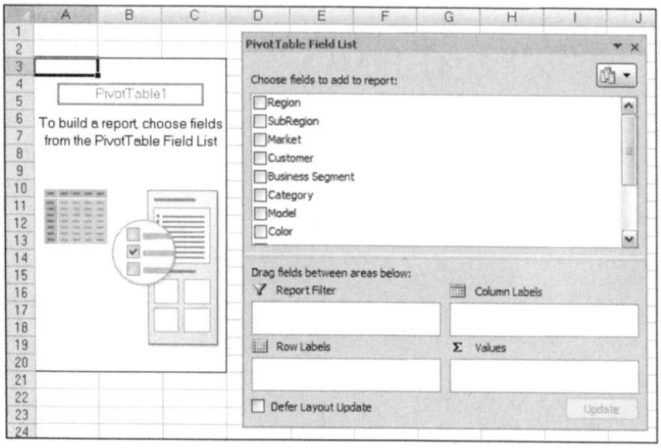

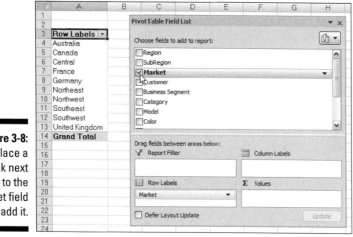

Figure 3-7: The PivotTable Field List dialog box.

Figure 3-8: Place a check next to the Market field to add it.

5. Find the Sales Amount field in field selector and place a check next to it, as demonstrated in Figure 3-9.

Figure 3-9:
Add the
Sales
Amount
field.

Placing a check next to any field that is *non-numeric* (text or date) automatically places that field into the row area of the pivot table. Placing a check next to any field that is *numeric* automatically places that field in the values area of the pivot table.

What happens if you need fields in the other areas of the pivot table? Well, instead of checking the field, you can drag any field directly to the different drop zones.

One more thing; when you add fields to the drop zones, you may find it difficult to see all the fields in each drop zone. You can expand the PivotTable Field List dialog box by clicking and dragging the borders of the dialog box.

As you can see, you have just analyzed the sales for each market in just five steps! That's an amazing feat considering you start with over 60,000 rows of data. With a little formatting, this modest pivot table can become the starting point for a management dashboard or report.

Changing and rearranging your pivot table

Now here's the wonderful thing about pivot tables. You can add as many layers of analysis as made possible by the fields in your source data table. Say that you want to show the dollar sales each market earned by business segment. Because your pivot table already contains the Market and Sales Amount fields, all you have to add the Business Segment field.

So simply click anywhere on your pivot table to reactivate the PivotTable Field List dialog box and then place a check next to the Business Segment field. Figure 3-10 illustrates what your pivot table should look like now.

If clicking the pivot table doesn't activate the PivotTable Field List dialog box, you can manually activate it by right-clicking anywhere inside the pivot table and selecting Show Field List.

Imagine that your manager says that this layout doesn't work for him. He wants to see business segments going across the top of the pivot table report. No problem. Simply drag the Business Segment field from the Row Labels drop zone to the Column Labels drop zone. As you can see in Figure 3-11, this instantly restructures the pivot table to his specifications.

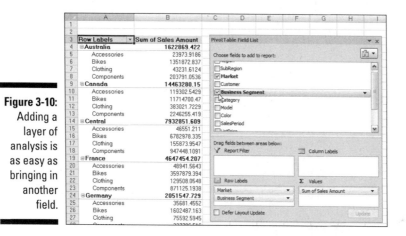

Figure 3-10: Adding a layer of analysis is as easy as bringing in another field.

Figure 3-11: Your business segments are now column oriented.

Adding a report filter

Often times, you're asked to produce reports for one particular region, market, product, and so on. Instead of working hours and hours building separate reports for every possible analysis scenario, you can leverage pivot tables to help create multiple views of the same data. For example, you can do so by creating a region filter in your pivot table.

Click anywhere on your pivot table to reactivate the PivotTable Field List dialog box and then drag the Region field to the Report Filter drop zone. This adds a drop-down selector to your pivot table, shown in Figure 3-12. You can then use this selector to analyze one particular region at a time.

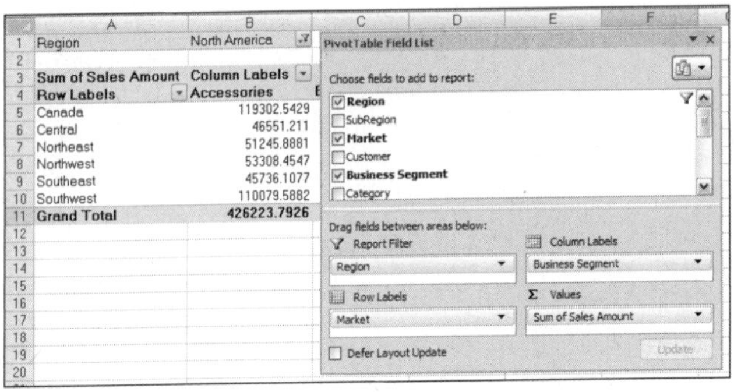

Figure 3-12:
Using pivot tables to analyze regions.

Keeping your pivot table fresh

In Hollywood, it's important to stay fresh and relevant. As boring as your pivot tables may seem, they'll eventually become the stars of your reports and dashboards. So it's just as important to keep your pivot tables fresh and relevant.

As time goes by, your data may change and grow with newly-added rows and columns. The action of updating your pivot table with these changes is *refreshing* your data.

Your pivot table report can be refreshed by simply right-clicking inside your pivot table report and selecting Refresh, as demonstrated in Figure 3-13.

Sometimes, *you're* the data source that feeds your pivot table changes in structure. For example, you may have added or deleted rows or columns from your data table. These types of changes affect the range of your data source, not just a few data items in the table.

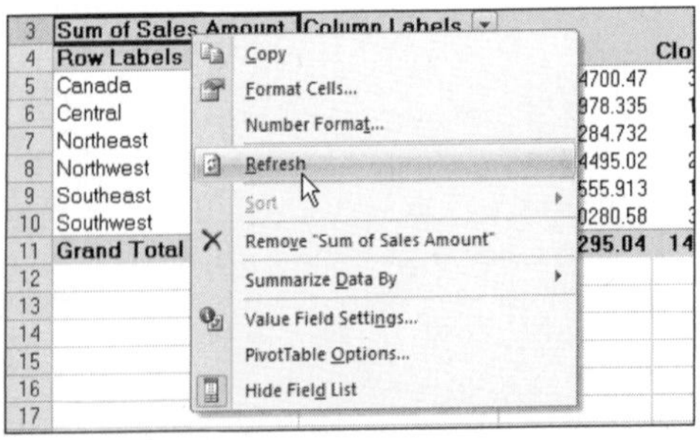

Figure 3-13:
Refreshing your pivot table captures changes made to your data.

Pivot tables and spreadsheet bloat

It's important to understand that pivot tables do come with space and memory implications for your reporting processes. When you create a pivot table, Excel takes a snapshot of your dataset and stores it in a pivot cache. A *pivot cache* is essentially a memory container that holds this snapshot of your dataset. Each pivot table report you create from a separate data source creates its own pivot cache, which increases your workbook's memory usage and file size. The increase in memory usage and file size depends on the size of the original data source that is being duplicated to create the pivot cache.

Simple enough, right? Well here's the rub: You often need to create separate pivot tables from the same data source in order to analyze the same data in different ways. If you create two pivot tables from the data source, a new pivot cache is automatically created even though one may already exist for the dataset being used. This means that you're bloating your spreadsheet with redundant data each time you create a new pivot table using the same dataset.

To work around this potential problem, you can employ Copy and then Paste. That's right; simply copying a pivot table and pasting it somewhere else will create another pivot table, *without* duplicating the pivot cache. This allows you to create multiple pivot tables that use the same source data, with negligible increase in memory and file size.

In these cases, performing a simple Refresh of your pivot table won't do. You have to update the range being captured by the pivot table. Here's how:

1. **Click anywhere inside your pivot table to activate the PivotTable Tools context tab in the Ribbon.**

2. **Select the Options tab in the Ribbon.**

3. **Click the Change Data Source button, as demonstrated in Figure 3-14.**

   The Change PivotTable Data Source dialog box appears.

4. **Change the range selection to include any new rows or columns. (See Figure 3-15.)**

5. **Click OK to apply the change.**

Figure 3-14: Changing the range that feeds your pivot table.

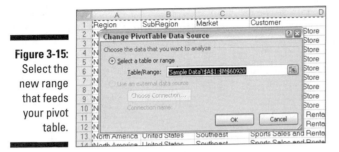

Figure 3-15: Select the new range that feeds your pivot table.

Customizing Your Pivot Table Reports

The pivot tables you create often need to be tweaked in order to get the look and feel you're looking for. In this section, I cover some of the options you can adjust to customize your pivot tables to suit your reporting needs.

Changing the pivot table layout

Unlike the previous versions of Excel, Excel 2007 gives you a choice in the layout of your data in a pivot table. The three layouts, shown side by side in Figure 3-16, are the Compact Form, Outline Form, and Tabular Form. Although no layout stands out as being better than the others, I prefer using the Tabular Form layout because it seems easiest to read, and it's the layout that most people who have seen pivot tables in the past are used to.

Compact Form Layout

Row Labels	Sales
Australia	1622869.422
Accessories	23973.9186
Bikes	1351872.837
Clothing	43231.6124
Components	203791.0536
Canada	14463280.15
Accessories	119302.5429
Bikes	11714700.47
Clothing	383021.7229
Components	2246255.419
Central	7932851.609
Accessories	46551.211
Bikes	6782978.335
Clothing	155873.9547
Components	947448.1091
France	4647454.207
Accessories	48941.5643
Bikes	3597879.394
Clothing	129508.0548
Components	871125.1938
Germany	2051547.729
Accessories	35681.4552
Bikes	1602487.163
Clothing	75592.5945
Components	337786.516

Outline Form Layout

Market	Segment	Sales
Australia		1622869.422
	Accessories	23973.9186
	Bikes	1351872.837
	Clothing	43231.6124
	Components	203791.0536
Canada		14463280.15
	Accessories	119302.5429
	Bikes	11714700.47
	Clothing	383021.7229
	Components	2246255.419
Central		7932851.609
	Accessories	46551.211
	Bikes	6782978.335
	Clothing	155873.9547
	Components	947448.1091
France		4647454.207
	Accessories	48941.5643
	Bikes	3597879.394
	Clothing	129508.0548
	Components	871125.1938
Germany		2051547.729
	Accessories	35681.4552
	Bikes	1602487.163
	Clothing	75592.5945
	Components	337786.516

Tabular Form Layout

Market	Segment	Sales
Australia	Accessories	23973.9186
	Bikes	1351872.837
	Clothing	43231.6124
	Components	203791.0536
Australia Total		1622869.422
Canada	Accessories	119302.5429
	Bikes	11714700.47
	Clothing	383021.7229
	Components	2246255.419
Canada Total		14463280.15
Central	Accessories	46551.211
	Bikes	6782978.335
	Clothing	155873.9547
	Components	947448.1091
Central Total		7932851.609
France	Accessories	48941.5643
	Bikes	3597879.394
	Clothing	129508.0548
	Components	871125.1938
France Total		4647454.207
Germany	Accessories	35681.4552
	Bikes	1602487.163
	Clothing	75592.5945
	Components	337786.516
Germany Total		2051547.729

Figure 3-16: The three layouts for a pivot table report.

The layout you choose not only affects the look and feel of your reporting mechanisms, but it may also affect the way you build and interact with any dashboard models based on your pivot tables.

Changing the layout of a pivot table is easy. Follow these steps:

1. **Click anywhere inside your pivot table to activate the PivotTable Tools context tab in the Ribbon.**

2. **Select the Design tab in the Ribbon.**

3. **Click the Report Layout icon and choose the layout you like. (See Figure 3-17.)**

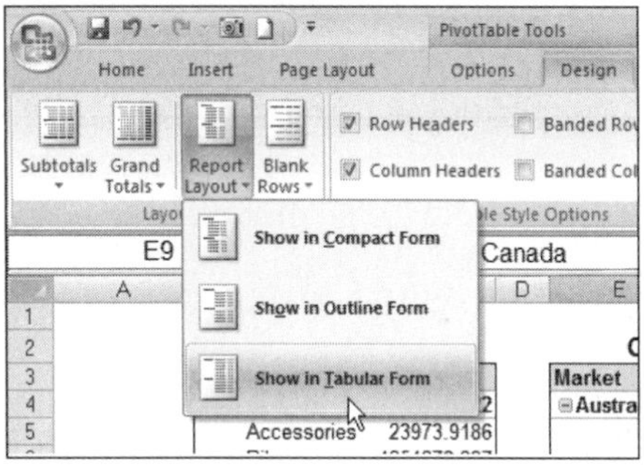

Figure 3-17: Changing the layout for your pivot table.

Customizing field names

Notice that every field in your pivot table has a name. The fields in the row, column, and filter areas inherit their names from the data labels in your source table. The fields in the Values area are given a name, such as Sum of Sales Amount.

There will often be times when you might prefer the name Total Sales instead of the unattractive default name, like Sum of Sales Amount. In these situations, the ability to change your field names is handy. To change a field name, do the following:

1. **Right-click any value within the target field.**

   For example, if you want to change the name of the field Sum of Sales Amount, you right-click any value under that field.

2. **Select Value Field Settings. (See Figure 3-18.)**

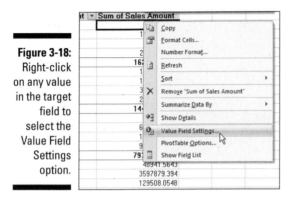

Figure 3-18:
Right-click
on any value
in the target
field to
select the
Value Field
Settings
option.

The Value Field Settings dialog box appears.

Note that if you were changing the name of a field in the row or column area, this selection is Field Settings.

3. Enter the new name in the Custom Name input box. (See Figure 3-19.)

Figure 3-19:
Use the
Custom
Name input
to change
the name of
the field.

4. Click OK to apply the change.

If you use the name of the data label used in your source table, you receive an error. For example, if you rename Sum of Sales Amount as Sales Amount, you get an error message because there's already a Sales Amount field in the source data table. Well, this is kinda lame, especially if Sales Amount is exactly what you want to name the field in your pivot table.

To get around this, you can name the field and add a space to the end of the name. Excel considers Sales Amount (followed by a space) to be different from Sales Amount. This way you can use the name you want, and no one will notice it's any different.

Applying numeric formats to data fields

Numbers in pivot tables can be formatted to fit your needs (that is, formatted as currency, percentage, or number). You can easily control the numeric formatting of a field using the Value Field Settings dialog box. Here's how:

1. **Right-click any value within the target field.**

   For example, if you want to change the format of the values in the Sales Amount field, right-click any value under that field.

2. **Select Value Field Settings.**

   The Value Field Settings dialog box appears.

3. **Click the Number Format.**

   The Format Cells dialog box opens.

4. **Apply the number format you desire, just as you normally would on your spreadsheet.**

5. **Click OK to apply the changes.**

   After you set the formatting for a field the applied formatting will persist even if you refresh or rearrange your pivot table.

Changing summary calculations

When creating your pivot table report, Excel will, by default, summarize your data by either counting or summing the items. Instead of Sum or Count, you might want to choose functions, such as Average, Min, Max, and so on. In all, 11 options are available, including

- ✔ **Sum:** Adds all numeric data.
- ✔ **Count:** Counts all data items within a given field, including numeric-, text-, and date-formatted cells.
- ✔ **Average:** Calculates an average for the target data items.
- ✔ **Max:** Displays the largest value in the target data items.
- ✔ **Min:** Displays the smallest value in the target data items.
- ✔ **Product:** Multiplies all target data items together.
- ✔ **Count Nums:** Counts only the numeric cells in the target data items.
- ✔ **StdDevP and StdDev:** Calculates the standard deviation for the target data items. Use StdDevP if your dataset contains the complete population. Use StdDev if your dataset contains a sample of the population.

✔ **VarP** and **Var:** Calculates the statistical variance for the target data items. Use `VarP` if your data contains a complete population. If your data contains only a sampling of the complete population, use `Var` to estimate the variance.

You can easily change the summary calculation for any given field by taking the following actions:

1. **Right-click any value within the target field.**

2. **Select Value Field Settings.**

   The Value Field Settings dialog box appears.

3. **Choose the type of calculation you want to use from the list of calculations. (See Figure 3-20.)**

4. **Click OK to apply the changes.**

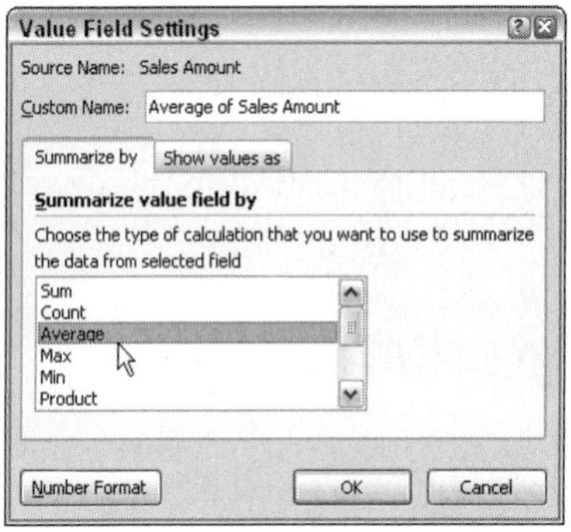

Figure 3-20:
Changing
the type of
summary
calculation
used in
a field.

Did you know that a single blank cell causes Excel to count instead of sum? That's right. If all the cells in a column contain numeric data, Excel chooses Sum. If just one cell is either blank or contains text, Excel chooses Count.

Be sure to pay attention to the fields that you place into the values area of the pivot table. If the field name starts with Count Of, Excel's counting the items in the field instead of summing the values.

Suppressing subtotals

Notice that each time you add a field to your pivot table, Excel adds a subtotal for that field. There may be, however, times when the inclusion of subtotals either doesn't make sense or just hinders a clear view of your pivot table report. For example, Figure 3-21 shows a pivot table where the subtotals inundate the report with totals that serve only to hide the real data you're trying to report.

Region	SubRegion	Market	Business Segment	Sum of Sales Amount
North America	United States	Central	Accessories	$46,551
			Bikes	$6,782,978
			Clothing	$155,874
			Components	$947,448
		Central Total		$7,932,852
		Northeast	Accessories	$51,246
			Bikes	$5,690,285
			Clothing	$163,442
			Components	$1,051,702
		Northeast Total		$6,956,674
		Northwest	Accessories	$53,308
			Bikes	$10,484,495
			Clothing	$201,052
			Components	$1,784,207
		Northwest Total		$12,523,063
		Southeast	Accessories	$45,736
			Bikes	$6,737,556
			Clothing	$165,689
			Components	$959,337
		Southeast Total		$7,908,318
		Southwest	Accessories	$110,080
			Bikes	$15,430,281
			Clothing	$364,099
			Components	$2,693,568
		Southwest Total		$18,598,027
	United States Total			$53,918,934
North America Total				$53,918,934
Grand Total				$53,918,934

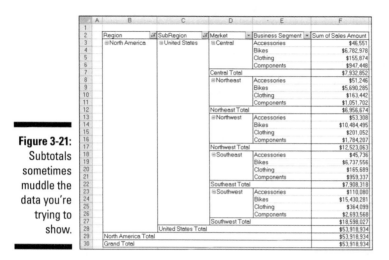

Figure 3-21: Subtotals sometimes muddle the data you're trying to show.

Removing all subtotals at one time

You can remove all subtotals at once by taking these actions:

1. **Click anywhere inside your pivot table to activate the PivotTable Tools context tab in the Ribbon.**
2. **Select the Design tab in the Ribbon.**
3. **Click the Subtotals icon and select Do Not Show Subtotals. (See Figure 3-22.)**

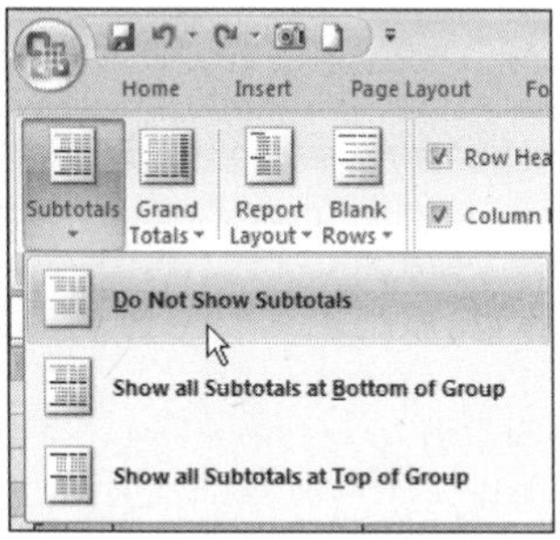

Figure 3-22: Use the Do Not Show Subtotals option to remove all subtotals at once.

As you can see in Figure 3-23, the same report without subtotals is much more pleasant to review.

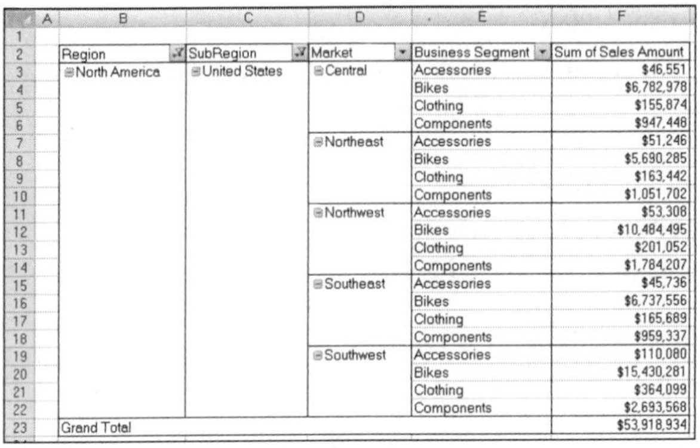

	A	B	C	D	E	F
1						
2		Region	SubRegion	Market	Business Segment	Sum of Sales Amount
3		North America	United States	Central	Accessories	$46,551
4					Bikes	$6,782,978
5					Clothing	$155,874
6					Components	$947,448
7				Northeast	Accessories	$51,246
8					Bikes	$5,690,285
9					Clothing	$163,442
10					Components	$1,051,702
11				Northwest	Accessories	$53,308
12					Bikes	$10,484,495
13					Clothing	$201,052
14					Components	$1,784,207
15				Southeast	Accessories	$45,736
16					Bikes	$6,737,556
17					Clothing	$165,689
18					Components	$959,337
19				Southwest	Accessories	$110,080
20					Bikes	$15,430,281
21					Clothing	$364,099
22					Components	$2,693,568
23		Grand Total				$53,918,934

Figure 3-23:
The same
report
without
subtotals.

Removing the subtotals for only one field

Maybe you want to remove the subtotals for only one field? In such a case, you can take the following actions:

1. **Right-click any value within the target field.**

2. **Select Field Settings.**

   The Field Settings dialog box appears.

3. **Choose the None button under the Subtotals option, as demonstrated in Figure 3-24.**

4. **Click OK to apply the changes.**

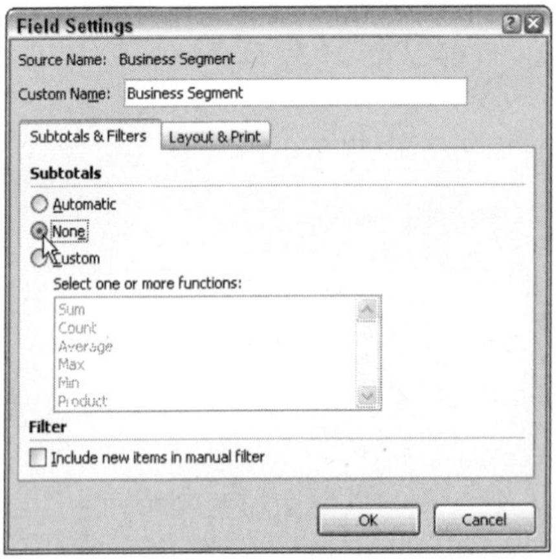

Figure 3-24:
Choose the
None option
to remove
subtotals for
one field.

Removing Grand Totals

There may be instances when you want to remove the Grand Totals from your pivot table.

1. **Right-click anywhere on your pivot table.**

2. **Select PivotTable Options.**

   The Options dialog box appears.

3. **Click the Totals & Filters tab.**

4. **Remove the check from Show Grand Totals for Rows.**

5. **Remove the check from Show Grand Totals for Columns.**

Showing and hiding data items

A pivot table summarizes and displays all the records in your source data table. There may, however, be situations when you want to inhibit certain data items from being included in your pivot table summary. In these situations, you can choose to hide a data item.

In terms of pivot tables, hiding doesn't just mean preventing the data item from being shown on the report, hiding a data item also prevents it from being factored into the summary calculations.

In the pivot table illustrated in Figure 3-25, I show sales amounts for all Business Segments by Market. In this example, however, I want to show totals without taking sales from the Bikes segment into consideration. In other words, I want to hide the Bikes segment.

Figure 3-25: I want to remove Bikes from this analysis.

	A	B	C
1			
2	Market	Business Segment	Sum of Sales Amount
3	⊟Australia	Accessories	$23,974
4		Bikes	$1,351,873
5		Clothing	$43,232
6		Components	$203,791
7	Australia Total		$1,622,869
8	⊟Canada	Accessories	$119,303
9		Bikes	$11,714,700
10		Clothing	$383,022
11		Components	$2,246,255
12	Canada Total		$14,463,280
13	⊟Central	Accessories	$46,551
14		Bikes	$6,782,978
15		Clothing	$155,874
16		Components	$947,448
17	Central Total		$7,932,852

I can hide the Bikes Business Segment by clicking the Business Segment drop-down list arrow and removing the check next to Bikes (see Figure 3-26).

After choosing OK to close the selection box, the pivot table instantly recalculates, leaving out the Bikes segment. As you can see in Figure 3-27, the Market totals sales now reflect the sales without Bikes.

I can just as quickly reinstate all hidden data items for my field. I simply click the Business Segment drop-down list arrow and place a check next to the Select All selection (see Figure 3-28).

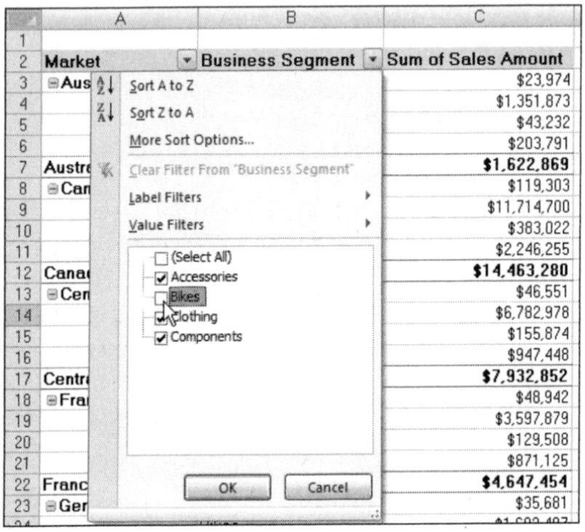

Figure 3-26: Removing the check from the Bikes item hides the Bikes segment.

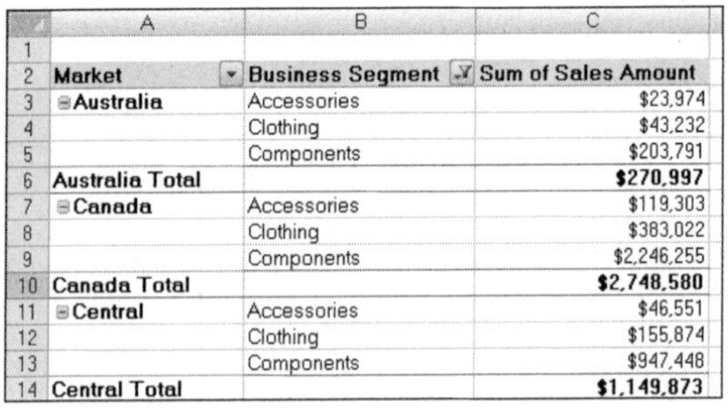

Figure 3-27: Segment analysis without the Bikes segment.

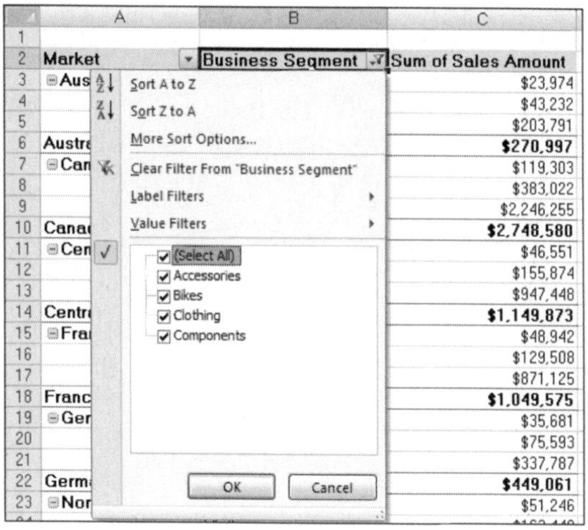

Figure 3-28: Placing a check next to Select All forces all data items in that field to become unhidden.

Hiding or showing items without data

By default, your pivot table shows only data items that have data. This inherent behavior may cause unintended problems for your data analysis.

Look at Figure 3-29, which shows a pivot table with the SalesPeriod field in the row area and the Region field in the filter area. Note that the Region field is set to (All), and every sales period appears in the report.

Region	(All)
SalesPeriod	**Sum of Sales Amount**
1/1/2004	$1,670,606
2/1/2004	$2,708,046
3/1/2004	$2,742,965
4/1/2004	$2,219,217
5/1/2004	$3,329,835
6/1/2004	$1,575,999
7/1/2004	$2,341,748
8/1/2004	$1,540,073
9/1/2004	$1,166,333
10/1/2004	$844,833
11/1/2004	$2,325,757
12/1/2004	$1,703,437
Grand Total	**$24,168,848**

Figure 3-29: All sales periods are showing.

If I choose to filter for only Europe in the filter area, you will notice that only a portion of all the sales periods are now showing. (See Figure 3-30.) The pivot table suddenly shows only those sales periods that apply to the Europe region.

Figure 3-30:
Filtering for
the Europe
region
causes
some of the
sales
periods to
disappear.

	A	B
1		
2	Region	Europe
3		
4	SalesPeriod	Sum of Sales Amount
5	1/1/2004	$240,541
6	2/1/2004	$769,615
7	3/1/2004	$536,571
8	4/1/2004	$333,899
9	5/1/2004	$1,002,925
10	6/1/2004	$275,767
11	7/1/2004	$407,807
12	Grand Total	$3,567,125
13		

The behavior of displaying only those items with data could cause trouble if I plan on using this pivot table as the feeder for my charts or other dashboard components. From a dashboarding-and-reporting perspective, it isn't ideal if half the year disappeared each time customers selected Europe.

Here's how you can prevent Excel from hiding pivot items without data:

1. **Right-click any value within the target field.**

   In this example, the target field is the SalesPeriod field.

2. **Select Field Settings.**

   The Field Settings dialog box appears.

3. **Select the Layout & Print tab in the Field Settings dialog box.**

4. **Place a check next to the Show Items with No Data option. (See Figure 3-31.)**

5. **Click OK to apply the change.**

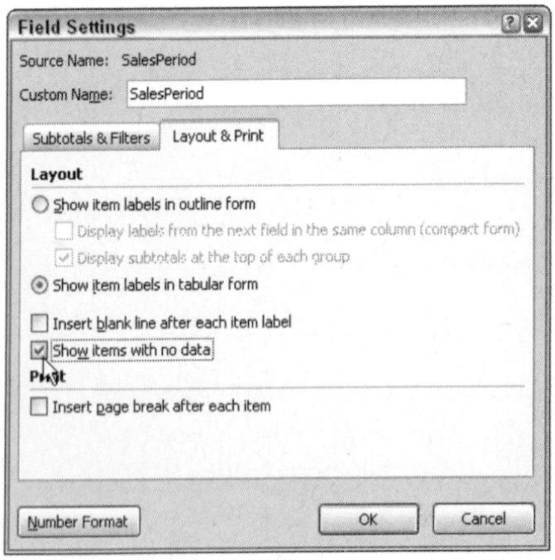

Figure 3-31:
Click the
Show Items
with No
Data option
to force the
display all
data items.

As you can see in Figure 3-32, after choosing the Show Items with No Data option, all the sales periods appear whether the selected region had sales that period or not.

Now that I'm confident that the structure of the pivot table is locked, I can use it to feed charts and other components in my dashboard.

Figure 3-32:
All sales
periods are
now
displayed
even if there
is no data to
be shown.

Sorting your pivot table

By default, items in each pivot field are sorted in ascending sequence based on the item name. Excel gives you the freedom to change the sort order of the items in your pivot table.

Like many actions you can perform in Excel, there are lots of different ways to sort data within a pivot table. The easiest way, and the way that I use the most, is to apply the sort directly in the pivot table. Here's how:

1. **Right-click any value within the *target field* (the field you need to sort).**

   In the example shown in Figure 3-33, I want to sort by Sales Amount.

2. **Select Sort and then select the sort direction.**

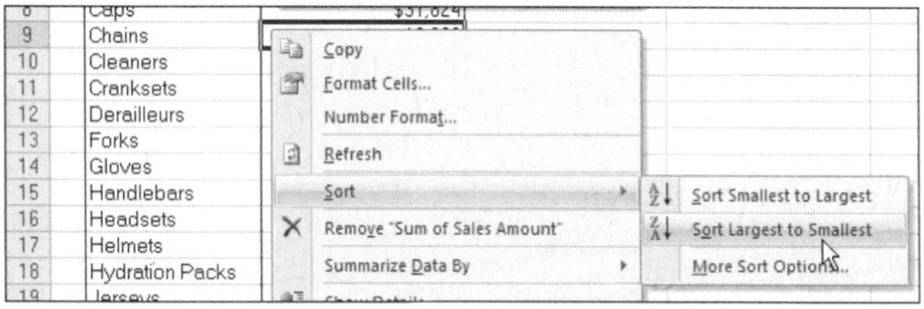

Figure 3-33:
Applying a
sort to a
pivot table
field.

The changes take effect immediately and persist while you work with your pivot table.

Creating Useful Pivot-Driven Views

At this point in your exploration of pivot tables, you have covered enough of the fundamentals to start creating your own pivot table reports. In this last section, I share with you a few of the techniques I use to create some of the more useful report views. Although you could create these views by hand, creating them with pivot tables helps save you hours of work and allows you to more easily update and maintain them.

Producing top and bottom views

You'll often find that managers are interested in the top and bottom of things: the top 50 customers, the bottom 5 sales reps, the top 10 products. Although you may think this is because managers have the attention span of a four-year-old, there's a more logical reason for focusing on the outliers.

Dashboarding and reporting is often about showing actionable data. If you, as a manager, know who the bottom ten revenue-generating accounts are, you could apply your effort and resources in building up those accounts. Because you most likely wouldn't have the resources to focus on all accounts, viewing a manageable subset of accounts would be more useful.

Luckily, pivot tables make it easy to filter your data for the top five, the bottom ten, or any conceivable combination of top or bottom records. Here's an example.

Imagine that in your company, the Accessories Business Segment is a high-margin business — you make the most profit for each dollar of sales in the Accessories segment. To increase sales, your manager wants to focus on the 50 customers who spend the least amount of money on Accessories. He obviously wants to spend his time and resources on getting those customers to buy more accessories. Here's what to do:

1. **Build a pivot table with Business Segment in the filter area, Customer in the row area, and Sales Amount in the values area (see Figure 3-34.) For cosmetic value, change the layout to Tabular Form.**

    You can find the sample file for this chapter on this book's companion Web site.

2. **Right-click any customer name in the Customer field, select Filter, and then Top 10 — as demonstrated in Figure 3-35.**

REMEMBER

Don't let the label *Top 10* confuse you. You can use the Top 10 option to filter both top and bottom records.

3. **In the Top 10 Filter dialog box, as illustrated in Figure 3-36, you simply have to define the view you're looking for. In this example, you want the bottom 50 items (customers), as defined by the Sum of Sales Amount field.**

4. **Click OK to apply the filter.**

	A	B
1	Business Segment	(All)
2		
3	Customer	Sum of Sales Amount
4	A Bike Store	85177.0812
5	A Great Bicycle Company	9055.2903
6	A Typical Bike Shop	83457.1089
7	Acceptable Sales & Service	1258.3767
8	Accessories Network	2215.8975
9	Acclaimed Bicycle Company	7682.28
10	Ace Bicycle Supply	3749.1338
11	Action Bicycle Specialists	328503.1613
12	Active Cycling	1805.454
13	Active Life Toys	200013.366
14	Active Systems	643.3457
15	Active Transport Inc.	88245.8727
16	Activity Center	42804.2561
17	Advanced Bike Components	363131.3817
18	Aerobic Exercise Company	2676.654
19	Affordable Sports Equipment	311446.431

Figure 3-34: Build this pivot table to start.

Figure 3-35: Select the Top 10 filter option.

	A	B	C	D
1	Business Segment	MS Sans ▾ 10 ▾ A̅ A̅ $ ✎		
2		B I ≡ ⊞ ▾ 🖌 ▾ A ▾ 📊		
3	Customer	Sum of Sales Amt		
4	A Bike Store	85177		
5	A Great Bicycle Company	📋 Copy		
6	A Typical Bike Shop	🖋 Format Cells...		
7	Acceptable Sales & Service			
8	Accessories Network	🔄 Refresh		
9	Acclaimed Bicycle Company	Sort ▸		
10	Ace Bicycle Supply			
11	Action Bicycle Specialists	Filter ▸	✎ Clear Filter From "Customer"	
12	Active Cycling	✓ Subtotal "Customer"	Keep Only Selected Items	
13	Active Life Toys		Hide Selected Items	
14	Active Systems	Expand/Collapse ▸		
15	Active Transport Inc.		Top 10...	
16	Activity Center	Group...	Label Filters...	
17	Advanced Bike Components	Ungroup...	Value Filters...	
18	Aerobic Exercise Company	Move ▸		

Figure 3-36: Specify the filter you want to apply.

Top 10 Filter (Customer)	? ✕
Show	
Bottom ▾	50 ⬍	Items ▾	by	Sum of Sales Amount ▾
	OK	Cancel

5. **In the filter area, click the drop-down button for the Business Segment field and select Change the Filter area. (See Figure 3-37.)**

   At this point, you have exactly what your manager has asked for — the 50 customers who spend the least amount of money on Accessories. You can go a step further and format the report a bit by sorting on the Sum of Sales Amount and applying a currency format to the numbers. (See Figure 3-38.)

Note that because you built this view using a pivot table, you can easily adapt your newly created report to create a whole new view. For example, you can add the Market field to the filter area to get the 50 United Kingdom customers who spend the least amount of money on Accessories. This, my friends, is the power of using pivot tables for the basis of your dashboards and reports. Continue to play around with the Top 10 Filter option to see what kind of reports you can come up with.

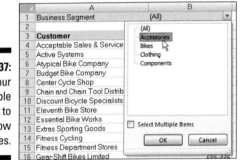

Figure 3-37: Filter your pivot table report to show Accessories.

	A	B
1	Business Segment	Accessories
2		
3	Customer	Sum of Sales Amount
4	Mobile Outlet	$1.37
5	Efficient Cycling	$1.37
6	Racing Bike Outlet	$1.37
7	Bike Goods	$1.37
8	Cycle Merchants	$1.37
9	Purchase Mart	$1.37
10	Vigorous Sports Store	$2.75
11	Closest Bicycle Store	$2.99
12	This Area Sporting Goods	$2.99
13	The Bicycle Accessories Company	$2.99
14	Novelty Bikes	$4.12
15	Bike Products and Accessories	$4.12
16	Roadway Bicycle Supply	$4.77
17	Transport Bikes	$4.77
18	Pretty Bikes and Toys	$4.77
19	Exemplary Cycles	$4.77
20	Executive Gift Store	$5.99

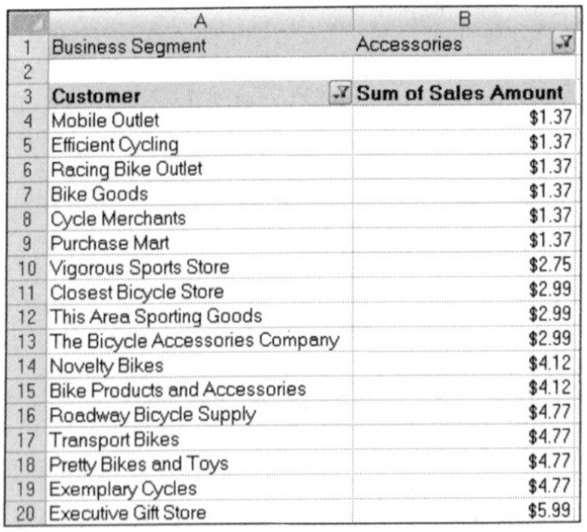

Figure 3-38: Your final report.

You may notice that in Figure 3-39, the bottom 50 report is showing only 23 records. This is because there are fewer than 50 customers in the United Kingdom market that have Accessories sales. Because I asked for the bottom 50, Excel shows up to 50 accounts, but fewer if there are fewer than 50. If there's a tie for any rank in the bottom 50, Excel shows you all the tied records.

You can remove the applied filters in your pivot tables by taking these actions:

1. **Click anywhere inside your pivot table to activate the PivotTable Tools context tab in the Ribbon.**

2. **Select the Options tab in the Ribbon.**

3. **Click the Clear icon and select Clear Filters, as demonstrated in Figure 3-40.**

Figure 3-39:
You can easily adapt this report to produce any combination of views.

	A	B
1	Market	United Kingdom
2	Business Segment	Accessories
3		
4	**Customer**	**Sum of Sales Amount**
5	Vigorous Sports Store	$2.75
6	Closest Bicycle Store	$2.99
7	Exclusive Bicycle Mart	$15.00
8	Extended Tours	$20.19
9	Instruments and Parts Company	$20.99
10	Tachometers and Accessories	$23.18
11	Metropolitan Bicycle Supply	$25.76
12	Number One Bike Co.	$29.73
13	Nearby Cycle Shop	$35.99
14	Metro Metals Co.	$46.11
15	Cycles Wholesaler & Mfg.	$375.53
16	Cycling Goods	$432.54
17	Exceptional Cycle Services	$757.72
18	Channel Outlet	$918.44
19	Express Bike Services	$1,718.19
20	Downhill Bicycle Specialists	$1,915.21
21	Uttermost Bike Shop	$3,806.93
22	Bulk Discount Store	$4,067.01
23	Commerce Bicycle Specialists	$4,435.70
24	Action Bicycle Specialists	$4,861.49
25	Exhibition Showroom	$5,723.12
26	Riding Cycles	$6,459.01
27	Prosperous Tours	$7,486.63
28	**Grand Total**	**$43,180.22**

Figure 3-40:
Select Clear Filters to clear the applied filters in a field.

Creating views by month, quarter, and year

Raw transactional data is rarely aggregated by month, quarter, or year for you. This type of data is often captured by the day. However, managers often want reports by month or quarters instead of detail by day. Fortunately, pivot tables make it easy to group date fields into various time dimensions. Here's how:

1. **Build a pivot table with Sales Date in the row area and Sales Amount in the values area; similar to the one in Figure 3-41.**

2. **Right-click any date and select Group, as demonstrated in Figure 3-42.**

	A	B
1		
2	SalesDate	Sum of Sales Amount
3	1/1/2002	$22,889.25
4	1/2/2002	$26,793.61
5	1/3/2002	$14,118.40
6	1/4/2002	$19,904.81
7	1/5/2002	$26,170.15
8	1/6/2002	$11,549.93
9	1/7/2002	$47,135.86
10	1/8/2002	$9,646.18
11	1/9/2002	$25,336.52
12	1/10/2002	$12,577.32
13	1/11/2002	$31,988.04
14	1/12/2002	$33,923.14
15	1/13/2002	$37,343.01

Figure 3-41: Build this pivot table to start.

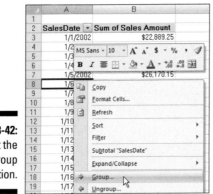

Figure 3-42: Select the Group option.

The Grouping dialog box appears, as shown in Figure 3-43.

3. **Select the time dimensions you want.**

In this example, you can select Months, Quarters, and Years.

4. **Click OK to apply the change.**

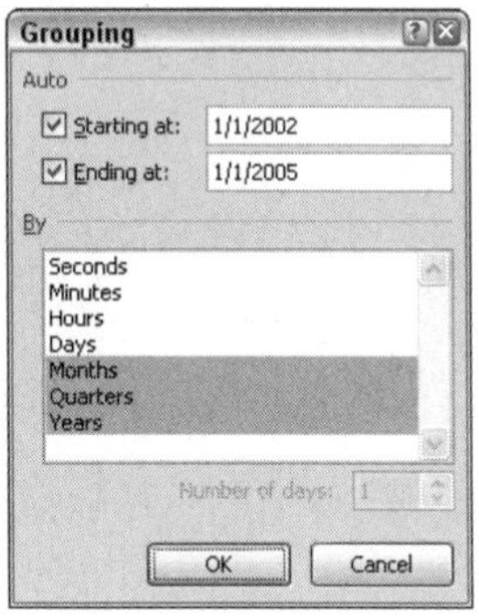

Figure 3-43:
Select the
time
dimensions
that suit
your needs.

Here are several interesting things to note about the resulting pivot table. First, notice that Quarters and Years have been added to your field list. Keep in mind that your source data hasn't changed to include these new fields; instead, these fields are now part of your pivot table. Another interesting thing to note is that by default, the Years and Quarters fields are automatically added next to the original date field in the pivot table layout, as shown in Figure 3-44.

After your date field is grouped, you can use each added time grouping just as you would any other field in your pivot table. In Figure 3-45, I use the newly created time groupings to show sales for each market by quarter for 2004.

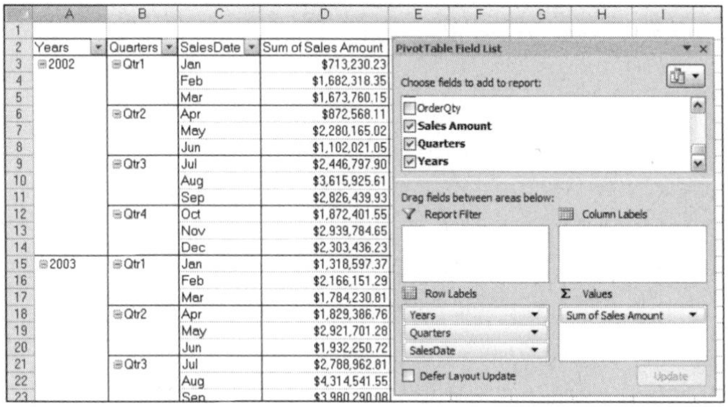

Figure 3-44:
Adding
Years and
Quarters
fields.

Figure 3-45: You can use your newly created time dimensions just like a normal pivot field.

	A	B	C	D	E	F
1						
2	Sum of Sales Amount	Years	Quarters			
3		2004				2004 Total
4	Market	Qtr1	Qtr2	Qtr3	Qtr4	
5	Australia	$340,521.71	$236,578.01	$170,142.42		$747,242.14
6	Canada	$1,024,563.94	$1,114,588.51	$884,515.64	$886,390.73	$3,910,058.83
7	Central	$626,423.96	$481,199.50	$565,002.03	$608,210.36	$2,280,835.85
8	France	$597,772.96	$680,722.44	$101,900.89		$1,380,396.29
9	Germany	$406,366.75	$399,498.00	$100,772.43		$906,637.18
10	Northeast	$475,563.24	$508,589.07	$288,912.08	$353,647.68	$1,626,712.07
11	Northwest	$1,166,060.82	$1,162,232.16	$931,870.76	$1,072,927.37	$4,333,091.10
12	Southeast	$500,399.17	$532,449.38	$719,665.56	$872,692.49	$2,625,206.61
13	Southwest	$1,441,357.21	$1,457,835.15	$1,069,881.55	$1,109,502.48	$5,078,576.39
14	United Kingdom	$542,586.65	$511,904.93	$225,600.34		$1,280,091.93
15						

Creating a percent distribution view

A percent distribution (or percent contribution) view allows you to see how much of the total is made up of a specific data item. This view is useful when you're trying to measure the general impact of a particular item.

The pivot table, as shown in Figure 3-46, gives you a view into the percent of sales that comes from each business segment. Here, you can tell that Bikes make up 81 percent of Canada's sales whereas only 77 percent of France's sales come from Bikes.

Figure 3-46: This view shows percent of total for the row.

	A	B	C	D	E	F
1	Region	(All)				
2						
3	Sales Amount	Segment				
4	Market	Accessories	Bikes	Clothing	Components	Grand Total
5	Australia	1%	83%	3%	13%	100%
6	Canada	1%	81%	3%	16%	100%
7	Central	1%	86%	2%	12%	100%
8	France	1%	77%	3%	19%	100%
9	Germany	2%	78%	4%	16%	100%
10	Northeast	1%	82%	2%	15%	100%
11	Northwest	0%	84%	2%	14%	100%
12	Southeast	1%	85%	2%	12%	100%
13	Southwest	1%	83%	2%	14%	100%
14	United Kingdom	1%	80%	3%	17%	100%
15	Grand Total	1%	82%	2%	15%	100%

Value Field Settings dialog box: Source Name: Sales Amount; Custom Name: Sales Amount; tabs: Summarize by, Show values as; Show values as: % of row (options: Normal, Difference From, % Of, % Difference From, Running Total in, % of row); Number Format, OK, Cancel.

You'll also notice in Figure 3-46 that this view was created by selecting the % of Row option in the Value Field Settings dialog box. Here are the steps to create this type of view:

1. **Right-click any value within the target field.**

   For example, if you want to change the settings for the Sales Amount field, right-click any value under that field.

2. **Select Value Field Settings.**

   The Value Field Settings dialog box appears.

3. **Click the Show Values As tab.**

4. Select % of Row from the drop-down list.

5. Click OK to apply your change.

The pivot table in Figure 3-47 gives you a view into the percent of sales that comes from each market. Here, you have the same type of view, but this time, you use the % of Column option.

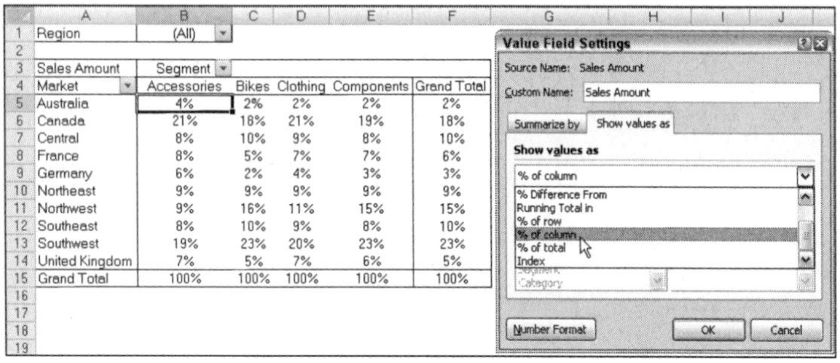

Figure 3-47: This view shows percent of total for the column.

Again, remember that because you built these views in a pivot table, you have the flexibility to slice the data by region, bring in new fields, rearrange data, and most importantly, refresh this view when new data comes in.

Creating a YTD totals view

Sometimes, it's useful to capture a running-totals view to analyze the movement of numbers on a year-to-date (YTD) basis. Figure 3-48 illustrates a pivot table that shows a running total of revenue by month for each year. In this view, you can see where the YTD sales stand at any given month in each year. For example, you can see that in August 2004, revenues were about a million dollars lower than the same point in 2003.

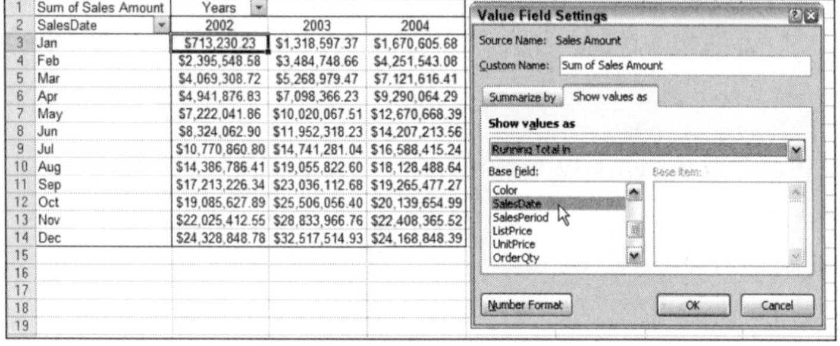

Figure 3-48: This view shows a running total of sales for each month.

In the sample data for this chapter, you don't see Months and Years. You have to create them by grouping the SalesDate field. Feel free to review the section, "Creating views by month, quarter, and year," earlier in this chapter to find out how.

To create this type of view, take these actions:

1. **Right-click any value within the target field.**

   For example, if you want to change the settings for the Sales Amount field, right-click any value under that field.

2. **Select Value Field Settings.**

   The Value Field Settings dialog box appears.

3. **Click the Show Values As tab.**

4. **Select Running Total In from the drop-down list.**

5. **In the Base Field list, select the field that you want the running totals to be calculated against.**

   In most cases, this would be a time series such as, in this example, the SalesDate field.

6. **Click OK to apply your change.**

Creating a month-over-month variance view

Another commonly requested view is a month-over-month variance. How did this month's sales compare to last month's sales? The best way to create these types of views is to show the raw number and the percent variance together.

In that light, you can start creating this view by building a pivot table similar to the one shown in Figure 3-49. Notice that you bring in the Sales Amount field twice. One of these remains untouched, showing the raw data. The other is changed to show the month-over-month variance.

Figure 3-49:
Build a pivot
table that
contains the
Sum of
Sales
Amount
twice.

	A	B	C
1		Years	Values
2		2004	
3	SalesDate	Sum of Sales Amount	Sum of Sales Amount2
4	Jan	$1,670,606	$1,670,606
5	Feb	$2,580,937	$2,580,937
6	Mar	$2,870,073	$2,870,073
7	Apr	$2,168,448	$2,168,448
8	May	$3,380,604	$3,380,604
9	Jun	$1,536,545	$1,536,545
10	Jul	$2,381,202	$2,381,202
11	Aug	$1,540,073	$1,540,073
12	Sep	$1,136,989	$1,136,989
13	Oct	$874,178	$874,178
14	Nov	$2,268,711	$2,268,711
15	Dec	$1,760,483	$1,760,483

Figure 3-50 illustrates the settings that convert the second Sum of Sales Amount field into a month-over-month variance calculation.

Figure 3-50:
Configure the second Sum of Sales Amount field to show month over month variance.

	A	B	C	D	E	F	G
1			Years	Values			
2			2004				
3		SalesDate	Sum of Sales Amount	Sum of Sales Amount2			
4		Jan	$1,670,606				
5		Feb	$2,580,937	54.49%			
6		Mar	$2,870,073	11.20%			
7		Apr	$2,168,448	-24.45%			
8		May	$3,380,604	55.90%			
9		Jun	$1,536,545	-54.55%			
10		Jul	$2,381,202	54.97%			
11		Aug	$1,540,073	-35.32%			
12		Sep	$1,136,989	-26.17%			
13		Oct	$874,178	-23.11%			
14		Nov	$2,268,711	159.53%			
15		Dec	$1,760,483	-22.40%			
16							
17							
18							
19							

Value Field Settings

Source Name: Sales Amount

Custom Name: Count of Sales Amount2

Summarize by | Show values as

Show values as

% Difference From

Base field: | Base item:
Model | (previous)
Color | (next)
SalesDate | <1/1/2002
SalesPeriod | Jan
ListPrice | Feb
UnitPrice | Mar

Number Format | OK | Cancel

As you can see, after the settings are applied, the pivot table gives you a nice view of raw sales dollar and the variance over last month. You can obviously change the field names (see the section, "Customizing field names," earlier in this chapter) to reflect the appropriate labels for each column.

In the sample data for this chapter, you don't see Months and Years. You have to create them by grouping the SalesDate field. Feel free to review the section, "Creating views by month, quarter, and year," earlier in this chapter to find out how.

To create the view in Figure 3-50, take these actions:

1. **Right-click any value within the target field.**

   In this case, the target field is the second Sum of Sales Amount field.

2. **Select Value Field Settings.**

   The Value Field Settings dialog box appears.

3. **Click the Show Values As tab.**

4. **Select % Difference From from the drop-down list.**

5. **In the Base Field list, select the field that you want the running totals to be calculated against.**

   In most cases, this is a time series like, in this example, the SalesDate field.

6. **In the Base Item list, select the item you want to compare against when calculating the percent variance.**

   In this example, you want to calculate each month's variance to the previous month. Therefore, select the (previous) item.

Chapter 4

Excel Charts for the Uninitiated

• •

• •

*N*o other tool is more synonymous with dashboards and reports than your old friend, the *chart.* Fast-paced business environments and new technologies have helped move charts from nice-to-have to a vital part of most business analyses. Charts offer instant gratification, allowing users to immediately see relationships, point out differences, and observe trends. No doubt about it; few mechanisms allow you to absorb data faster than a chart.

For those of you who have not yet been initiated to the world of Excel 2007 charting, this chapter gives you the basics of creating and customizing charts in Excel. This chapter also gives you a few best practices when it comes to creating charts for use in dashboards.

Chart Building Basics

Building a chart in Excel in and of itself is not a terribly difficult thing to do. The hard part is getting your mind around what types of chart to use and how best to display your data in a chart. While you go through each chapter of this book, you discover various imaginative ways to give these charts utility and functionality. For now, I start this look at building basic charts by reviewing the most-commonly-used chart types and discussing the customary ways each chart type is employed.

A review of the most-commonly-used chart types

Excel has 11 major chart types with variations on each type. For most business dashboards and reports, you need only a handful of the chart types available in Excel. Take a moment to review some of the chart types most commonly used for reporting:

- ✔ **Line chart:** The line chart is one of the most-frequently-used chart types, typically used to show trends over a period of time. Figure 4-1 demonstrates a line chart being used to show revenue by year for three different regions.

- ✔ **Pie chart:** Another frequently used chart is the old pie chart. A pie chart represents the distribution or proportion of each data item over a total value (represented by the overall pie). For example, in the pie chart shown in Figure 4-2, you can easily see how much of the total value is made up by each region.

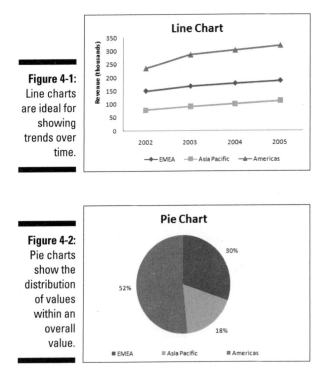

Figure 4-1:
Line charts
are ideal for
showing
trends over
time.

Figure 4-2:
Pie charts
show the
distribution
of values
within an
overall
value.

✔ **Column chart:** Column charts are typically used to compare several items in a specific range of values. Figure 4-3 demonstrates how a column chart could be used to compare the overall revenue performance for each region.

✔ **Stacked column chart:** A stacked column chart allows you to compare items in a specific range of values as well as show the relationship of the individual sub-items with the whole. For instance, the stacked column chart in Figure 4-4 shows not only the overall revenue for each year but also the proportion of the total revenue made up by each region.

✔ **Bar chart:** Bar charts are typically used to compare several items in a specific range of values. Figure 4-5 demonstrates how a bar chart could be used to compare the overall revenue performance for a given set of years.

Figure 4-3:
Use a column chart to visually compare the values of items.

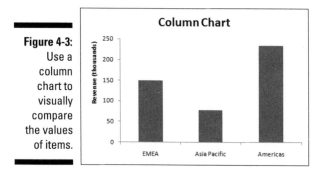

Figure 4-4:
Use stacked column charts to show the relationship of sub-items within the compared data values.

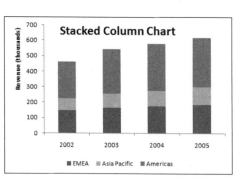

✔ **Stacked bar chart:** Like a bar chart, the stacked bar chart is used for illustrating comparisons between data items. The difference is that a stacked bar chart allows you to show the relationship of individual sub-items in the overall bar that is compared with other bars. For instance, the bar chart in Figure 4-6 shows not only the revenue for each year but also the proportion of the total revenue made up by each region.

✔ **XY scatter plot chart:** Scatter charts in Excel (also known as XY scatter plot charts) are ideal for showing correlations between two sets of values. The *x* and *y* axes work together to represent data plots on the chart based on the intersection of *x* and *y* values. Figure 4-7 illustrates the correlation between employee performance and competency, demonstrating that employee performance rises when competency improves.

✔ **Area chart:** Area charts are ideal for clearly illustrating the magnitude of change between two or more data points. For instance, the chart in Figure 4-8 effectively gives a reader a visual feel for the degree of variance between the high and low price for each month.

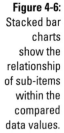

Figure 4-5:
Bar charts are ideal for showing differences between data items.

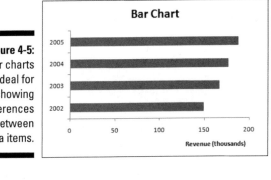

Figure 4-6:
Stacked bar charts show the relationship of sub-items within the compared data values.

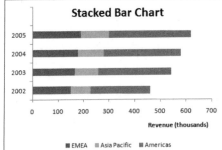

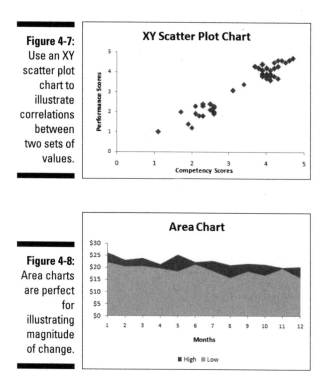

Figure 4-7:
Use an XY
scatter plot
chart to
illustrate
correlations
between
two sets of
values.

Figure 4-8:
Area charts
are perfect
for
illustrating
magnitude
of change.

To get a detailed review of all chart types available in Excel 2007, pick up a copy of *Excel 2007 Charts* by John Walkenbach (Wiley). This book provides an excellent introduction to every aspect of charting with Excel.

Preparing data for different chart types

The trick to creating a data table to feed your charts is knowing where each value in your table will be used by Excel in the chart. In this section, I show you the appropriate data setup for each chart type and how Excel plots each value in data tables.

Preparing data for line, column, bar, and area charts

Figure 4-9 illustrates the ideal data table for basic line, column, bar, and area charts.

As you can see in Figure 4-9, the ideal data table is laid out in rows and columns — with no blanks within the data range. Also notice that there are both column headers that label each year and row headers that label each region.

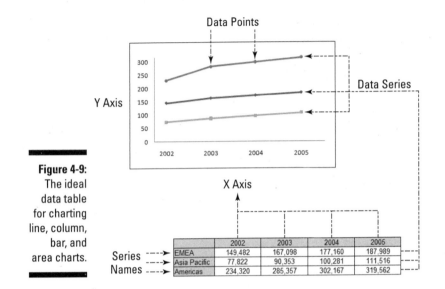

Figure 4-9:
The ideal
data table
for charting
line, column,
bar, and
area charts.

Here is how Excel uses each value in the data table:

- ✔ Each **row** in the table becomes a separate data series.

- ✔ Each **data value** in the rows is used to create the data point in its respective data series. Excel also creates the *y*-axis scaling based on the data values in your table.

- ✔ The **row headers** are used for series names, identifying each series in the legend and other places in the chart.

Preparing data for pie charts

For pie charts, the table setup is a bit different. Because you can have only one data series in a pie chart, the data table would consist of only one column of data with column and row headers. Figure 4-10 illustrates the ideal data table for a pie chart and how each value is used by Excel.

Here's how Excel uses each value in the data table:

- ✔ Each **data value** in the table becomes a data point (or slice) in the pie chart.

- ✔ The **row headers** are used for category names, identifying each pie slice in the legend and other places in the chart.

- ✔ The **column header** is used as the series name.

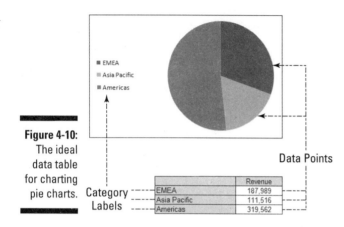

Figure 4-10:
The ideal
data table
for charting
pie charts.

Data Points

Category
Labels

	Revenue
EMEA	187,989
Asia Pacific	111,516
Americas	319,562

Preparing data for XY scatter charts

For XY charts, the table setup consists of two columns, as shown in Figure 4-11. Together, the two columns make up a data point in the scatter chart. The first column holds the *x*-axis coordinates for the data point whereas the second column holds the *y*-axis coordinates for the data point.

Here's how Excel uses each value in this table:

- ✓ The **first column** defines the *x*-axis coordinates for each data point.
- ✓ The **second column** defines the *y*-axis coordinates for each data point.
- ✓ Each **row** in the table is used to plot a data point on the chart.

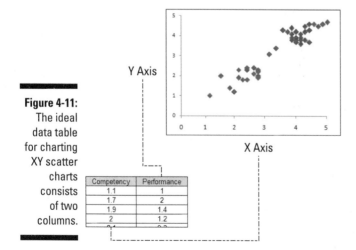

Figure 4-11:
The ideal
data table
for charting
XY scatter
charts
consists
of two
columns.

Y Axis

X Axis

Competency	Performance
1.1	1
1.7	2
1.9	1.4
2	1.2

Creating a chart from scratch

Enough chitchat. Let's walk through the creation of a basic line chart. Follow these steps:

1. **Start with a data table similar to the one shown in Figure 4-12 (which is conducive to creating line charts, as I discuss earlier in this chapter) and then select the entire range of data.**

2. **Select the Insert tab in the Ribbon.**

3. **In the Charts group, click the drop-down arrow under the Line chart icon and select your desired chart type. (See Figure 4-13.)**

   As soon as you select your desired chart type, Excel creates an embedded chart directly on the same worksheet your data is on. (See Figure 4-14.) From here, you can move, size, and format the chart to suit your needs.

Figure 4-12:
Select all the data in your data table.

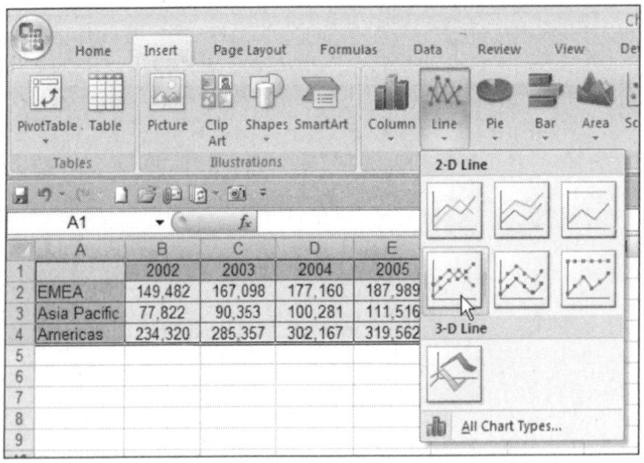

	A	B	C	D	E
1		2002	2003	2004	2005
2	EMEA	149,482	167,098	177,160	187,989
3	Asia Pacific	77,822	90,353	100,281	111,516
4	Americas	234,320	285,357	302,167	319,562

Figure 4-13:
Select the desired chart type.

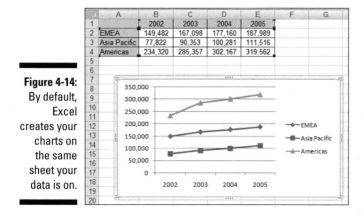

Figure 4-14:
By default,
Excel
creates your
charts on
the same
sheet your
data is on.

Charting disparate data

It may not always be convenient to force your data into clean contiguous tables for charting. For example, Figure 4-15 illustrates a table that displays quarter totals along with annual totals for the years 2002, 2003, and 2004.

Imagine you want to use this table to chart only the annual totals (not the quarter totals). It'd be downright inconvenient to create another table that shows only annual totals. That would be one more table you'd have to create and maintain processes for.

The answer to dilemmas like this is to manually select the data you need to chart while holding down the Ctrl key on your keyboard. When you hold down the Ctrl key while you select data ranges, Excel automatically strings the ranges together, recognizing them as one contiguous range.

Figure 4-15:
What do
you do
when your
data table
isn't ideal
for
charting?

	A	B	C	D	E	F	G	H	I	J	K	L	M	N	O	P
1				2002					2003					2004		
2		Qtr1	Qtr2	Qtr3	Qtr4	CY 2002	Qtr1	Qtr2	Qtr3	Qtr4	CY 2003	Qtr1	Qtr2	Qtr3	Qtr4	CY 2004
3	USA	1,010	1,037	2,423	1,861	6,331	1,354	1,821	2,242	1,772	7,188	1,441	1,461	1,078	1,098	5,079

Here are the steps to create a chart using non-standard, disparate data:

1. **Hold down the Ctrl key on your keyboard while you select the data you need to chart.**

   Your goal is to select data that will get you as close to a table that is conducive to charting as possible. Figure 4-16 demonstrates the selection of non-contiguous values.

   From here, you can continue creating your chart as normal.

2. **Select the Insert tab in the Ribbon.**

3. **In the Charts group, select your desired chart type.**

Figure 4-16:
Holding
down the
Ctrl key on
your
keyboard
while
selecting
data allows
you to
define a
dataset
Excel can
use for
charting.

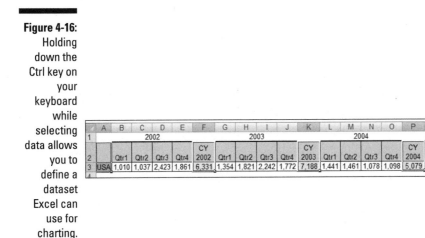

Common Chart Tasks

It's rare that Excel creates charts so perfect that you don't have to touch them after they're created. In fact, you often have to perform various tasks on your chart to get them looking the way you want them to. This section covers some of those tasks.

Resizing and moving charts

The most common tasks you perform on your charts are to resize and to move them. Here, you find some of the ways you can resize and move your charts.

✔ **Resizing a chart:** After you create your chart, click it once and a border of sorts appears around it. At certain points around the border, you see chart handles (identified with arrows in Figure 4-17), which you can click and drag to resize your chart in various directions.

✔ **Moving a chart within the same worksheet:** To move your chart in the same sheet, you can click between the chart handle, as illustrated in Figure 4-17, and drag the chart where you need it.

✔ **Moving a chart to a different worksheet:** If you need your chart to be placed on a different worksheet within the same workbook, you can use the Move Chart button on the Ribbon. Here's how:

1. *Click your chart to reveal the Chart Tools context tabs, as shown here in Figure 4-18.*

   These context tabs contain all the commands and functions used to create and format charts.

2. *Select the Design tab and click the Move Chart.*

   This opens the Move Chart dialog box, as shown in Figure 4-19.

3. *Use the Object In drop-down list to select the worksheet where you want to move the chart.*

Figure 4-17:
Use the chart handles to resize your charts. Click between the handles to move your chart within the same worksheet.

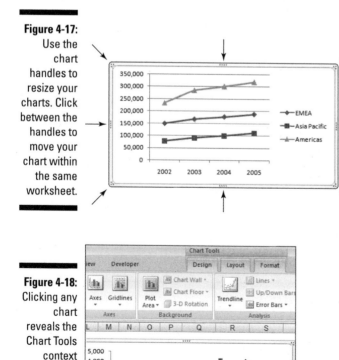

Figure 4-18:
Clicking any chart reveals the Chart Tools context tabs.

You can also activate the Move Chart dialog box by right-clicking your chart and selecting Move Chart.

✔ **Making multiple charts the same size:** When creating multiple charts for a dashboard, you often want to make all charts the same size. Excel makes it easy to resize multiple charts at one time. Here's how:

1. *Press and hold down the Ctrl key on your keyboard and select all your charts.*

    Interestingly enough, selecting multiple charts activates the Drawing Tools context menu, which exposes formatting options for shapes.

2. *Under the Format tab, find and adjust the height and width selectors under the Size group, as demonstrated in Figure 4-20.*

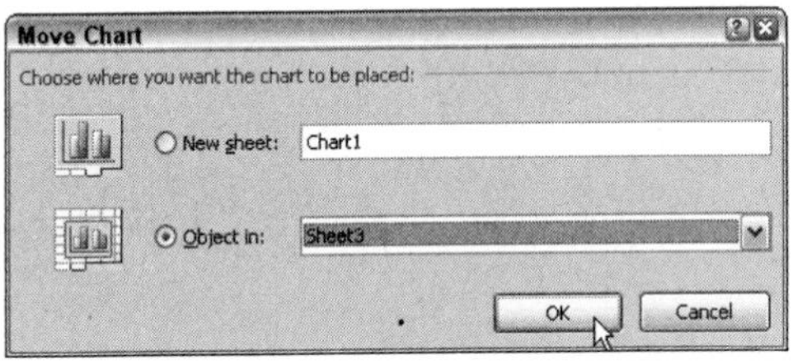

Figure 4-19:
Use the Move Chart dialog box to move a chart from one sheet to another.

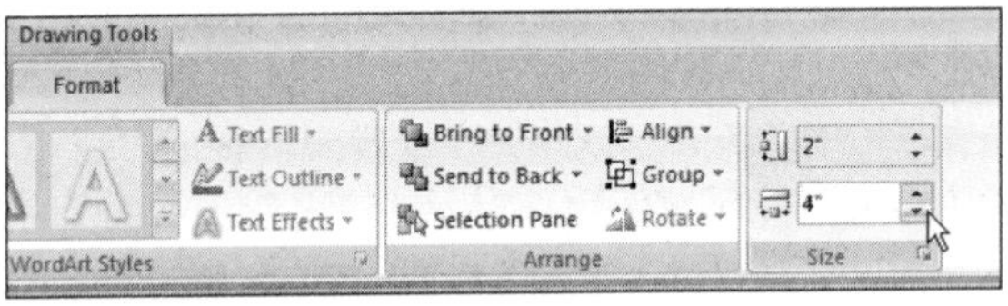

Figure 4-20:
Adjust the height and width selectors to resize multiple charts at one time.

Changing chart type

When you create charts, you'll find that it's useful to test how your data looks in various chart types. For example, you may initially create a bar chart but decide a line chart would better display your data. You can easily change the chart type without having to create the chart from scratch.

1. **Click your chart to activate the Chart Tools context tabs.**

2. **Under the Design tab, find and click the Change Chart Type button, as demonstrated in Figure 4-21.**

   The Change Chart Type dialog box appears. (See Figure 4-22.)

   You can also activate the Change Chart Type dialog box by right-clicking your chart and selecting Change Chart Type.

3. **Select the type of chart you want to switch to.**

Figure 4-21:
Use the
Change
Chart Type
button to
change your
chart's type.

Figure 4-22:
The Change
Chart Type
dialog box.

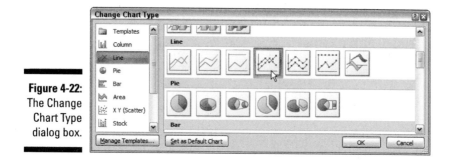

Creating a combination chart

A *combination chart* is essentially two or more chart types melded into one chart. For example, Figure 4-23 illustrates a combination chart that shows number of households with a computer (column chart) and the number of households with Internet access (line chart).

Why bother with a combination chart? Sometimes showing a data series in a in a different chart type makes it stand out, getting the message across faster and in a more effective way.

Take the example shown in Figure 4-23. The original chart for that example is shown here in Figure 4-24. This chart is okay, but the growth trend for Internet usage is subdued when shown as bars.

To create a combination chart, follow these steps:

1. **Right-click the data you want changed and select Change Series Chart Type. (See Figure 4-25.)**

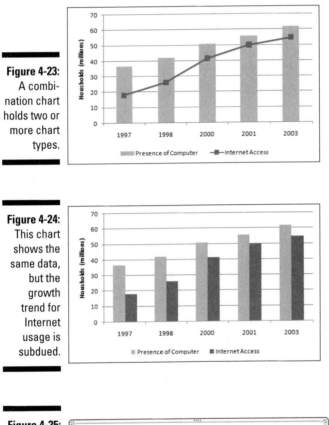

Figure 4-23:
A combination chart holds two or more chart types.

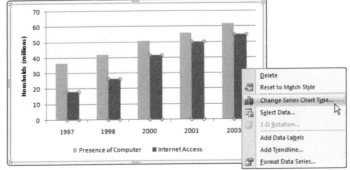

Figure 4-24:
This chart shows the same data, but the growth trend for Internet usage is subdued.

Figure 4-25:
To change the chart type of only one data series, right-click that series and select Change Series Chart Type.

The Change Chart Type dialog box appears.

2. Select the type of chart you want to switch to.

Selecting and formatting chart elements

All your charts have elements that you can format and customize. Take a moment to review the various ways to get to the formatting options for the elements in your charts.

Selecting elements

The first step in formatting an element of your chart is selecting that element. The easiest way to select an element is to simply right-click it. Why right-click? This way, the shortcut menu that activates gives you a clue to which element you selected and exposes the formatting options for that element. For example, Figure 4-26 demonstrates what you'd get if you right-clicked the gridlines in a chart.

It may sometimes be difficult to physically right-click the chart element you need to format. In this case, you can use Excel's nifty little element selector. To get to it, click your chart and select the Layout tab.

As Figure 4-27 demonstrates, you can use the drop-down list provided to select hard-to-reach elements.

When the desired element is selected, click the Format Selection button (see Figure 4-28) to activate the formatting dialog box for the selected element.

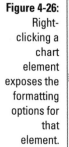

Figure 4-26:
Right-clicking a chart element exposes the formatting options for that element.

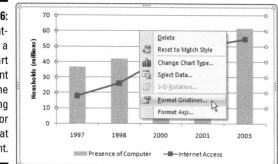

Figure 4-27:
Use the
Chart
Elements
drop-down
box to
select hard-
to-reach
elements.

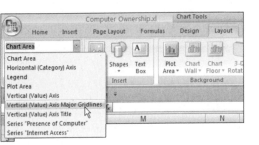

Figure 4-28:
The Format
Selection
button
activates the
formatting
dialog box
for the
selected
chart
element.

Each data element has its own formatting dialog box that provides various formatting options (that is, fill color, border color, line style, shadow options, 3D options, and so on). Alas, the scope and focus of this book isn't on charting per se, so I don't go through detailed explanations of every formatting option available. To get a detailed review of all formatting options available in Excel 2007, pick up a copy of *Excel 2007 Charts For Dummies* by Ken Bluttman (Wiley). In his book, Ken does an excellent job of reviewing every aspect of charting with Excel.

Using the chart tools context tabs to apply formatting

As I discuss earlier in this chapter, clicking a chart activates the Chart Tools context tabs. In these tabs, a plethora of formatting options allows you to easily customize your charts. Here's a high-level overview of the options on each tab:

✔ **The Design Tab:** The Design tab (see Figure 4-29) provides tools that allow you to quickly apply predefined layouts and styles to your charts. Although some the available layouts and styles don't comply with standard dashboarding best practices (see Chapter 16), the ability to apply predefined settings can often give you a one-touch head start on applying formatting that can be adjusted appropriately.

✔ **The Layout Tab:** The Layout tab provides tools that allow for one-touch formatting of major chart elements, such as axes, labels, and backgrounds. For instance, Figure 4-30 demonstrates how you can turn off gridlines simply by using the options under the Gridlines button. Here, you can practically format your entire chart with just a few clicks of the mouse.

✔ **The Format Tab:** The Format tab (see Figure 4-31) is based on the Format tab used for shapes in Office. The idea behind the Format tab is to choose any chart element and format it as if it was an independent shape, applying effects, such as Glow, Chiseled, and Soft Edges. This tab also holds WordArt effects, allowing you to apply effects to your chart titles and labels. As a matter of design principle, many of the options on the Format tab don't comply with standard charting best practices (see Chapter 16). It's best to avoid this tab when building charts for use in dashboards.

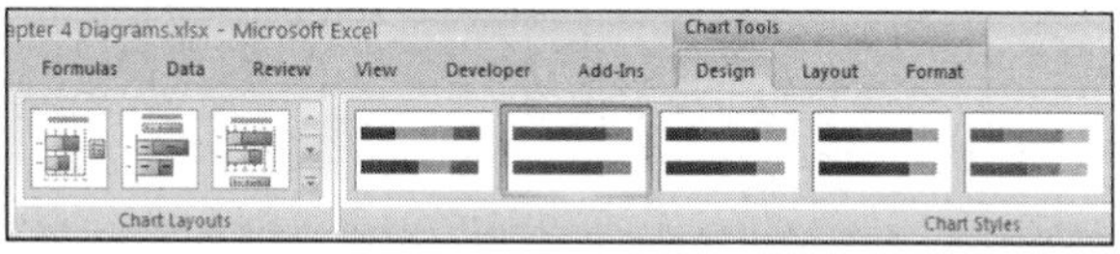

Figure 4-29:
The Design tab holds predefined layouts and styles, which you can apply to your charts.

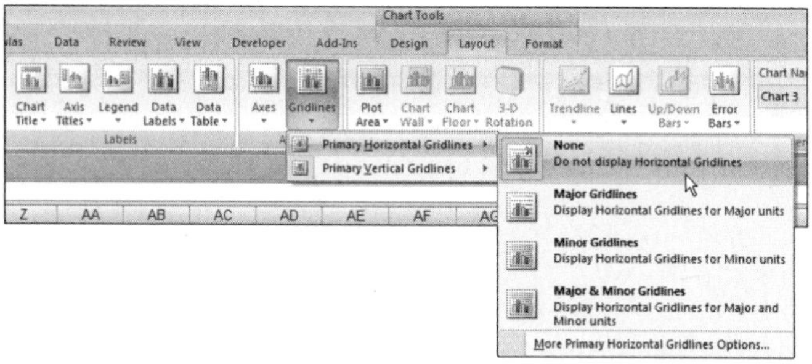

Figure 4-30:
The Layout tab allows for one-touch formatting of your charts.

Figure 4-31:
The Format
tab holds the
cosmetic
formatting
options for
shapes and
WordArt.

Working with Pivot Charts

No chapter on Excel charts would be complete without a look at one of the more amazing charts in Excel — the pivot chart. As the name implies, a *pivot chart* is a graphical representation of the data in a pivot table. What makes a pivot chart so amazing is that it's directly tied to a pivot table, allowing you to *interactively* add, remove, filter, and refresh data fields inside the chart just as you would do in your pivot table. There's no easier way to create a dynamic reporting tool in Excel than using the powerful combination of pivot tables and pivot charts.

In this section, you explore pivot charts and discover just how easy it can be to build interactive charting into your reporting mechanisms.

If you're unfamiliar with pivot tables, you may find this section on pivot charts a bit confusing. Feel free to visit Chapter 3 for a detailed look at pivot tables and how they work.

Pivot chart fundamentals

To demonstrate how simple it is to create a pivot chart, look at the pivot table in Figure 4-32.

As you can see, this pivot table provides for a simple view of sales by market. The Region and Segment fields in the Filter Area let you parse out sales by region and business segment.

Building a pivot chart on top of this pivot table would do two things. First, it'd allow for an instant view of the performance of each market. Second, it'd create an interactive charting mechanism that allows you to filter by region and business segment.

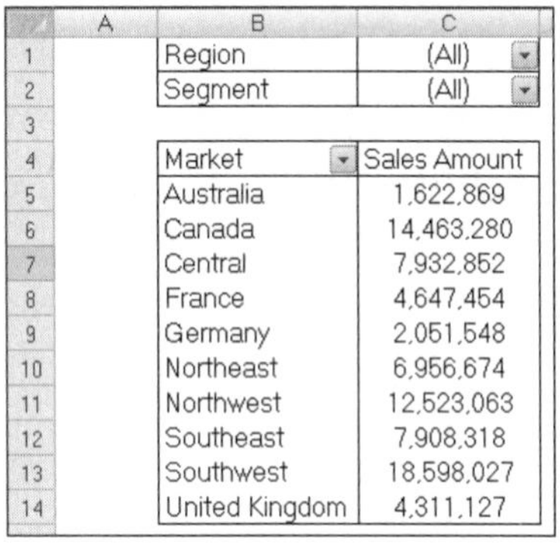

	A	B	C
1		Region	(All)
2		Segment	(All)
3			
4		Market	Sales Amount
5		Australia	1,622,869
6		Canada	14,463,280
7		Central	7,932,852
8		France	4,647,454
9		Germany	2,051,548
10		Northeast	6,956,674
11		Northwest	12,523,063
12		Southeast	7,908,318
13		Southwest	18,598,027
14		United Kingdom	4,311,127

Figure 4-32:
Start with
an existing
pivot table.

You can find the sample file for this chapter on this book's companion
Web site.

Follow these steps to create the pivot chart:

1. **Place your cursor anywhere inside the pivot table and click the Insert
   tab on the Ribbon.**

2. **In the Charts group, choose the chart type you want to use for your
   pivot chart, just as you would when charting standard data. (In this
   example, click the Column chart icon and select the first 2D
   column chart.)**

   As you can see in Figure 4-33, choosing the chart type immediately
   causes a column chart to appear on the same sheet as your pivot table.

You now have a chart that's a visual representation of your pivot table. More
than that, because the pivot chart is tied to the underlying pivot table,
changing the pivot table in any way changes the chart.

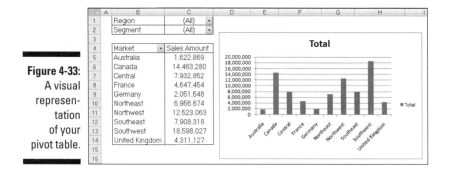

Figure 4-33:
A visual
represen-
tation
of your
pivot table.

For instance, try sorting the pivot table by Sales Amount and filtering for Accessories in the Segment field. Figure 4-34 illustrates how your pivot chart keeps up with those changes.

Again, if you're unfamiliar with actions such as sorting and filtering in a pivot table, you may find it valuable to check out Chapter 3 for a refresher.

In addition to being able to reflect the existing data in a pivot table, a pivot chart also captures any new data you add to the pivot table. For example, Figure 4-35 demonstrates how adding the Region field to the pivot table adds a region dimension to your chart.

Notice that pivot charts don't display the subtotals shown in their underlying pivot tables. Pivot charts ignore all subtotals and the grand total.

The cool thing is that your pivot table doesn't even have to be visible. Take a look at Figure 4-36. Notice that rows 3–15 are hidden. Those rows hold the pivot table. All I have showing here is the Filter Area and the pivot chart. This gives me the look and feel of an interactive reporting tool.

Figure 4-34:
Your pivot chart reflects what's in your pivot table.

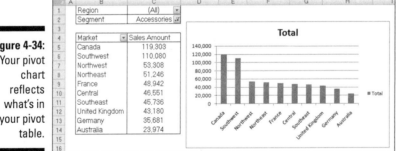

Figure 4-35:
Your pivot chart displays the same fields your underlying pivot table displays, even if the fields are layered.

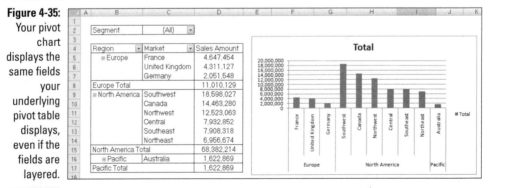

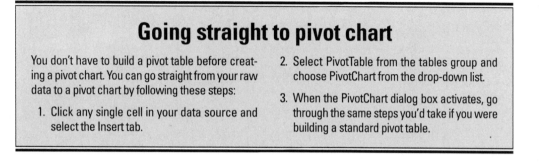

Going straight to pivot chart

You don't have to build a pivot table before creating a pivot chart. You can go straight from your raw data to a pivot chart by following these steps:

1. Click any single cell in your data source and select the Insert tab.

2. Select PivotTable from the tables group and choose PivotChart from the drop-down list.

3. When the PivotChart dialog box activates, go through the same steps you'd take if you were building a standard pivot table.

And remember, because pivot charts are essentially a graphical representation of their source pivot tables, they automatically update when you refresh your pivot tables. Think about the possibilities. On the power of pivot tables and pivot charts alone, you can create a fairly robust reporting mechanism without one line of programming.

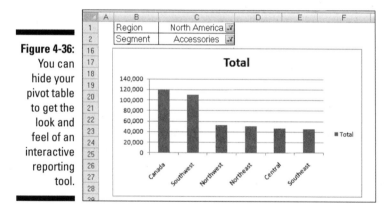

Figure 4-36: You can hide your pivot table to get the look and feel of an interactive reporting tool.

Pivot charts and the x and y axes

One mistake most people naturally make with pivot charts is to assume Excel places the values in the column area of the pivot table in the *x*-axis of the pivot chart. After all, the column area of a pivot table is oriented to go across like the *x*-axis of a chart.

Take Figure 4-37, for instance. The structure chosen shows the SalesPeriods in the column area and the Region in the row area. This structure works fine in the pivot table view.

Now, you would instinctively expect to see sales periods across the *x*-axis and lines of business along the *y*-axis. However, as shown in Figure 4-38, building a pivot chart on top of this format results in the Region in the *x*-axis and the SalesPeriod in the *y*-axis.

So why does the structure in your pivot table not translate to a clean pivot chart? Well in a pivot chart, both the *x*-axis and the *y*-axis correspond to specific areas in your pivot table.

- **x-axis:** Corresponds to the row area in your pivot table and makes up the *x*-axis of your pivot chart.
- **y-axis:** Corresponds to the column area in your pivot table and makes up the *y*-axis of your pivot chart.

Although it may seem counterintuitive at times, following these guidelines ensures you have a clean pivot chart. Figure 4-39 shows the same pivot table rearranged to show SalesPeriod in the row area and Region in the column area. Although this format isn't ideal for a pivot table view, it does allow your pivot chart to give you the effect you're looking for.

This new arrangement generates the pivot chart shown in Figure 4-40.

	B	C	D	E	F	G	H	I	J	K	L	M	N
1	Segment	(All)											
2	Market	(All)											
3													
4	Sales Amount	SalesPeriod											
5	Region	1/1/2004	2/1/2004	3/1/2004	4/1/2004	5/1/2004	6/1/2004	7/1/2004	8/1/2004	9/1/2004	10/1/2004	11/1/2004	12/1/2004
6	North America	1,366,685	1,861,930	2,005,753	1,826,503	2,210,842	1,235,782	1,766,552	1,540,073	1,166,333	844,833	2,325,757	1,703,437
7													

Figure 4-37: The placement of data works in a pivot table.

	B	C	D	E	F	G	H	I	J	K	L	M	N
1	Segment	(All)											
2	Market	(All)											
3													
4	Sales Amount	SalesPeriod											
5	Region	1/1/2004	2/1/2004	3/1/2004	4/1/2004	5/1/2004	6/1/2004	7/1/2004	8/1/2004	9/1/2004	10/1/2004	11/1/2004	12/1/2004
6	North America	1,366,685	1,861,930	2,005,753	1,826,503	2,210,842	1,235,782	1,766,552	1,540,073	1,166,333	844,833	2,325,757	1,703,437

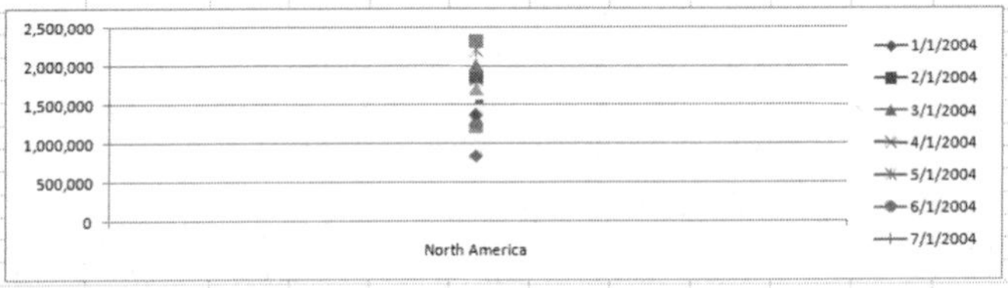

Figure 4-38: Although the pivot table is nicely structured, it doesn't work in a pivot chart.

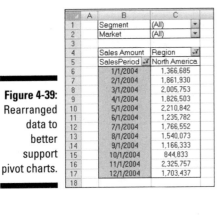

Figure 4-39:
Rearranged
data to
better
support
pivot charts.

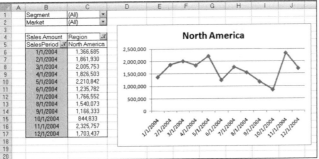

Figure 4-40:
You now
have a pivot
chart that
makes
sense.

Pivot charts formatting limitations

Microsoft has worked hard to ensure that the overall look and feel of pivot charts in Excel 2007 are very much that of standard charts. As a result, you can customize your pivot charts just as you would a standard chart, formatting each element of a pivot chart using the same actions and commands outlined earlier in this chapter.

That being said, keep in mind a few formatting limitations when working with pivot charts:

✔ **Chart types:** You can't use XY (scatter) charts, bubble charts, or stock charts when creating a pivot chart.

✔ **Trend lines:** Applied trend lines are lost when the underlying pivot table changes.

✔ **Data label:** The data labels in the pivot chart can't be resized. However, you can change the font of a data label, and making the font bigger or smaller indirectly resizes the data label.

Chapter 5

The New World of Conditional Formatting

In This Chapter

▶ Using predefined formatting scenarios

▶ Creating custom formatting rules

▶ Useful ways to implement conditional formatting

▶ Applying conditional formatting to pivot tables

*C*onditional formatting is the term given to the functionality whereby Excel dynamically changes the formatting of a value, a cell, or a range of cells based on a set of conditions you define. Conditional formatting allows you to look at your Excel reports and make split-second determinations as to which values are *good* and which are *bad*, all based on formatting.

Microsoft has dramatically enhanced this functionality in Excel 2007. In Excel 2007, conditional formatting includes a more robust set of visualizations and predefined formatting rules. These enhancements allow you to quickly and easily build dashboard-style reporting that goes far beyond the traditional red, yellow, and green designations.

In this chapter, you're introduced to the new world of conditional formatting in Excel 2007, discovering how to leverage this functionality to enhance your dashboards and reports.

Applying Basic Conditional Formatting

Thanks to the many predefined scenarios offered with Excel 2007, you can literally apply some basic conditional formatting with a few mouse clicks. To get a first taste of what you can do with this functionality, click the Conditional Formatting button found on the Home tab of the Ribbon. (See Figure 5-1.)

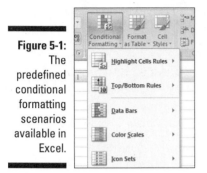

Figure 5-1:
The predefined conditional formatting scenarios available in Excel.

As you can see, there are five categories of predefined scenarios: Highlight Cells Rules, Top/Bottom Rules, Data Bars, Color Scales, and Icon Sets.

Take a moment to review what each category of predefined scenarios allows you to do.

Highlight Cells Rules

The formatting scenarios under the Highlight Cells Rules category, as shown in Figure 5-2, allow you to highlight those cells whose values meet a specific condition.

The thing to remember about these scenarios is that they work very much like an `If ... then ... else` statement. That is to say if the condition is met, the cell is formatted; if the condition is not met, the cell is not touched.

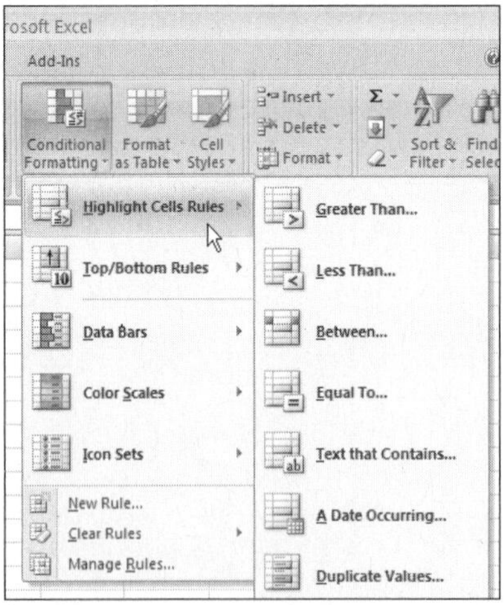

Figure 5-2:
The Highlight Cells Rules scenarios apply formats if specific conditions are met.

The scenarios under the Highlight Cells Rules category are pretty self-explanatory. Here's a breakdown of each scenario:

- ✔ **Greater Than:** This scenario allows you to conditionally format a cell whose value is greater than a specified amount. For instance, you can tell Excel to format those cells that contain a value greater than 50.

- ✔ **Less Than:** This scenario allows you to conditionally format a cell whose value is less than a specified amount. For instance, you can tell Excel to format those cells that contain a value less than 100.

- ✔ **Between:** This scenario allows you to conditionally format a cell whose value is between two given amounts. For example, you can tell Excel to format those cells that contain a value between 50 and 100.

- ✔ **Equal To:** This scenario allows you to conditionally format a cell whose value is equal to a specified amount. For instance, you can tell Excel to format those cells whose values are exactly 100.

- ✔ **Text That Contains:** This scenario allows you to conditionally format a cell that contains any form of a given text you specify as a criterion. For example, you can tell Excel to format those cells that contain the text *North*.

- ✔ **A Date Occurring:** This scenario allows you to conditionally format a cell whose contents contain a date occurring in a specified period relative to today's date. For example, Yesterday, Last Week, Last Month, Next Month, Next Week, and so on.

- ✔ **Duplicate Values:** This scenario allows you to conditionally format both duplicate values and unique values in a given range of cells. This rule was designed more for data cleanup than dashboarding, enabling you to quickly identify either duplicates or unique values in your dataset.

For your first encounter with conditional formatting, take a moment to go through an example of how to apply one of these scenarios. In this example, you highlight all values greater than a certain amount. Follow these steps:

1. **Start with a set of data similar to the one illustrated in Figure 5-3 and select the range of cells to which you need to apply the conditional formatting.**

Figure 5-3: Select the cells you need formatted.

	A	B
1		
2	Jan	100
3	Feb	150
4	Mar	200
5	Apr	250
6	May	300
7	Jun	350
8	Jul	400
9	Aug	450
10	Sep	500
11	Oct	550
12	Nov	600
13	Dec	650

TIP

Be sure to select all the cells to which you want to apply the conditional formatting rule. Selecting one cell results in only that one cell being conditionally formatted.

2. **Choose the Greater Than scenario found under the Highlight Cells Rules category. (Refer to Figure 5-2.)**

   The Greater Than dialog box appears. (See Figure 5-4.)

3. **Define a value that triggers the conditional formatting.**

   You can either type the value (400 in this example) or you can reference a cell that contains the trigger value. Also in this dialog box, you can use the drop-down list to specify the format you want applied.

4. **Click OK and you immediately see the formatting rule applied to the selected cells. (See Figure 5-5.)**

Now you may be thinking, what's the point? Wouldn't it have been just as easy to manually format the cells greater than zero? Sure, but the benefit of a conditional formatting rule is that Excel automatically re-evaluates the rule each time a cell is changed (provided that cell has a conditional formatting rule applied to it).

Figure 5-4:
Each scenario has its own dialog box that you can use to define the trigger values and the format for each rule.

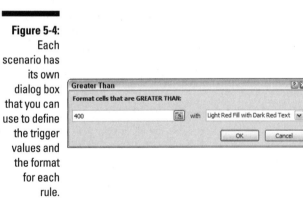

Figure 5-5:
Cells greater than 400 are now formatted.

For instance, if I changed a value in the example dataset to 450, as in the value for May in Figure 5-6, the formatting would automatically change because all the cells in the dataset have the conditional formatting applied to them.

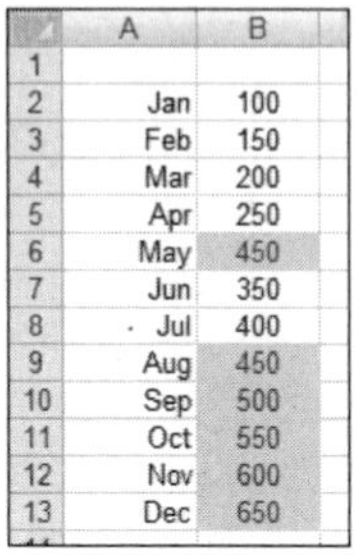

Figure 5-6:
Cells with a
conditional
formatting
rule applied
are re-
evaluated
each time
their value
changes.

	A	B
1		
2	Jan	100
3	Feb	150
4	Mar	200
5	Apr	250
6	May	450
7	Jun	350
8	Jul	400
9	Aug	450
10	Sep	500
11	Oct	550
12	Nov	600
13	Dec	650

Top/Bottom Rules

The formatting scenarios under the Top/Bottom Rules category, as shown in Figure 5-7, allow you to highlight those cells whose values meet a given threshold.

Figure 5-7:
The
Top/Bottom
Rules
scenarios
apply
formats if
specific
thresholds
are met.

Like the Highlight Cells Rules scenarios, these scenarios work like If . . . then . . . else statements — if the condition is met, the cell is formatted; if the condition is not met, the cell remains untouched.

Here's a breakdown of each scenario under the Top/Bottom Rules category:

✔ **Top 10 Items:** Although the name doesn't suggest it, this scenario allows you to specify any number of cells to highlight based on individual cell values (not just ten). For example, you can highlight the top five cells whose values are among the five largest numbers of all the cells selected.

✔ **Top 10 %:** This scenario is similar to the Top 10 Items scenario, except the selected cells are evaluated on a percentage basis. Again, don't let the name fool you; the percent selection doesn't have to be ten. For instance, you can highlight the cells whose values make up the top 20 percent of the total values of all the selected cells.

✔ **Bottom 10 Items:** This scenario allows you to specify the number of cells to highlight based on the lowest individual cell values. Again, don't let the name fool you. You can specify any number of cells to highlight — not just ten. For example, you can highlight the bottom 15 cells whose values are within the 15 smallest numbers among all the cells selected.

✔ **Bottom 10 %:** This scenario is similar to the Bottom 10 Items scenario, expect the selected cells are evaluated on a percentage basis. For instance, you can highlight the cells whose values make up the bottom 15 percent of the total values of all the selected cells.

✔ **Above Average:** This scenario allows you to conditionally format each cell whose value is above the average of all cells selected.

✔ **Below Average:** This scenario allows you to conditionally format each cell whose value is below the average of all cells selected.

In this example, you conditionally format all cells whose values are within the top 40 percent of the total values of all cells.

To avoid overlapping different conditional formatting scenarios, you may want to clear any conditional formatting you have previously applied before applying a new scenario. That is to say, you can delete the conditional formatting you may have already applied.

To clear the conditional formatting for a given range of cells, select the cells and then select Conditional Formatting from the Home tab of the Ribbon. Here you find the Clear Scenarios selection. Click Clear Scenarios and select whether you want to clear conditional formatting for the entire sheet or only the selected cells.

Then follow these steps to apply your first Top/Bottom Rules scenario:

1. **Start with a set of data similar to the one illustrated in Figure 5-8 and select the range of cells to which you need to apply the conditional formatting.**

2. **Choose the Top 10 % scenario found under the Top/Bottom Scenarios category. (Refer to Figure 5-7.)**

   The Top 10% dialog box appears. (See Figure 5-9.)

3. **Define the threshold that triggers the conditional formatting.**

   In this example, I enter **40**. Also, in this dialog box, you can use the drop-down list to specify the format you want applied.

4. **Click OK and you immediately see the formatting scenario applied to the selected cells. (See Figure 5-10.)**

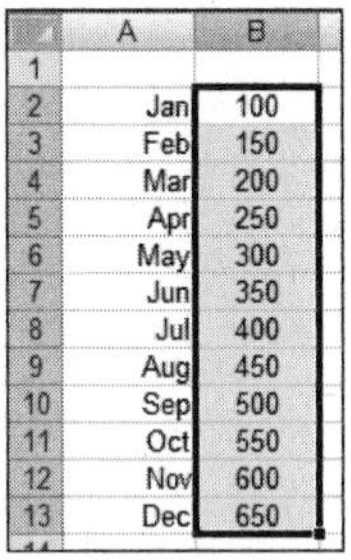

Figure 5-8:
Select the cells you need formatted.

Figure 5-9:
Each scenario has its own dialog box that you can use to define the trigger values and the format for each scenario.

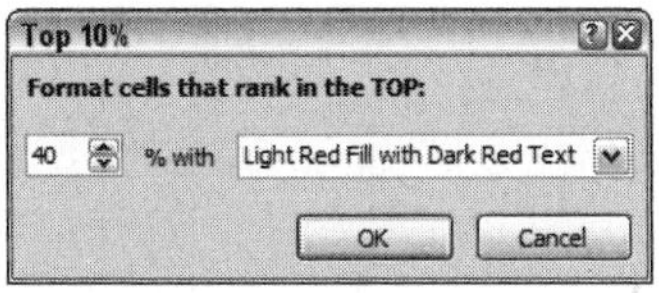

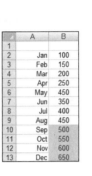

Figure 5-10:
With
conditional
formatting,
you can
easily see
that
September
through
December
makes up 40
percent of
the total
value in this
dataset.

Data Bars, Color Scales, and Icon Sets

Data Bars, Color Scales, and Icon Sets are new to Excel and present you with some new and interesting ways to highlight data. Here are a few examples of the types of formatting you can get from these scenarios:

✓ **Data Bars:** Data Bars fill each cell you're formatting with mini-bars in varying length, indicating the value in each cell relative to other formatted cells. Excel essentially takes the largest and smallest values in the selected range and calculates the length for each bar. To apply Data Bars to a range, do the following:

   1. Select the target range of cells to which you need to apply the conditional formatting.

   2. Choose Data Bars from the Conditional Formatting menu in the Home tab on the Ribbon. (See Figure 5-11.)

As you can see in Figure 5-12, the result is essentially a mini-chart within the cells you selected.

✓ **Color Scales:** Color Scales fill each cell you're formatting with a color, varying in scale based on the value in each cell relative to other formatted cells. Excel essentially takes the largest and smallest values in the selected range and determines the color for each cell. To apply Color Scales to a range, do the following:

   1. Select the target range of cells to which you need to apply the conditional formatting.

> 2. *Choose Color Scales from the Conditional Formatting menu in the Home tab on the Ribbon. (See Figure 5-13.)*

As you can see in Figure 5-14, the result is a kind of heat-map within the cells you selected.

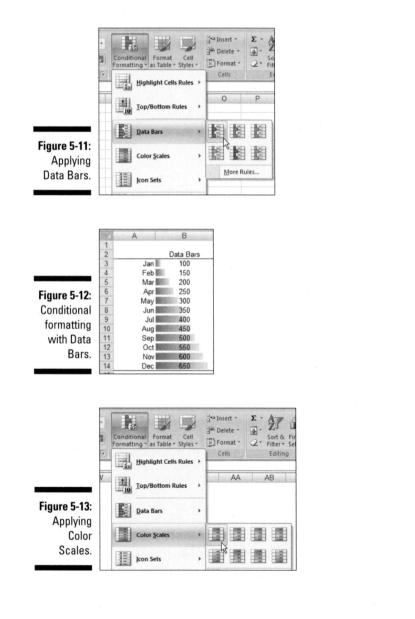

Figure 5-11:
Applying
Data Bars.

Figure 5-12:
Conditional
formatting
with Data
Bars.

Figure 5-13:
Applying
Color
Scales.

✔ **Icon Sets:** Icon Sets are sets of symbols that are inserted in each cell you're formatting. Excel determines which symbol to use based on the value in each cell relative to other formatted cells. To apply an Icon Set to a range, do the following:

1. *Select the target range of cells to which you need to apply the conditional formatting.*

2. *Choose Icon Set from the Conditional Formatting menu in the Home tab on the Ribbon.*

As you can see in Figure 5-15, you can choose from a menu of Icon Sets varying in shape and colors.

Figure 5-16 illustrates how each cell is formatted with a symbol indicating each cell's value based on the other cells.

Figure 5-14:
Conditional
formatting
with Color
Scales.

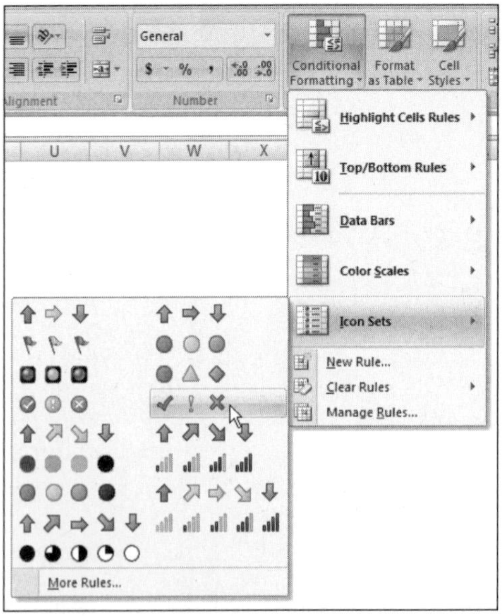

Figure 5-15:
Applying
Icon Sets.

Figure 5-16:
Conditional
formatting
with Icon
Sets.

Icon Sets		
Jan	✗	100
Feb	✗	150
Mar	✗	200
Apr	✗	250
May	!	300
Jun	!	350
Jul	!	400
Aug	!	450
Sep	✓	500
Oct	✓	550
Nov	✓	600
Dec	✓	650

Conditional formatting is one of those functions in Excel that offers countless ways of achieving a result. The examples you just covered only scratch the surface of the myriad of things you can do with conditional formatting. Alas, the focus of this book doesn't include a detailed look into every aspect of conditional formatting.

For a more comprehensive treatment of conditional formatting, take a gander at *Excel 2007 For Dummies* by Greg Harvey (Wiley). There, you find a whole chapter dedicated to the ins and outs of conditional formatting.

Getting Fancy with Conditional Formatting

The title says it all, folks. In this section, you explore a few techniques that allow you to get fancy with your conditional formatting. The next few examples are geared toward using conditional formatting to enhance your dashboards and reports.

Adding your own formatting rules manually

In this first example, I want to show you that you can create your own formatting rules manually. That is to say, you don't have to use one of the predefined scenarios offered by Excel. Why would you want to go through manually creating a formatting rule? Well, creating your own formatting rules helps you better control how cells are formatted and allows you to do things you couldn't do with the predefined scenarios.

For example, a useful conditional formatting rule is to tag all above average values with a check icon, and all below average values get an X icon. Figure 5-17 demonstrates this.

Now, the *above average* and *below average* scenarios built into Excel allow you to format only cell and font attributes; they don't enable the use of Icon Sets. You can imagine why Icon Sets would be better on a dashboard than just color variances. Icons and shapes do a much better job at conveying your message, especially when your dashboard is printed in black and white.

To get started in creating your first custom formatting rule, open the Chapter 5 Sample File found among the sample files on this book's companion Web site. When the file is open, go to the Create Rule by Hand tab. Then follow these steps:

1. **Select the target range of cells to which you need to apply the conditional formatting, select** the Conditional Formatting button found on the Home tab of the Ribbon, then **select New Rule (see Figure 5-18).**

   This opens the New Formatting Rule dialog box, as shown in Figure 5-19. When you look through the rule types at the top of this dialog box, you'll recognize some of them from the predefined scenario choices that I discuss earlier in this chapter.

Figure 5-17: With custom formatting, you can tag above-average values with a check and the below-average values with an X.

	A	B	C
1	REGION	MARKET	Sales
2	North	Great Lakes	✖ 70,261
3	North	New England	✔ 217,858
4	North	New York North	✖ 157,774
5	North	New York South	✖ 53,670
6	North	North Carolina	✖ 124,600
7	North	Ohio	✖ 100,512
8	North	Shenandoah Valley	✖ 149,742
9	South	Florida	✖ 111,606
10	South	Gulf Coast	✔ 253,703
11	South	Illinois	✖ 129,148
12	South	Indiana	✖ 152,471
13	South	Kentucky	✔ 224,524
14	South	South Carolina	✔ 249,535
15	South	Tennessee	✔ 307,490
16	South	Texas	✔ 180,167
17	West	California	✔ 190,264
18	West	Central	✖ 133,628
19	West	Colorado	✖ 134,039
20	West	North West	✖ 120,143
21	West	Southwest	✔ 248,098
22	West	Topeka	✔ 222,389

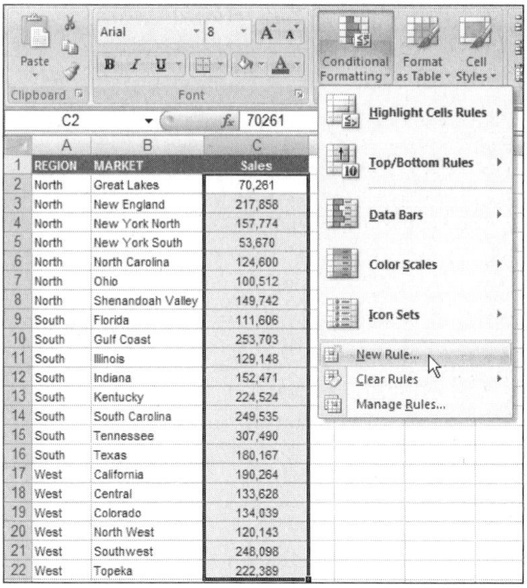

Figure 5-18:
Select the target range and then select New Rule.

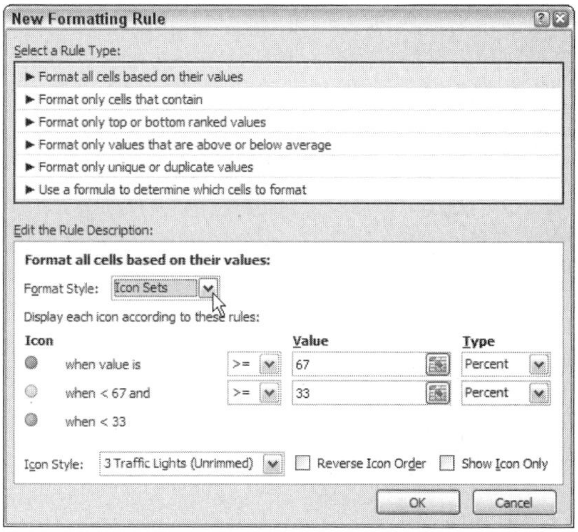

Figure 5-19:
Select Icon Sets from the Format Style drop-down list.

Format All Cells Based On Their Values: This selection measures the values in the selected range against each other. This selection is handy for finding general anomalies in your dataset.

Format Only Cells That Contain: This selection applies conditional formatting to those cells that meet a specific criterion you define. This selection is perfect for comparing values against a defined benchmark.

Format Only Top or Bottom Ranked Values: This selection applies conditional formatting to those cells that are ranked in the top or bottom *n*th number or percent of all the values in the range.

Format Only Values That are Above or Below the Average: This applies conditional formatting to those values that are mathematically above or below the average of all values in the selected range.

Format Only Unique and or Duplicate Values: This selection allows you to highlight unique and/or duplicate values in the selected range. This rule comes in handy in the data-cleanup and analysis phase of reporting.

Use a Formula to Determine Which Cells to Format: This selection evaluates values based on a formula you specify. If a particular value evaluates to true, the conditional formatting is applied to that cell. This selection is used typically when applying conditions based on the results of an advanced formula or mathematical operation.

Data Bars, Color Scales, and Icon Sets can be used only with the Format All Cells Based On Their Values rule type.

2. **Ensure that the Format All Cells Based On Their Values rule type is selected and then use the Format Style drop-down list to switch to Icon Sets. (Refer to Figure 5-19.)**

   Use the various inputs and drop-down lists to define exactly what you're looking for, as follows.

3. **Click the Icon Style drop-down list to select your desired Icon Set.**

   In this example, select 3 Symbols (Uncircled).

4. **Change both Type drop-down lists to Formula.**

   At this point, your dialog box should look similar to Figure 5-20.

5. **Put a formula in each of the Value boxes, as shown in Figure 5-20.**

   Let me explain the idea here. Excel assesses every cell in your target range to see if its contents match the logic in each Value box in order (top box first). If a cell contains a number or text that evaluates true to the first Value box, the first icon is applied and Excel moves on to the next cell in your range. If not, Excel continues down each Value box until one of them evaluates to true. If the cell being assessed doesn't fit any of the logic placed in the Value boxes, Excel automatically tags that cell with the last icon.

   In this example, you want your cells to get a check icon only if the value of that cell is greater than (or equal to) the average of the total values. Otherwise, you want Excel to skip right to the X icon and apply the X.

6. **In each Value Box, enter** =Average($C$2:$C$22).

TIP

This tells Excel that the value in each cell must be greater than the average of the entire dataset in order to get the check icon.

When a condition is met for a cell, Excel stops evaluating that cell and moves on to the next one.

At this point, your dialog box should look like the one shown in Figure 5-21.

7. **Press OK to apply your conditional formatting.**

If all went well, your table should look like Figure 5-17.

Figure 5-20:
The New
Formatting
Rule dialog
box,
completed
to the end of
step 4.

New Formatting Rule

Select a Rule Type:

▶ Format all cells based on their values
▶ Format only cells that contain
▶ Format only top or bottom ranked values
▶ Format only values that are above or below average
▶ Format only unique or duplicate values
▶ Use a formula to determine which cells to format

Edit the Rule Description:

Format all cells based on their values:

Format Style: Icon Sets

Display each icon according to these rules:

Icon			Value		Type	
✔	when value is	>=			Formula	
!	when < Formula and	>=			Formula	
✖	when < Formula					

Icon Style: 3 Symbols (Uncircled)   ☐ Reverse Icon Order   ☐ Show Icon Only

OK   Cancel

Figure 5-21:
Add a
formula to
check if the
value of that
cell is
greater than
(or equal to)
the average
of the total
values.

New Formatting Rule

Select a Rule Type:

▶ Format all cells based on their values
▶ Format only cells that contain
▶ Format only top or bottom ranked values
▶ Format only values that are above or below average
▶ Format only unique or duplicate values
▶ Use a formula to determine which cells to format

Edit the Rule Description:

Format all cells based on their values:

Format Style: Icon Sets

Display each icon according to these rules:

Icon			Value		Type	
✔	when value is	>=	=Average($C$2:$C$2		Formula	
!	when < Formula and	>=	=Average($C$2:$C$2		Formula	
✖	when < Formula					

Icon Style: 3 Symbols (Uncircled)   ☐ Reverse Icon Order   ☐ Show Icon Only

OK   Cancel

Showing only one icon

In many cases, you may not need to show all icons when applying the Icon Set. In fact, showing too many icons at one time may only serve to obstruct the data you're trying to convey in your dashboard.

Here's a simple example. The table in Figure 5-22 shows a table that has conditional formatting already applied. Here, all values less than zero are tagged with an X whereas values greater than zero are tagged with a check. Imagine that you only want to show the X icons because those are the ones you want to draw attention to.

	A		B
1			
2	**Markets**		**2003 vs 2002**
3	Connecticut	✖	(22,976)
4	Maine	✔	1,068
5	Massachusetts	✔	8,230
6	New Hampshire	✖	(74,195)
7	Rhode Island	✖	(21,130)
8	Vermont	✖	(2,830)
9	Delaware	✖	(10,759)
10	District of Columbia	✔	3,428
11	Maryland	✖	(6,506)
12	New Jersey	✔	31,452
13	New York	✖	(25,166)
14	Pennsylvania	✖	(5,170)
15	Illinois	✔	58,156
16	Indiana	✖	(56,991)
17	Michigan	✔	1,936
18	Ohio	✖	(6,430)
19	Wisconsin	✖	(2,217)

Figure 5-22: Too many icons can hide the items you want to draw attention to.

The trick to showing only one icon is to add a second conditional formatting rule where the items you don't want formatted are given a blank formatting rule.

In this example, you want to remove the check icons. The cells that contain those icons all have values above zero. Therefore, you first need to add a condition for all cells whose values are greater than zero.

1. **Highlight all the cells in the table.**

2. **Choose the Greater Than scenario found under the Highlight Cells Rules category.**

   Refer to Figure 5-2 if you have trouble finding the Greater Than scenario.

   The Greater Than dialog box opens.

3. **Enter 0 in the input, select Custom Format from the drop-down list, and click OK twice to close all dialog boxes.**

4. **Select the target range of cells and then select Manage Rules, as demonstrated in Figure 5-23.**

   This opens the Conditional Formatting Rules Manager dialog box, as shown in Figure 5-24. Here notice that both rules are shown. The idea is to tell Excel to stop evaluating those cells that meet the first condition. This way, they'll never be evaluated by the second condition.

5. **Place a check in the Stop if True check box. (See Figure 5-24.)**

6. **Click OK to apply your changes.**

   As you can see in Figure 5-25, only the X icons are now shown.

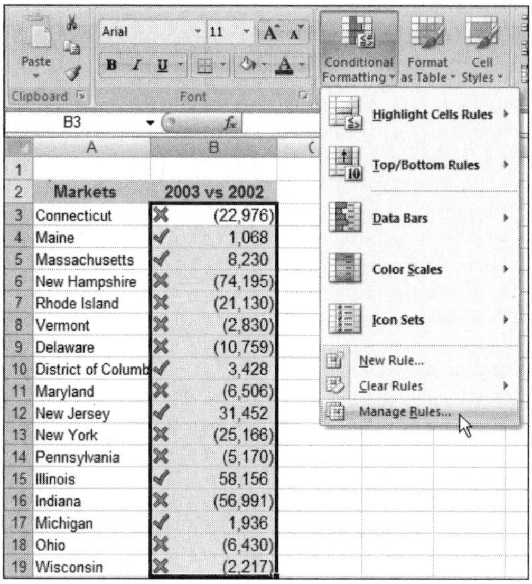

Figure 5-23: Select the target range and then select Manage Rules.

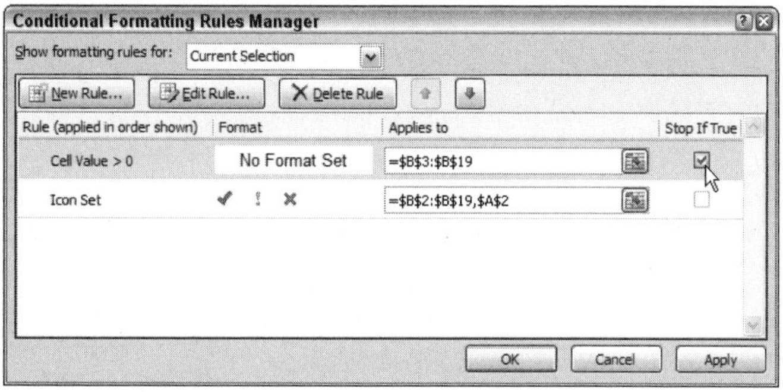

Figure 5-24: Select Stop if True to tell Excel to stop evaluating those cells that meet the first condition.

	A	B
1		
2	**Markets**	**2003 vs 2002**
3	Connecticut	✖ (22,976)
4	Maine	1,068
5	Massachusetts	8,230
6	New Hampshire	✖ (74,195)
7	Rhode Island	✖ (21,130)
8	Vermont	✖ (2,830)
9	Delaware	✖ (10,759)
10	District of Columb	3,428
11	Maryland	✖ (6,506)
12	New Jersey	31,452
13	New York	✖ (25,166)
14	Pennsylvania	✖ (5,170)
15	Illinois	58,156
16	Indiana	✖ (56,991)
17	Michigan	1,936
18	Ohio	✖ (6,430)
19	Wisconsin	✖ (2,217)

Figure 5-25: This table is now formatted to show only one icon.

Showing Data Bars and icons outside cells

Although Data Bars and Icon Sets give you a snazzy way of adding visualizations to your dashboards, you don't have a lot of say in where they appear within your cell. Take a look at Figure 5-26 to see what I mean.

	A	B
1	**MARKET**	**Sales**
2	Great Lakes	70,261
3	New England	217,858
4	New York North	157,774
5	New York South	53,670
6	Ohio	100,512
7	Shenandoah Valley	149,742
8	South Carolina	249,535
9	Florida	111,606
10	Gulf Coast	253,703
11	Illinois	129,148
12	Indiana	152,471
13	Kentucky	224,524
14	North Carolina	124,600
15	Tennessee	307,490
16	Texas	180,167
17	California	190,264
18	Central	133,628
19	Colorado	134,039
20	North West	120,143
21	Southwest	248,098
22	Topeka	222,389

Figure 5-26: Showing Data Bars inside the same cell as your values can make it difficult to analyze the data.

The Data Bars are, by default, placed directly inside each cell, almost obfuscating the data. From a dashboarding perspective, this is less than ideal for two reasons. First, the numbers themselves can get lost in the colors of the Data Bars, making them difficult to read — especially when printed in black and white. Second, it's difficult to see the ends of each bar. It's bad enough that Data Bars end in a gradient, you don't need overlapping numbers to compound the problem.

The solution to this problem is to show the Data Bars outside the cell that contains the value. Let's start with a fresh table with all conditional formatting removed and walk through a few steps:

1. **To the right of each cell, enter a formula that references the cell that contains your data value.**

   For example, if your data is in B2, go to cell C2 and enter =**B2**.

2. **Apply the Data Bars conditional formatting to the formulas you just created.**

   At this point, you have something that looks like Figure 5-27.

3. **Select the formatted range of cells and then select Manage Rules under the Conditional Formatting button in the Home tab of the Ribbon.**

4. **In the dialog box that opens, click the Edit Rule button.**

   The Edit Formatting Rule dialog box appears.

	A	B	C
1	MARKET	Sales	
2	Great Lakes	70,261	70,261
3	New England	217,858	217,858
4	New York North	157,774	157,774
5	New York South	53,670	53,670
6	Ohio	100,512	100,512
7	Shenandoah Valley	149,742	149,742
8	South Carolina	249,535	249,535
9	Florida	111,606	111,606
10	Gulf Coast	253,703	253,703
11	Illinois	129,148	129,148
12	Indiana	152,471	152,471
13	Kentucky	224,524	224,524
14	North Carolina	124,600	124,600
15	Tennessee	307,490	307,490
16	Texas	180,167	180,167
17	California	190,264	190,264
18	Central	133,628	133,628
19	Colorado	134,039	134,039
20	North West	120,143	120,143
21	Southwest	248,098	248,098
22	Topeka	222,389	222,389

Figure 5-27:
Create a new column of data and apply Data Bars to the new column.

5. **Place a check in the Show Bar Only option box, as demonstrated in Figure 5-28.**

6. **Click OK to apply your change.**

The reward for your efforts is a view that is cleaner and much better suited for reporting in a dashboard environment. Figure 5-29 illustrates the improvement gained with this technique.

Using the same technique, you can separate Icon Sets from the data, allowing you to position the icons where they best suit your dashboard. Here in Figure 5-30, the icons are shown to the right of the data.

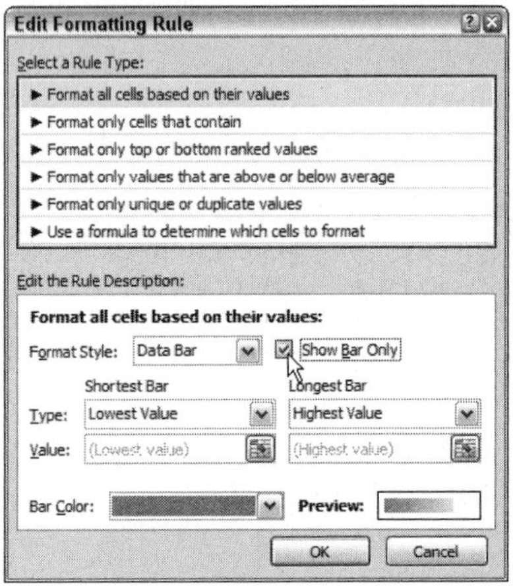

Figure 5-28: Edit the formatting rule to show only the Data Bars, not the data.

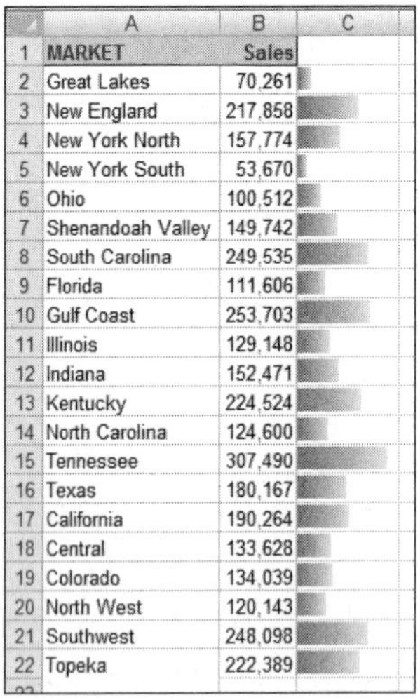

Figure 5-29: Your Data Bars are now outside the cell, making them much easier to see.

	A	B	C
1	MARKET	Sales	
2	Great Lakes	70,261	✖
3	New England	217,858	!
4	New York North	157,774	!
5	New York South	53,670	✖
6	Ohio	100,512	✖
7	Shenandoah Valley	149,742	!
8	South Carolina	249,535	✔
9	Florida	111,606	✖
10	Gulf Coast	253,703	✔
11	Illinois	129,148	✖
12	Indiana	152,471	!
13	Kentucky	224,524	✔
14	North Carolina	124,600	✖
15	Tennessee	307,490	✔
16	Texas	180,167	!
17	California	190,264	!
18	Central	133,628	✖
19	Colorado	134,039	✖
20	North West	120,143	✖
21	Southwest	248,098	✔
22	Topeka	222,389	!

Figure 5-30:
The same technique can be applied to Icon Sets.

Representing trends with Icon Sets

In a dashboard environment, there may not always be enough space available to add a chart that shows trending. In these cases, Icon Sets are an ideal replacement, enabling you to visually represent the overall trending without taking up a lot of space. Take a moment to walk through a simple example of how Icon Sets help display overall trends.

Trending refers to the measuring of variances over some defined interval — typically time periods like days, months, or years.

In the `Chapter 5 Sample File` found among the sample files on this book's companion Web site, you'll find the Represent Trending with Icons tab. In this tab, you'll see a table (as shown in Figure 5-31) that shows numbers for the previous and current months. As you can see by looking at the formula bar, a simple formula calculates the variance between the two months.

In some situations, you'll want to do the same type of thing. The key is to create a formula that gives you a variance or trending of some sort.

Follow these steps to create that formula:

1. **Select the target range of cells to which you need to apply the conditional formatting.**

   In this case, the target range is the cells that hold your variance formulas.

2. **Choose Icon Set from the Conditional Formatting menu in the Home tab and then choose the most appropriate icons for your situation.**

   In this example, the set with three arrows works. (See Figure 5-32.)

Figure 5-31:
Ensure you have a column containing a formula that calculates a variance or trend of some sort.

	E2		f_x	=D2/C2-1	
	A	B	C	D	E
1	REGION	MARKET	Previous Month	Current Month	Variance
2	North	Great Lakes	70,261	72,505	3.2%
3	North	New England	217,858	283,324	30.0%
4	North	New York North	157,774	148,790	-5.7%
5	North	New York South	53,670	68,009	26.7%
6	North	Ohio	100,512	98,308	-2.2%
7	North	Shenandoah Valley	149,742	200,076	33.6%
8	South	South Carolina	249,535	229,473	-8.0%
9	South	Florida	111,606	136,104	22.0%
10	South	Gulf Coast	253,703	245,881	-3.1%
11	South	Illinois	129,148	131,538	1.9%
12	South	Indiana	152,471	151,699	-0.5%
13	South	Kentucky	224,524	225,461	0.4%
14	North	North Carolina	124,600	130,791	5.0%
15	South	Tennessee	307,490	268,010	-12.8%

Figure 5-32:
The up arrow indicates an upward trend, a down arrow indicates a downward trend, and a right-pointing arrow indicates a flat trend.

	A	B	C	D	E
1	REGION	MARKET	Previous Month	Current Month	Variance
2	North	Great Lakes	70,261	72,505	⇨ 3.2%
3	North	New England	217,858	283,324	⬆ 30.0%
4	North	New York North	157,774	148,790	⬇ -5.7%
5	North	New York South	53,670	68,009	⬆ 26.7%
6	North	Ohio	100,512	98,308	⇨ -2.2%
7	North	Shenandoah Valley	149,742	200,076	⬆ 33.6%
8	South	South Carolina	249,535	229,473	⬇ -8.0%
9	South	Florida	111,606	136,104	⬆ 22.0%
10	South	Gulf Coast	253,703	245,881	⬇ -3.1%
11	South	Illinois	129,148	131,538	⇨ 1.9%
12	South	Indiana	152,471	151,699	⇨ -0.5%
13	South	Kentucky	224,524	225,461	⇨ 0.4%
14	North	North Carolina	124,600	130,791	⇨ 5.0%
15	South	Tennessee	307,490	268,010	⬇ -12.8%
16	South	Texas	180,167	195,791	⇨ 8.7%
17	West	California	190,264	176,648	⬇ -7.2%
18	West	Central	133,628	132,262	⇨ -1.0%
19	West	Colorado	134,039	106,361	⬇ -20.6%
20	West	North West	120,143	125,260	⇨ 4.3%
21	West	Southwest	248,098	235,494	⬇ -5.1%
22	West	Topeka	222,389	265,720	⬆ 19.5%

In most case, you'll want to adjust the thresholds that define what up, down, and flat mean. Imagine that you need any variance above 3 percent to be tagged with an up arrow, any variance below 3 percent to be tagged with a down arrow, and all others to show flat.

3. **Select the target range of cells and then select Manage Rules under the Conditional Formatting button in the Home tab of the Ribbon.**

4. **In the dialog box that opens, click the Edit Rule button.**

   The Edit Formatting Rule dialog box appears.

5. **Adjust the properties, as shown in Figure 5-33.**

   In Figure 5-33, notice the Type property for the formatting rule is set to Number even though the data (the variance) you're working with are percentages. You'll find that working with the Number setting gives you more control and predictability when setting thresholds.

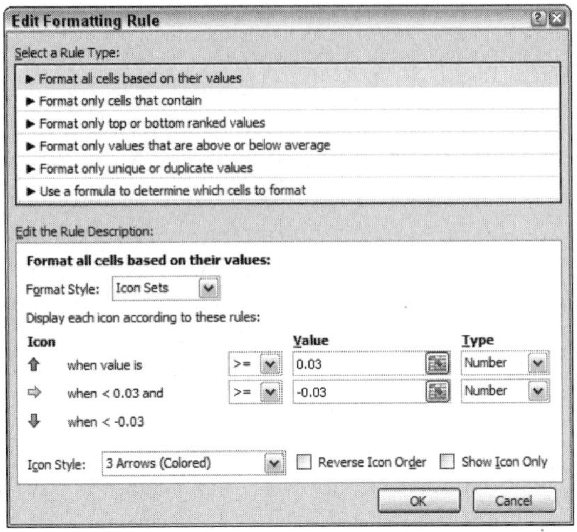

Figure 5-33: You can adjust the thresholds that define what up, down, and flat mean.

Building a legend for your conditional formatting

Many of the icons offered in Excel 2007 are self-describing — you can tell what they mean by virtue of their color or shape. The meaning of some icons, however, will leave your clients confused unless you tell them explicitly. When building a dashboard or report that uses any kind of Icon Set, it's generally good practice to add some sort of legend defining what each icon means. Figure 5-34 demonstrates how a legend can help clear up confusion. Here's how you do it:

1. **Build a legend table.**

   This table should contain a description for each icon in the set you're using and a number that triggers the icon for that description. Confused? Look at Figure 5-35 to see what I mean.

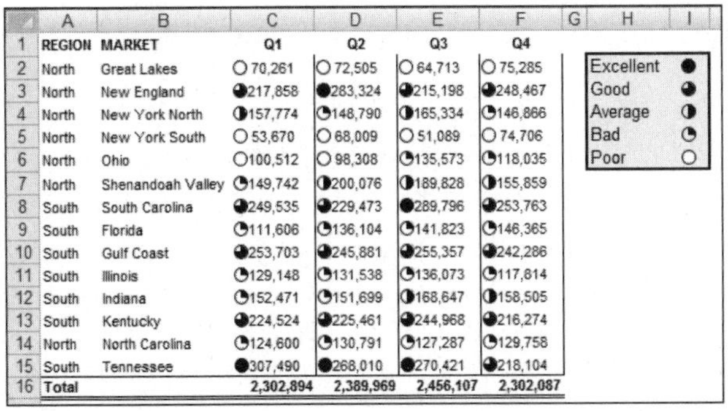

	A	B	C	D	E	F	G	H	I
1	REGION	MARKET	Q1	Q2	Q3	Q4			
2	North	Great Lakes	70,261	72,505	64,713	75,285		Excellent	
3	North	New England	217,858	283,324	215,198	248,467		Good	
4	North	New York North	157,774	148,790	165,334	146,866		Average	
5	North	New York South	53,670	68,009	51,089	74,706		Bad	
6	North	Ohio	100,512	98,308	135,573	118,035		Poor	
7	North	Shenandoah Valley	149,742	200,076	189,828	155,859			
8	South	South Carolina	249,535	229,473	289,796	253,763			
9	South	Florida	111,606	136,104	141,823	146,365			
10	South	Gulf Coast	253,703	245,881	255,357	242,286			
11	South	Illinois	129,148	131,538	136,073	117,814			
12	South	Indiana	152,471	151,699	168,647	158,505			
13	South	Kentucky	224,524	225,461	244,968	216,274			
14	North	North Carolina	124,600	130,791	127,287	129,758			
15	South	Tennessee	307,490	268,010	270,421	218,104			
16	Total		2,302,894	2,389,969	2,456,107	2,302,087			

Figure 5-34: A legend can shed light on what your icons mean.

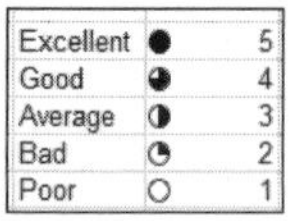

Figure 5-35:
Build a
legend table
and apply
the same
conditional
format you
applied to
your dataset.

Excellent	●	5
Good	◕	4
Average	◑	3
Bad	◔	2
Poor	○	1

2. **Apply the same conditional formatting to the legend you applied to your dataset.**

   The numbers you use in the legend table don't really matter. The idea is just to trigger the icon that matches associated description. When the conditional formatting is applied to the legend table, you can adjust the numbers to force a match.

   You then want to hide the numbers because they don't really mean anything.

3. **Select the formatted range of cells in the legend table and choose Manage Rules under the Conditional Formatting button in the Home tab of the Ribbon.**

4. **In the dialog box that opens, click the Edit Rule button.**

5. **Place a check in the Show Icon Only option and click OK to apply your change.**

   Voilà! You now have an instant legend for your conditional formatting.

Using conditional formatting with pivot tables

In previous versions of Excel, conditional formatting couldn't be cleanly and predictably used with pivot tables. Oh, you could apply conditional formatting to the cells in and around the pivot table, but if something changed or the pivot table was rearranged, your conditional formatting wouldn't be applied to the correct cells.

In Excel 2007, Microsoft has made a brilliant effort to integrate conditional formatting into pivot tables. This gives you the ability to tie conditional formatting to the actual pivot table itself, not just the cells it occupies. This means you can rearrange, refresh, sort, and adjust your pivot table without affecting the integrity of your conditional formatting. The best part is that you can apply conditional formatting to your pivot table just as you would with standard cells — no special processes.

In the sample file for this chapter on this book's companion Web site, you'll find a simple example of conditional formatting applied to a pivot table. (See Figure 5-36.)

In this example, an Icon Set has been applied to easily pick the most popular colors for each region. As you can see, blue and yellow are the most popular product colors. The Pacific Region Manager may want to take this into account when planning for next year's product line.

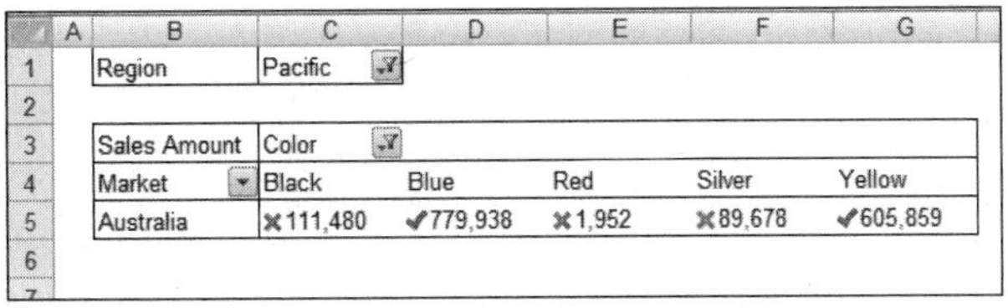

Figure 5-36:
Conditional
formatting
applied to a
pivot table.

	A	B	C	D	E	F	G
1		Region	Pacific ☑				
2							
3		Sales Amount	Color ☑				
4		Market ▾	Black	Blue	Red	Silver	Yellow
5		Australia	✖111,480	✔779,938	✖1,952	✖89,678	✔605,859
6							
7							

And because this is a pivot table, you get the benefit of interactively changing regions (via the Filter Area drop-down list) and applying the same conditional formatting to a different set of data without having to adjust the formatting rule.

Chapter 6

The Art of Dynamic Labeling

Up to this point, I've covered the major tools you can use to build basic dashboard components: pivot tables, charts, and conditional formatting. In this chapter, I focus on functionality that is less apparent — *dynamic labeling*.

Dynamic labeling is less a function in Excel than it is a concept. *Dynamic labels* are labels that change to correspond to the data you're viewing. With dynamic labeling, you can interactively change the labeling of data, consolidate many pieces of information into one location, and easily add layers of analysis.

In this chapter, you explore the various techniques that can be used to create dynamic labels.

Creating a Basic Dynamic Label

A common use for dynamic labels is labeling interactive charts. In Figure 6-1, I have a pivot chart that shows the Top 10 Categories by market. When the market is changed in the Filter drop-down list, the chart changes. Now, it'd be nifty to have a label on the chart itself that shows the market for which the data is currently being displayed.

Don't know what a pivot chart is? Feel free to take a gander at Chapter 4 for a discussion of pivot charts.

Figure 6-1:
Interactive
charts, such
as this pivot
chart, are
ideal places
to use
dynamic
labels that
change
based on
current
selection.

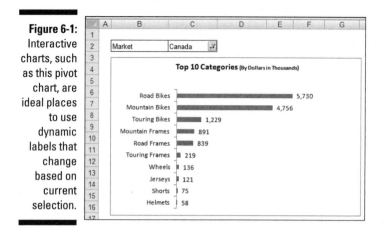

To create a dynamic label within your chart, follow these steps:

1. **On the Insert tab in the Ribbon, select the Text Box icon, as shown in Figure 6-2.**

Figure 6-2:
Select the
Text Box
Icon.

2. **Click inside the chart to create an empty text box.**

3. **While the text box is selected, go up to the formula bar, type the equal sign (=), and then click the cell that contains the text for your dynamic label.**

   Again, type the formula into the formula bar, *not* directly into the text box.

   In the example shown in Figure 6-3, the text box is linked to cell C2. You'll notice that cell C2 holds the Filter drop-down list for the pivot table.

4. **Format the text box so that it looks like any other label.**

   You can format the text box using the standard formatting options found on the Home tab.

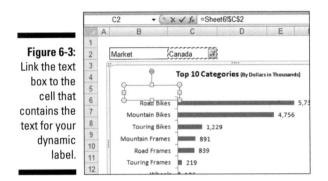

Figure 6-3:
Link the text
box to the
cell that
contains the
text for your
dynamic
label.

If all goes well, you'll have a label on your chart that changes to correspond
with the cell to which it's linked. Figure 6-4 illustrates how the dynamic label
can be made to blend in with your chart.

Be aware that text boxes can't display any more than 255 characters.

Figure 6-4:
The France
label within
the chart is
actually a
dynamic
label that
changes
when a new
market is
selected in
the drop-
down list.

Adding Layers of Analysis with Dynamic Labels

What would happen if you were to link your text boxes to cells that contained
formulas instead of simple labels? A whole new set of opportunities would
open up. With text boxes linked to formulas, you could add a layer of analysis
into your charts and dashboards without a lot of complex hocus pocus.

Figure 6-5 illustrates a simple example. Here, you see two views of the same pivot chart. On the top, the Northwest market is selected, and you see that the pivot chart is labeled with a layer of analysis around Q4 variance. On the bottom, Southeast is selected, and you can see that the label changes to correspond with the analysis around Q4 variance for the Southeast market.

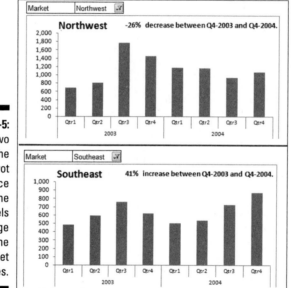

Figure 6-5:
This is two views of the same pivot chart; notice how the chart labels change when the market changes.

This example can be found in the Chapter 6 sample file on this book's companion Web site.

The example shown in Figure 6-5 actually uses three dynamic labels. One to display the current selected market, one to display the actual calculation of Q4-2003 versus Q4-2003, and one to add some contextual text that describes the analysis.

Figure 6-6 illustrates the behind-the-scenes links. Take a moment to examine what's happening here. The label showing 41% is linked to cell B13, which contains a formula returning the variance analysis. The label showing the contextual text is linked to cell C13, which contains an IF formula that returns a different sentence, depending on whether the variance percent is an increase or decrease.

Together, these labels provide your audience with a clear message about the variance for the selected market. This is one of countless ways you can implement this technique.

Figure 6-6:
This pivot
chart
actually
uses three
dynamic
labels; each
linked to a
different
cell.

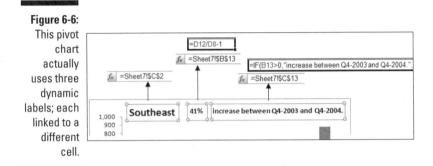

Excel's Mysterious Camera Tool

Excel's Camera tool enables you to take a live picture of a range of cells that updates dynamically while the data in that range updates. I call it the *mysterious* Camera tool because it's been hidden away in the last few versions of Excel. Although Microsoft has chosen not to include this tool in the mainstream Ribbon, it's actually quite useful for those of us endeavoring to build dashboards and reports.

Finding the Camera tool

Before you can use the Camera tool, you have to find it and add it to your Quick Access Toolbar (QAT).

The *Quick Access Toolbar* is a customizable toolbar in which you can store frequently used commands so that they're always accessible with just one click. You can add commands to the QAT by dragging them directly from the Ribbon or by going through the Customize menu.

Follow these steps to add the Camera tool to the QAT:

1. **Click the Office icon in the upper-left corner of Excel.**

2. **Select the Excel Options button to activate the Excel Options dialog box.**

3. **Click the Customize button.**

4. **In the Choose Commands From drop-down list, select Commands Not in the Ribbon.**

5. **Scroll down the alphabetical list of commands (see Figure 6-7) and find Camera; double-click to add it to QAT.**

6. **Click OK to close the Excel Options dialog box.**

When you've taken these steps, you'll see the Camera tool in your Quick Access Toolbar, as shown in Figure 6-8.

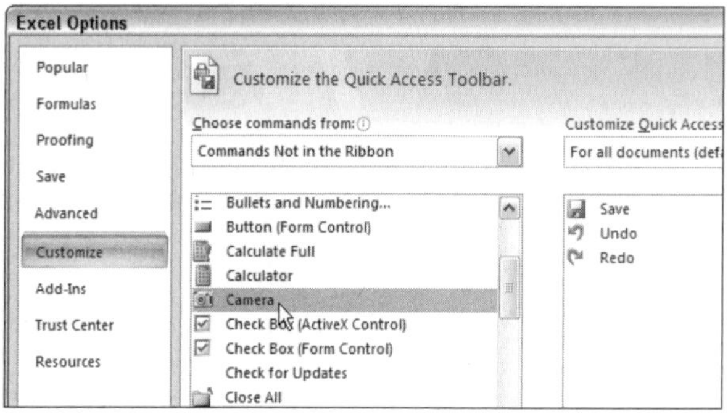

Figure 6-7:
Add the
Camera tool
to the Quick
Access
Toolbar.

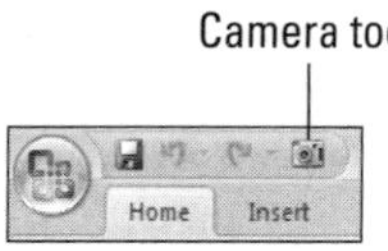

Figure 6-8:
Not
surprisingly,
the icon for
the Camera
tool looks
like a
camera.

Camera tool

The basics of using the Camera tool

The idea behind the Camera tool is simple. You highlight a range of cells, and everything in that range is captured in a live picture. When I say "everything," I mean *everything:* charts, conditional formatting, shapes, whatever you see in that range of cells, and so on. The cool thing about the Camera tool is that you're not limited to showing a single cell's value like you are with a linked text box. And because the picture is live, any updates made to the source range automatically change the picture.

Enough chitchat. Let me walk you through a basic example using the Camera tool. In Figure 6-9, I entered some simple numbers and created a chart based on those numbers — nothing fancy. The goal here is to create a live picture of the range that holds both the numbers and the chart.

Figure 6-9:
Enter some
simple
numbers in
a range and
create a
basic chart
from those
numbers.

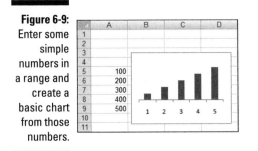

1. **Highlight the entire range containing all the information you want to capture.**

   In this scenario, I highlight the range spanning from A3–D11.

2. **Click the Camera tool icon (added to the QAT in the preceding section, "Finding the Camera tool").**

3. **Click the spreadsheet in the location where you want the picture to be placed.**

   Excel immediately creates a live picture of the entire range, as shown in Figure 6-10.

Figure 6-10:
A live
picture is
created via
the Camera
tool.

Changing any number in the original range automatically causes the picture to update.

By default, the picture that's created has a border around it. To remove the border, simply right-click the picture and select Format Picture. This activates the Format Picture dialog box. In the Colors and Lines tab, you see a Line Color drop-down list. Here you can select No Color, thereby removing the border.

On a similar note, to get a picture without gridlines, simply remove the gridlines from the source range.

Creating a live picture without the Camera tool

Did you know you can create a live picture without actually using the Camera tool? That's right. Excel 2007 has made it relatively easy to mimic the Camera tool functionality manually.

1. Select the target range and copy it.

2. Go to the Home tab on the Ribbon and choose Paste⇨As Picture⇨Paste Picture Link.

Of course, the advantage of using the Camera tool is that you can do the same thing with two clicks. Call me lazy, but two-click functionality is just too good to pass up.

Cool uses for the Camera tool

In this section, I go beyond the basics and share with you a few of the ways you can use the Camera tool to enhance your dashboards and reports. You can use the Camera tool to perform the following functions:

- ✔ **Consolidate disparate ranges into one print area.**
- ✔ **Rotate objects to save time.**
- ✔ **Create small charts.**

All these are discussed in the following sections.

Consolidating disparate ranges into one print area

Sometimes a reporting model gets so complex that it's difficult to keep all the final data in one printable area. This often forces the printing of multiple pages that are inconsistent in layout and size. Given that dashboards are most effective when contained in a compact area that can be printed in a page or two, complex models prove to be problematic when it comes to layout and design.

The Camera tool can be used in these situations to create live pictures of various ranges that you can place on a single page. Figure 6-11 demonstrates a workbook that contains data from various worksheets. The secret here is that these are nothing more than linked pictures created by the Camera tool.

When you create pictures with the Camera Tool, you can size and move the pictures around freely. This gives you the freedom to test different layouts without the need to worry about column widths, hidden rows, or other such nonsense. In short, you can create and manage multiple analyses on different tabs and then bring together all your presentation pieces into a nicely formatted presentation layer.

Rotating objects to save time

Again, because the Camera tool outputs pictures, you can rotate the pictures in situations where placing the copied range on its side can help save time. A great example is a chart. Certain charts are relatively easy to create in a vertical orientation but extremely difficult to create in a horizontal orientation.

Figure 6-12 shows a vertical bullet graph (on the left). This graph is relatively easy to create in this vertical format. However, creating a horizontal bullet graph involves lots of intricate steps with multiple chart types. It's basically a pain to create a horizontal bullet graph.

The Camera tool to the rescue! When the live picture of the chart is created, all you have to do is rotate the picture using the rotate handle to create a horizontal version.

REGION	MARKET	Previous Month	Current Month	Variance
North	Great Lakes	70,261	72,505	3.2%
North	New England	217,858	283,324	30.0%
North	New York North	157,774	148,790	-5.7%
North	New York South	53,670	68,009	26.7%
North	Ohio	100,512	98,308	-2.2%
North	Shenandoah Valley	149,742	200,076	33.6%
South	South Carolina	249,535	229,473	-8.0%
South	Florida	111,606	136,104	22.0%
South	Gulf Coast	253,703	245,881	-3.1%
South	Illinois	129,148	131,538	1.9%
South	Indiana	152,471	151,699	-0.5%
South	Kentucky	224,524	225,461	0.4%
North	North Carolina	124,600	130,791	5.0%
South	Tennessee	307,490	268,010	-12.8%

REGION	MARKET	Last Month Sales
North	Great Lakes	70,261
North	New England	217,858
North	New York North	157,774
North	New York South	53,670
North	North Carolina	124,600
North	Ohio	100,512
North	Shenandoah Valley	149,742
South	Florida	111,606
South	Gulf Coast	253,703
South	Illinois	129,148
South	Indiana	152,471
South	Kentucky	224,524
South	South Carolina	249,535
South	Tennessee	307,490
South	Texas	180,167
West	California	190,264
West	Central	133,628
West	Colorado	134,039
West	North West	120,143
West	Southwest	248,098
West	Topeka	222,389

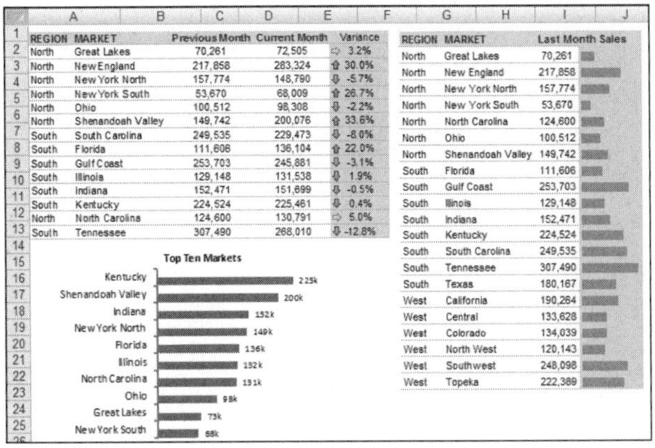

Figure 6-11: Use the Camera tool to get multiple disparate ranges into a compact area.

Figure 6-12: You can use the rotation handle to rotate your live pictures to a horizontal orientation, as seen here on the right.

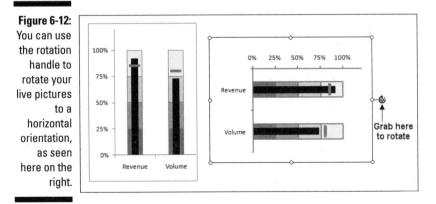

Creating small charts

Another useful thing you can do with the Camera tool is create small charts. Although you can resize charts easily enough through other means, you typically would have to spend time tweaking the scaling, font, and other elements on the chart after you get the chart small enough. Because the Camera tool creates a picture that keeps its pixel ratios intact while you resize, it allows you to achieve small chart sizes without tweaking a single chart element.

Formula-Driven Visualizations

A *formula-driven label* is a label or text resulting from a formula, which can be used to further analysis and reporting. The idea here is that you build some logic into a formula and then use the resulting value as a new dimension of data which can used to sort, conditionally format, and chart.

Take a look at the simple example illustrated in Figure 6-13. Beside each number is a formula that determines whether the number is above 300. If it is, the word *Above* is displayed, else the word *Below* is displayed. The results of the formula can be sorted, conditionally formatted, used in charting, and so on.

Figure 6-13:
Adding the
results of
the formula
next to each
number.

100	=IF(G4>300,"Above","Below")
275	Below
325	Above
280	Below
312	Above

Now I realize that even to the average Excel user this is a fairly intuitive concept. You hardly need me to point out various examples of how you can implement formulas in your analysis and reporting.

I do, however, want to take this concept further and show you a few examples of how you can add a visual element to your formulas, thereby creating a *formula-driven visualization.* That is, creating formulas which return visualizations instead of just text.

In-cell charting without charts or conditional formatting

Figure 6-14 shows a table that contains in-cell charting, providing a visualization of the numbers shown. The cool thing is that the in-cell charting achieved here is the result of a simple formula.

This effect was achieved by using Excel's REPT function. The REPT repeats a given character a specified number of times. For example, if you went to a cell and entered **=REPT("s",10)**, the returned value would be ssssssssss (the "s" character repeated ten times).

Figure 6-14:
The in-cell charting seen here is nothing more than formulas.

	A	B	C	D
1	REGION	MARKET	Last Month Sales	
2	North	Great Lakes	70,261	
3	North	New England	217,858	
4	North	New York North	157,774	
5	North	New York South	53,670	
6	North	North Carolina	124,600	
7	North	Ohio	100,512	
8	North	Shenandoah Valley	149,742	
9	South	Florida	111,606	
10	South	Gulf Coast	253,703	
11	South	Illinois	129,148	
12	South	Indiana	152,471	
13	South	Kentucky	224,524	
14	South	South Carolina	249,535	
15	South	Tennessee	307,490	
16	South	Texas	180,167	
17	West	California	190,264	
18	West	Central	133,628	
19	West	Colorado	134,039	
20	West	North West	120,143	
21	West	Southwest	248,098	
22	West	Topeka	222,389	

The idea is instead of using a letter, you use a character that, when repeated, looks kind of like a chart. The *pipe character* (the | shown above the backslash on your keyboard) is a perfect character for this kind of thing. If you went to a cell and entered **=REPT("|",10)**, the returned value would be ||||||||||. That looks very similar to a bar in a chart.

You may be wondering why you'd even use this. Why wouldn't you just use the Data Bars conditional formatting feature or for that matter, a chart?

First, Data Bars are not *backwards-compatible* — anyone who doesn't have Excel 2007 can't use them. Second, their gradient style may not conform to the overall look and feel of your dashboard. As for standard charts, they take up much more space than in-cell charting. Plus, they add overhead to your file.

In-cell charting gives you an easy-to-implement alternative that doesn't require a lot of real estate or setup.

To push this further, imagine that you had then number 30 in cell A1. You could, in cell B1, enter **=REPT(" | ", A1)**. This would show 30 pipe characters in cell B1, giving you a visualization of the number in A1.

This is all dandy until you get to really big numbers. For instance, you can imagine that repeating the pipe character 200 times just isn't that useful. In situations where you have large values, you can cut the number down to size by dividing it by 10, 100, 1000, or whatever makes sense.

So if Cell A1 contains 200, you can use `=REPT(" | ",A1/10)`. This effectively returns 20 pipe characters instead of 200. Figure 6-15 demonstrates this concept; note the formula being used in the formula bar.

Figure 6-15:
When using the REPT function with large values, divide the values into smaller increments that can be used in the REPT function.

	A	B	C	D
1		Good		
2	30	ⅼⅼⅼⅼ		
3	50	ⅼⅼⅼⅼⅼ		
4	56	ⅼⅼⅼⅼⅼ		
5	75	ⅼⅼⅼⅼⅼⅼⅼ		
6	90	ⅼⅼⅼⅼⅼⅼⅼⅼ		
7	100	ⅼⅼⅼⅼⅼⅼⅼⅼⅼ		
8	124	ⅼⅼⅼⅼⅼⅼⅼⅼⅼⅼⅼ		
9	200	ⅼⅼⅼⅼⅼⅼⅼⅼⅼⅼⅼⅼⅼⅼⅼⅼⅼⅼ		
10	143	ⅼⅼⅼⅼⅼⅼⅼⅼⅼⅼⅼⅼⅼ		
11				

B2 ▾ 𝑓ₓ =REPT("|",A2/10)

Another way to limit the number of times a character is repeated is to define a maximum for the formula. You can do this by getting a bit fancy and using Excel's MAX function. To understand this, take a look at Figure 6-16.

In Figure 6-16, note the formula in the formula bar:

```
=REPT(" | ",A2/MAX($A$2:$A$9)*25)
```

Be sure to make the range used in the MAX function an *absolute reference*. That is to say, be sure to include a dollar sign ($) in front of the column and row references, such as MAX($A$2:$A$9). With the $ character, you tell Excel to not increment the column and row references when you copy a range. This ensures that the range being referenced is locked when you copy the formula.

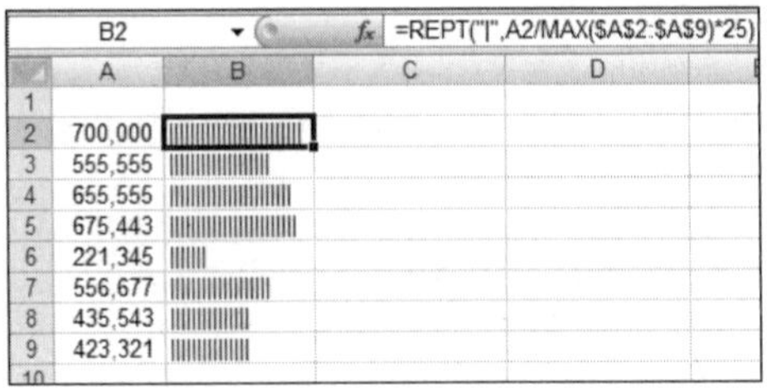

Figure 6-16:
You can incorporate a MAX function into your formula to limit the number of characters repeated.

This formula basically tells Excel to take the value being referenced and divide it by the maximum value for entire range. Then take that answer and multiply it by 25. The value shown in A2, 700000, is indeed the maximum value in the entire range. So in the case of Cell A2 the formula essentially translates to `=REPT("|",700000/700000*25)`. Mathematically, `700000/700000*25` gives you 25.

In the case of Cell A3, the formula would translate to `=REPT("|",555555/700000*25)`. Mathematically, `555555/700000*25` gives you 19.84.

Stand back and think about what this means. The maximum number of characters that can possibly be returned by this formula is 25. This formula essentially limits the number of pipe characters no matter how big your numbers are.

Because the value returned by the REPT function is nothing more than a text string, you can apply formatting to it just as you would any other text. You can change font, change pitch, add color, apply conditional formatting, and even change alignment. Figure 6-17 demonstrates how you can get fancy with in-cell charting to achieve some nifty looking analysis just by adjusting various formatting options.

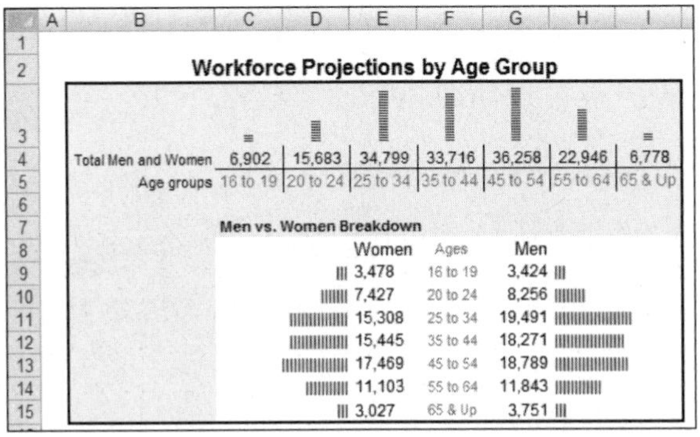

Figure 6-17:
Experiment with various formatting options to create different visualizations.

Creating visualizations with Wingdings and things

If you read Chapter 5, you know that Excel 2007 offers some new conditional formatting rules that allow you add icons to your cells. With icons, you can distinguish values from one another by using different shapes and colors. The problem is that Icon Sets aren't backwards-compatible — anyone who doesn't have Excel 2007 can't use them.

A creative alternative to using the Icon Sets offered with conditional formatting is to use the various symbol fonts that come with Office. The symbol fonts are Wingdings, Wingdings2, Wingdings3, and Webdings. These fonts display symbols for each character instead of the standard numbers and letters.

Take a look at Figure 6-18 to see what I mean. Columns A–C list numbers and letters in the standard Arial font. The same numbers and letters are shown in the various symbol fonts. As you can see, a few of the symbols (highlighted in Figure 6-18) look similar to the Icons Sets offered with conditional formatting.

The idea here is simple: Make a formula that returns a character and then change the font so that the symbol for that character is shown based on the font you select. For instance, if you entered the uppercase **P** in cell A1 and then change the font to Windings2, you get a checkmark symbol. Looking at the table in Figure 6-19, see that the equivalent of the uppercase P is indeed a checkmark in Windings2 font.

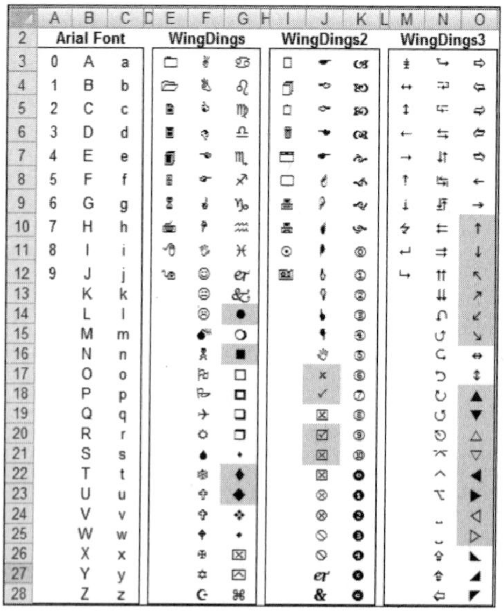

Figure 6-18: You can use symbol fonts to return symbols instead of numbers and letters.

Figure 6-19:
Adjust your
formulas
to return
characters
formatted
into a
symbol font.

	Q	R	S	T	U
1		=IF(Q3>50,"True","False")	=IF(Q3>50,"J","L")	=IF(Q3>50,"O","P")	=IF(Q3>50,"p","q")
2		Arial	Windings	Windings2	Windings3
3	10	False	☺	×	▼
4	20	False	☺	×	▼
5	30	False	☺	×	▼
6	40	False	☺	×	▼
7	50	False	☺	×	▼
8	60	True	☺	✓	▲
9	70	True	☺	✓	▲
10	80	True	☺	✓	▲
11	90	True	☺	✓	▲
12	100	True	☺	✓	▲
13					

Here's a simple example of how you use this concept. Imagine you have the number 55 in cell A1. In cell B1, you can enter **=IF(A1>50,"P","O")**. In a standard font, this formula returns the letter P because the value in cell A1 is indeed greater than 50. However, if you change the font to Windings2, you'd see a checkmark.

Figure 6-19 expands this concept, showing you how you can adjust your formulas to return characters that you can then format to show as a symbol.

To change the font, select the cell or range of cells in which you want the visualizations displayed, then choose the appropriate font from the Font group on the Home tab of the Ribbon. Remember that you only need to change the font for those cells in which you want the icons to be shown.

Be aware that not all fonts are available on all systems internationally. If you work for an international company where many people in different countries will use your dashboards, you will want to ensure that the font you use renders properly in each of your users' versions of Excel.

Part III
Building Advanced Dashboard Components

The 5th Wave   By Rich Tennant

"Well, shoot! This eggplant chart is just as confusing as the butternut squash chart and the gourd chart. Can't you just make a pie chart like everyone else?"

In this part . . .

The chapters in this section take you beyond the basics to take a look at some of the advanced components you can create with Excel 2007. This part consists of three chapters, starting with Chapter 7, in which I demonstrate how to represent time trending, seasonal trending, moving averages, and other types of trending in dashboards. That chapter also introduces you to Sparklines. In Chapter 8, I explore the many methods used to *bucket* data, or to put data into groups for reporting. Chapter 9 demonstrates some of the charting techniques that help you display and measure values versus goals.

Chapter 7

Components That Show Trending

*N*o matter what business you're in, you can't escape the tendency to trend. In fact, one of the most common concepts used in dashboards and reports is the concept of *trending*. A *trend* is a measure of variance over some defined interval — typically time periods, like days, months, or years.

The reason trending is so popular is that trending provides a rational expectation of what might happen in the future. If I know this book has sold 10,000 copies a month over the last 12 months (I wish), I have reasonable expectation to believe sales next month will be around 10,000 copies. In short, trending tells you where you've been and where you might be going.

In this chapter, you explore basic trending concepts and some of the advanced techniques you can use to take your trending components beyond simple line charts.

Trending Dos and Don'ts

As with all aspects of reporting with Excel, building trending components has some dos and don'ts. This section helps you avoid some common trending *faux pas*.

Using chart types appropriate for trending

Yes, you do have the freedom to use any chart type you want when building your trending components. After all, it's your data. But, the truth is, no chart type is the silver bullet for all situations. As overwhelming as it may sound, for effective trending, you'll want to understand which chart types are most effective in different trending scenarios.

Trending with line charts

Line charts are the kings of trending. In business reporting, a line chart almost always indicates movement across time. Even in areas not related to business, the concept of lines is used to indicate time — consider timelines, family lines, bloodlines, and so on. The benefit of using a line chart for trending is that it instantly is recognized as a trending component, avoiding any delay in information processing.

Line charts are especially effective in presenting trends with many data points — as the chart at the top of the Figure 7-1 shows. You can also use a line chart to present trends for more than one time period, as shown in the chart at the bottom of Figure 7-1.

Trending with area charts

An *area chart* is essentially a line chart that's been filled in. So, technically, area charts are appropriate for trending. They're particularly good at highlighting trends over a large time span. For example, the chart in Figure 7-2 trends over 120 days of data.

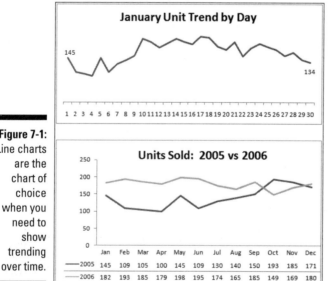

Figure 7-1: Line charts are the chart of choice when you need to show trending over time.

Trending with column charts

If you're trending one series of time, a line chart is absolutely the way to go. However, if you're comparing two or more time periods on the same chart, columns may best bring out the comparisons.

Figure 7-3 demonstrates how a combination chart can instantly call attention to the exact months when 2006 sales fell below 2005. A combination of line and column charts is an extremely effective way to show the difference in trending between two time periods. I show you how to create this type of chart later in this chapter (in the section, "Creating stacked time comparisons").

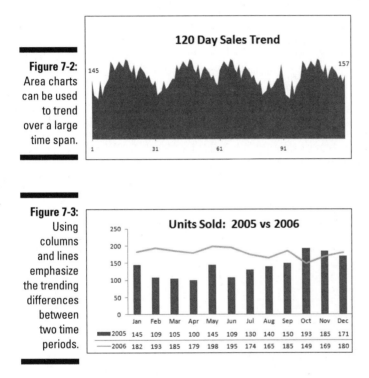

Figure 7-2:
Area charts can be used to trend over a large time span.

Figure 7-3:
Using columns and lines emphasize the trending differences between two time periods.

	Jan	Feb	Mar	Apr	May	Jun	Jul	Aug	Sep	Oct	Nov	Dec
2005	145	109	105	100	145	109	130	140	150	193	185	171
2006	182	193	185	179	198	195	174	165	185	149	169	180

Starting the vertical scale at zero

This point will no doubt cause a bit of controversy, but I am of the opinion that the vertical axis on trending charts should almost always start at zero. The reason I say *almost,* though, is because you may have trending data that contains negative values or fractions. In those situations, it's generally best to keep Excel's default scaling. However, in situations where there are only non-negative integers, ensure that your vertical axis starts at zero.

The reason is that the vertical scale of a chart can have a significant impact on the representation of a trend. For instance, the two charts shown in Figure 7-4 contain the same data. The only difference is that in the top chart, I did nothing to fix the vertical scale assigned by Excel (it starts at 96), but in the bottom chart, I fixed the scale to start at zero.

Now you may think the top chart is more accurate because it shows the ups and downs of the trend. However, if you look at the numbers closely, you see that the units represented went from 100 to 107 in 12 months. That's not exactly a material change, and it certainly doesn't warrant such a dramatic chart. In truth, the trend is relatively flat, yet the top chart makes it look as though the trend is way up.

The bottom chart more accurately reflects the true nature of the trend. I achieved this effect by locking the Minimum value on the vertical axis to zero.

To adjust the scale of your vertical axis, follow these simple steps:

1. **Right-click the vertical axis and choose Format Axis.**

   The Format Axis dialog box appears. (See Figure 7-5.)

2. **In the Format Axis dialog box, click the Fixed radio button next to the Minimum property, and then set the Minimum value to 0.**

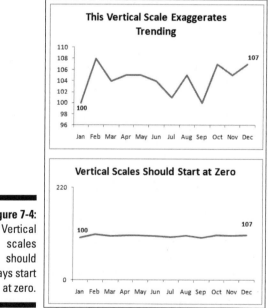

Figure 7-4:
Vertical scales should always start at zero.

Format Axis

Axis Options	
Number	Axis Options
Fill	Minimum: ○ Auto ⦿ Fixed `0`
Line Color	Maximum: ⦿ Auto ○ Fixed `110.0`
Line Style	Major unit: ○ Auto ⦿ Fixed `220`
Shadow	Minor unit: ⦿ Auto ○ Fixed `0.4`
3-D Format	☐ Values in reverse order
Alignment	☐ Logarithmic scale Base: `10`

Display units: None ⏷

☐ Show display units label on chart

Major tick mark type: Outside ⏷
Minor tick mark type: None ⏷
Axis labels: Next to Axis ⏷

Horizontal axis crosses:
⦿ Automatic
○ Axis value: `0.0`
○ Maximum axis value

Close

Figure 7-5:
Always
set the
Minimum
value of
your vertical
axis to zero.

3. **(Optional) You can set the Major Unit value to twice the Maximum value in your data.**

    This ensures that your trend line gets placed in the middle of your chart.

4. **Click the Close button to apply your changes.**

Many would argue that the bottom chart shown in Figure 7-4 hides the small-scale trending that may be important. That is to say, a seven unit difference may be very significant in some businesses. Well, if that's true, why use a chart at all? If each unit has such an impact on the analysis, why use a broad-sweep representation like a chart? A table with conditional formatting would do a better job at highlighting small-scale changes than any chart ever could.

Leveraging Excel's logarithmic scale

There may be situations when your trending starts with very small numbers and ends with very large numbers. In these cases, you'll end up with charts that don't accurately represent the true trend. Take Figure 7-6, for instance. In this figure, you see the unit trending for both 2006 and 2007. As you can see in the data table, 2006 started with a modest 50 units. As the months progressed, the monthly unit count increased to 11,100 units through December 2007. Because the two years are on such different scales, it's difficult to discern a comparative trending for the two years together.

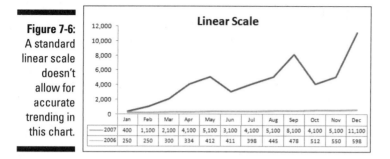

Figure 7-6:
A standard
linear scale
doesn't
allow for
accurate
trending in
this chart.

The solution is to use a logarithmic scale instead of a standard linear scale.

Without going into high school math, a logarithmic scale allows your axis to jump from 1 to 10, to 100 to 1000, and so on without changing the spacing between axis points. In other words, the distance between 1 and 10 is the same as the distance between 100 and 1000.

Figure 7-7 shows the same chart as that in Figure 7-6, but in a logarithmic scale. Notice that the trending for both years is now clear and accurately represented.

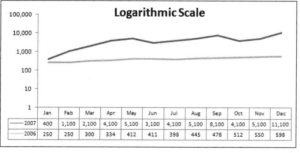

Figure 7-7:
Using the
logarithmic
scale helps
bring out
trending in
charts that
contain very
small and
very large
values.

To change the vertical axis of a chart to logarithmic scaling, follow these steps:

1. **Click anywhere on the chart.**

   This activates the Chart Tools tab on the Ribbon.

2. **Select the Layout tab found under the Chart Tools sub tab.**

3. **Click the Axis button and select Primary Vertical Axis.**

4. **Click the Show Axis with Log Scale option. (See Figure 7-8.)**

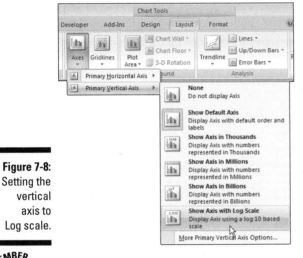

Figure 7-8:
Setting the
vertical
axis to
Log scale.

Logarithmic scales work only with positive numbers.

Applying creative label management

As silly as it may sound, one of the sticking points to creating trending components is the labeling. Trending charts tend to hold lots of data points, whose category axis labels take up lots of room. In this section, you find a few tips to help manage the labels in your trending components.

Abbreviating instead of changing alignment

Month names look and feel very long when you have to place them in a chart — especially when that chart has to fit on a dashboard. However, the solution isn't to change their alignment, as shown in Figure 7-9. Words that are placed on their sides inherently cause a reader to stop for a moment and read the labels. This isn't ideal when you want them to think about your data and not spend time reading with their heads tilted.

Although it's not always possible, the first option is always to keep your labels normally aligned. So instead of jumping right to the alignment option to squeeze them in, try abbreviating the month names. As you can see in Figure 7-9, even using the first letter of the month name is appropriate.

Implying labels to reduce clutter

When you're listing the same months over the course of multiple years, you may be able to imply the labels for months instead of labeling each and every one of them.

Take Figure 7-10, for example. In this figure, you see a chart that shows trending through two years. There are so many data points that the labels are forced to be vertically aligned. To reduce clutter, as you can see, only certain months are explicitly labeled. The others are implied by a dot. To achieve this effect, you can simply replace the label in the original data table with a dot (or whatever character you like).

Going vertical when you have too many data points for horizontal

Trending data by day is common, but it does prove to be painful if the trending extends to 30 days or more. In these scenarios, it becomes difficult to keep the chart to a reasonable size and even more difficult to effectively label it.

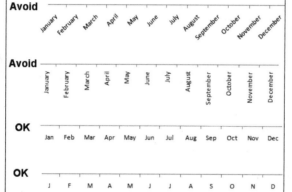

Figure 7-9:
Choose to abbreviate category names instead of changing alignment.

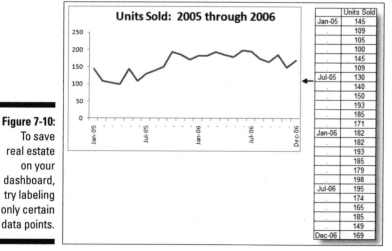

Figure 7-10:
To save real estate on your dashboard, try labeling only certain data points.

One solution is to show the trending vertically using a bar chart. (See Figure 7-11.) With a bar chart, you have room to label the data points and keep the chart to a reasonable size. This isn't something to aspire to, however. Trending vertically isn't as intuitive and may not convey your information in a very readable form. Nevertheless, this solution can prove to be just the workaround you need when the horizontal view proves to be impractical.

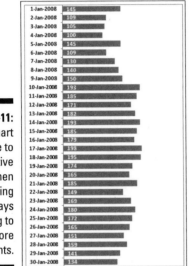

Figure 7-11:
A bar chart can prove to be effective when trending days extending to 30 or more data points.

Comparative Trending

Although the name is fancy, *comparative trending* is a simple concept. You chart two or more data series on the same chart so that the trends from those series can be visually compared. In this section, you walk through a few techniques that allow you to build components that present comparative trending.

Creating side-by-side time comparisons

Figure 7-12 shows a chart that presents a side-by-side time comparison of three time periods. With this technique, you can show different time periods in different colors without breaking the continuity of the overall trending.

Figure 7-12:
You can
show
trends for
difference
periods
side-by-
side.

Figure 7-12: You can show trends for difference periods side-by-side.

1. **To create this type of chart, you would structure a table similar to the one shown in Figure 7-13.**

   Note that instead of placing the all the data into one column, you're staggering the data into respective years. This tells the chart to create three separate lines (allowing for the three colors).

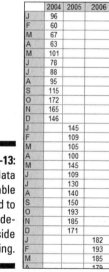

Figure 7-13: The data table needed to create side-by-side trending.

	2004	2005	2006
J	96		
F	60		
M	67		
A	63		
M	101		
J	78		
J	88		
A	95		
S	115		
O	172		
N	165		
D	146		
J		145	
F		109	
M		105	
A		100	
M		145	
J		109	
J		130	
A		140	
S		150	
O		193	
N		185	
D		171	
J			182
F			193
M			185
A			170

2. **When you have your data in the correct structure, simply highlight the entire table and create a line chart.**

   This automatically creates the chart shown in Figure 7-12.

3. **If you want to get a bit fancy, click the chart to select it, and then right-click. Choose Change Chart Type from the context menu that activates.**

4. **When the Change Chart Type dialog box opens, select Stacked Column Chart.**

As you can in Figure 7-14, your chart now shows the trending for each year in columns.

Would you like a space in between the years? Adding a space in the data table (between each 12 month sequence) adds a space in the chart. (See Figure 7-15.)

Figure 7-14:
Change the chart type to Stacked Column Chart to present columns instead of lines.

Figure 7-15:
If you want to separate each year with a space, simply add a space into the source data table.

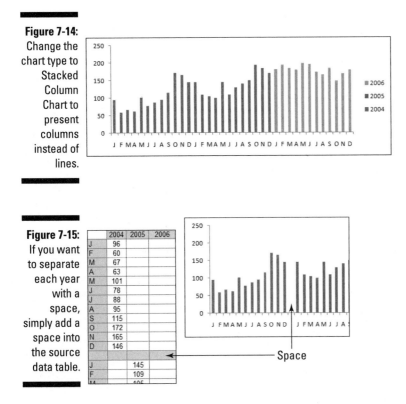

Creating stacked time comparisons

The stacked time comparison places two series on top of each other instead of side-by-side. Although this removes the benefit of having an unbroken overall trending, it replaces it with the benefit of an at-a-glance comparison within a compact space. Figure 7-16 illustrates a common stacked time comparison.

Figure 7-16:
A stacked
time
comparison
allows you
to view and
compare
two years of
data in a
compact
space.

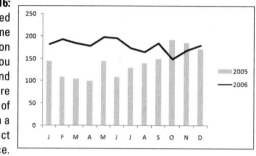

1. **To create this chart, create a new table and structure it like the one shown in Figure 7-17.**

Figure 7-17:
Start with
a table
containing
the data for
two time
periods.

	A	B	C
1		2005	2006
2	J	145	182
3	F	109	193
4	M	105	185
5	A	100	179
6	M	145	198
7	J	109	195
8	J	130	174
9	A	140	165
10	S	150	185
11	O	193	149
12	N	185	169
13	D	171	180
14			

2. **Highlight the entire table and create a column chart.**

3. **Select and right-click any of the bars for the 2006 data series and then choose Change Chart Type.**

4. **When the Change Chart Type dialog box opens, select the Line with Markers type.**

This technique works well with two time series. You generally want to avoid stacking any more than that. Stacking more than two series often muddies the view and causes users to constantly reference the legend to keep track of the series they're evaluating.

Trending with a secondary axis

In some trending components, you'll have series that trends two very different units of measure. For instance, in Figure 7-18, you have a table that shows a trend for People Count and a trend for % of Labor Cost.

Figure 7-18:
You often
need to
trend two
very
different
units of
measure,
such as
counts and
percentages.

	A	B	C
1		People Count	% Labor Cost
2	J	145	20%
3	F	109	21%
4	M	105	23%
5	A	100	23%
6	M	145	24%
7	J	109	25%
8	J	130	24%
9	A	140	25%
10	S	150	24%
11	O	193	26%
12	N	185	28%
13	D	171	29%
14			

These are two very different units of measure, that when charted, produce the unimpressive chart you see in Figure 7-19. Because Excel builds the vertical axis to accommodate the largest number, the percentage of labor cost trending gets lost at the bottom of the chart. Even a logarithmic scale doesn't help in this scenario.

Because the default vertical axis (or primary axis) doesn't work for both series, the solution is to create another axis to accommodate the series that doesn't fit into the primary axis. This other axis is the *secondary axis.*

To place a data series on the secondary axis, follow these steps:

1. Right-click the data series and choose Format Data Series.

The Format Data Series dialog box appears. (See Figure 7-20.)

Technically, it doesn't matter which data series you place on the secondary axis. A general rule is to place the problem data series on the secondary axis. In this scenario, because the data series for percentage of labor cost seems to be the problem, I place that series on the secondary axis.

Figure 7-19:
The trending for
percentage
of labor cost
gets lost at
the bottom
of the chart.

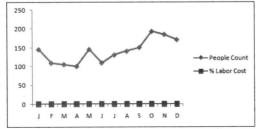

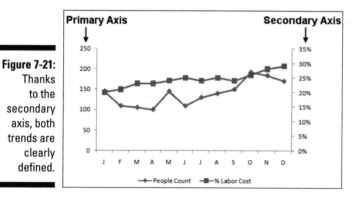

Figure 7-20:
Placing a
data series
on the
secondary
axis.

2. **In the Format Data Series dialog box, select the Series Options button in the left pane and then select the Secondary Axis radio button.**

In Figure 7-21, notice a newly-added axis to the right of the chart. Any data series on the secondary axis has its vertical axis labels shown on the right.

Figure 7-21:
Thanks
to the
secondary
axis, both
trends are
clearly
defined.

Again, changing the chart type of any one of the data series can help in comparing the two trends. In Figure 7-22, the chart type for the People Count trend has been changed to a column. Now you can easily see that although the number of people has gone down in November and December, the percentage of labor cost continues to rise.

To change the chart type of any data series, right-click the data series and then choose Change Chart Type.

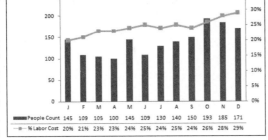

Figure 7-22:
Changing
the chart
type of
one data
series can
underscore
comparisons.

Highlighting Periods of Time

Some of your trending components may contain certain periods where a special event occurred, causing an anomaly in the trending pattern. For instance, you may have an unusually large spike or dip in the trend caused by some occurrence in your organization. Or maybe you need to mix actual data with forecasts in your charting component. In such cases, it could be helpful to highlight specific periods in your trending with special formatting.

Formatting specific periods

Imagine you just created the chart component illustrated in Figure 7-23 and you want to explain the spike in October. You could, of course, use a footnote somewhere, but that would force your audience to look for an explanation elsewhere on your dashboard. Calling attention to an anomaly directly on the chart helps give your audience context without the need to look away from the chart.

A simple solution is to format the data point for October to display in a different color and then add a simple text box that explains the spike.

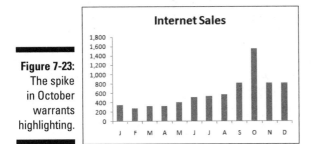

Figure 7-23:
The spike
in October
warrants
highlighting.

To format a single data point:

1. **Click the data point once.**

   This places dots on all the data points in the series.

2. **Click the data point again to ensure Excel knows you're formatting only that one data point.**

   The dots disappear from all but the target data point.

3. **Right-click and choose Format Data Point.**

   This opens the Format Data Point dialog box, as shown in Figure 7-24.

Figure 7-24: The Format Data Point dialog box gives you formatting options for a single data point.

The idea is to adjust the formatting properties of the data point as you see fit.

The dialog box shown in Figure 7-24 is for a column chart. Different chart types have different options in the Format Data Point dialog box. Nevertheless, the idea remains the same in that you can adjust the properties in the Format Data Point dialog box to change the formatting of a single data point.

After changing the fill color of the October data point and adding a text box with some context, the chart nicely explains the spike. (See Figure 7-25.)

Figure 7-25: The chart now draws attention to the spike in October and provides instant context via a text box.

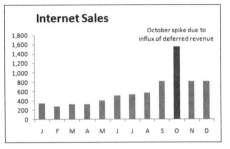

To add a text box to a chart, click the Insert tab in the Ribbon and select the Text Box icon. Then click inside the chart to create an empty text box, which you can fill with your words. Visit Chapter 6 for a detailed refresher on dynamic labeling.

Using dividers to mark significant events

Every now and then a particular event shifts the entire paradigm of your data permanently. A good example is a price increase. The trend shown in Figure 7-26 has permanently been affected by a price increase implemented in October. As you can see, a dividing line (along with some labeling) provides a distinct marker for the price increase, effectively separating the old trend from the new.

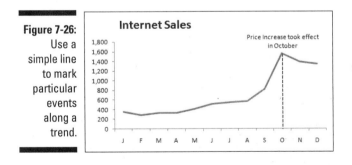

Figure 7-26: Use a simple line to mark particular events along a trend.

Although there are lots of fancy ways to create this effect, I find that I rarely need to get any fancier that manually drawing a line myself. To draw a dividing line inside a chart, take the following steps:

1. **Click the chart to select it.**

2. **Select the Insert tab on the Ribbon and click the Shapes button.**

3. **Select the line shape, go to your chart, and draw the line where you want it.**

4. **Right-click your newly-drawn line and choose Format Shape.**

5. **Use the Format Shape dialog box to format your line's color, thickness, and style.**

Representing forecasts in your trending components

It's common to be asked to show both actual data and forecast as a single trending component. When you do show the two together, you want to ensure that your audience can clearly distinguish where actual data ends and where forecasting begins. To see what I mean, take a look at Figure 7-27.

Figure 7-27: You can easily see where sales trending ends and forecast trending begins.

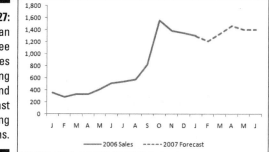

The best way to achieve this effect is to start with a data structure similar to the one shown in Figure 7-28. As you can see, sales and forecasts are in separate columns so that when charted, you get two distinct data series. Also note that the value in cell B14 is actually a formula referencing C14. This value serves to ensure a continuous trend line (with no gaps) when the two data series are charted together.

When you have the appropriately structured dataset, you can create a line chart. At this point, you can apply special formatting to the 2007 Forecast data series. Follow these steps:

1. **Click the data series that represents 2007 forecast.**

   This places dots on all the data points in the series.

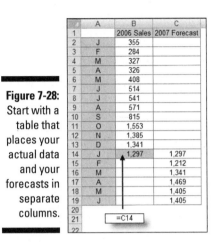

Figure 7-28:
Start with a
table that
places your
actual data
and your
forecasts in
separate
columns.

2. **Right-click and choose Format Data Series.**

   This opens the Format Data Series dialog box.

   When the Format Data Series dialog box activates, you can adjust the
   properties to format the series color, thickness, and style.

Other Trending Techniques

In this section, I show you a few techniques that go beyond the basic concepts I've covered so far.

Avoiding overload with directional trending

Do you work with a manager that's crazy for data? Are you getting headaches
from trying to squeeze three years of monthly data into a single chart?
Although it's understandable to want to see a three-year trend, placing too
much information on a single chart can make for a convoluted trending component that tells you almost nothing.

When you're faced with the need to display impossible amounts of data, step
back and think about the true purpose of the analysis. When your manager
asks for a three-year sales trend by month, what's he really looking for? It
could be that he's really asking whether current monthly sales are declining
versus history. Do you really need to show each and every month or can you
show the directional trend?

A *directional trend* is one that uses simple analysis to imply a relative direction of performance. The key attribute of a directional trend is that the data used is often a set of calculated values as opposed to actual data values. For instance, instead of charting each month's sales for a single year, you could chart the average sales for Q1, Q2, Q3, and Q4. With such a chart, you'd get a directional idea of monthly sales, without the need to look into detailed data.

Take a look at Figure 7-29, which shows two charts. The top chart trends each year's monthly data in a single trending component. You can see how difficult it is to discern much from this chart. It looks like monthly sales are dropping in all three years. The bottom chart shows the same data in a directional trend, showing average sales for key time periods. The trend really jumps at you, showing that sales have flattened out after healthy growth in 2004 and 2005.

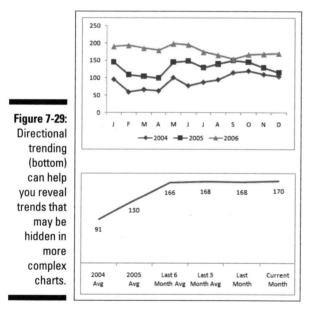

Figure 7-29: Directional trending (bottom) can help you reveal trends that may be hidden in more complex charts.

Smoothing data

Certain lines of business lend themselves to wide fluctuations in data from month to month. For instance, a consulting practice may go months without a steady revenue stream before a big contract comes along and spikes the sales figures for a few months. Some call these ups and downs *seasonality* or *business cycles*.

Whatever you call them, wild fluctuations in data can prevent you from effectively analyzing and presenting trends. Figure 7-30 demonstrates how highly volatile data can conceal underlying trends.

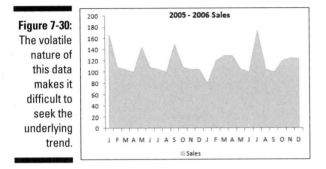

Figure 7-30: The volatile nature of this data makes it difficult to seek the underlying trend.

This is where the concept of *smoothing* comes in. Smoothing does just what it sounds like — it forces the range between the highest and lowest values in a dataset to smooth to a predictable range without disturbing the proportions of the dataset.

Now, you can use lots of different techniques to smooth a dataset. Take a moment to walk through one of the easier ways to apply smoothing.

Start a new column in the data source for the chart. In Figure 7-31, the new column is appropriately called Smoothing. In the second row of the smoothing column, create a simple average formula that averages the first data point and the second data point. Note that the reference to the first data point (cell D2) is locked as an absolute value with dollar ($) signs. This ensures that when this formula is copied down, the range grows to include all previous data points.

After you copy the formula down to fill the entire smoothing column, you can plot its data add a new data series to your chart. Figure 7-32 illustrates the smoothed data plotted as a line chart.

Figure 7-31: The smoothing column feeds a new series to your chart.

	B	C	D	E
1			Sales	Smoothing
2		J	167	
3		F	109	=AVERAGE($D$2:D3)
4		M	105	
5		A	100	
6		M	145	
7		J	109	
8		J	105	
9		A	100	
10		S	150	
11		O	100	

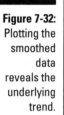

Figure 7-32:
Plotting the
smoothed
data
reveals the
underlying
trend.

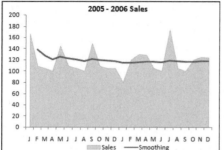

Catching sparkline fever

Sparklines, developed by visualization guru Edward Tufte, are mini word-sized charts placed in and among textual data, allowing you to see trends and patterns at a glance with minimal space. With the sparkline concept, Tufte provides a mechanism that allows you to get visual context for data without the need to take up a lot of real estate on your dashboards.

Figure 7-33 illustrates how trending sparklines help provide an additional layer of context to the month-over-month analysis provided. You can see that the month-over-month variance for the year 2006 is 8 percent. Without the sparkline, this variance would seem like cause for celebration. However, the 12-month trend provided by the sparkline allows you to quickly see that the data has been in a long, slow decline for some time.

Figure 7-33:
Sparklines
allow you to
see trends
and patterns
at a glance
with minimal
space.

	Last Month	This Month	Variance	12 Mo Trend
2005	179	186	4%	～～
2006	130	141	8%	～～

In terms of Excel, a sparkline is simply a miniature chart. The steps in creating a sparkline natively in Excel are relatively simple. Just follow these steps:

1. **Create a normal-sized chart that displays the trending you need to see.**

2. **Remove anything from the chart that isn't part of the data series: gridlines, labels, axes, titles, and so on.**

3. **Under the Format tab, find and adjust the height and width selectors under the Size group to resize the chart so that the height is about .50 inches wide and .25 inches tall.**

4. **Click and drag the chart where you want it displayed.**

If you really want to get fancy with sparklines, you may want to explore any one of the Excel add-in applications that specialize in creating sparklines. My favorite sparkline add-in is MicroCharts from BonaVista Systems. The MicroCharts add-in integrates directly into the Excel Ribbon and offers plenty of sparklines that are both effective and attractive. (See Figure 7-34.)

With MicroCharts, you can point to your data and then sparklines are placed where you specify. No need to create and maintain separate charts. When you have a data model prepared, creating a dashboard, like the one shown in Figure 7-35, becomes a matter of pointing the MicroCharts add-in to the data.

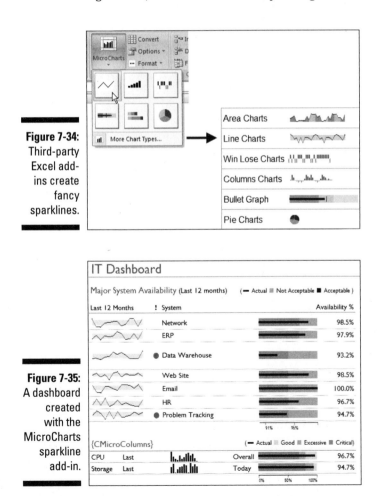

Figure 7-34: Third-party Excel add-ins create fancy sparklines.

Figure 7-35: A dashboard created with the MicroCharts sparkline add-in.

To take a test drive of the MicroCharts add-in, download the free trial from www.bonavistasystems.com/DownloadMicroCharts.html.

Chapter 8

Components That Group and Bucket Data

*I*t's often helpful to organize your analyses into logical groups of data. Grouping allows you to focus on manageable sets that have key attributes. For example, instead of looking at all customers in one giant view, you can analyze customers who buy only one product. This allows you to focus attention and resources on those customers who have the potential of buying more products.

The benefit of grouping data is that it allows you to more easily pick out groups that fall outside the norm for your business.

In this chapter, I explore some of the techniques you can use to create components that group and bucket data.

Creating Top and Bottom Displays

When I look at the list of Fortune 500 companies, I immediately look to see the top 20 companies. Then I look to see who just eked in at the bottom 20. I rarely check to see who's number 251. It's not because I don't care about number 251; it's just that I don't have the time or energy to process all 500 companies. So I process the top and bottom of the list.

This is the same concept behind creating top and bottom displays. Your audience has only a certain amount of time and resources to dedicate to solving any issues you can highlight in your reporting mechanism. Showing them the top and bottom values in a dataset can help them pinpoint where and how they can have the most impact with the time and resources they do have.

Incorporating top and bottom displays into dashboards

The top and bottom displays you create can be as simple as tables you incorporate into your dashboards. These tables are typically placed to the right of a dashboard to highlight some detailed data a manager can use to take action on a metric. For example, the simple dashboard shown in Figure 8-1 shows sales information with top and bottom Sales Reps.

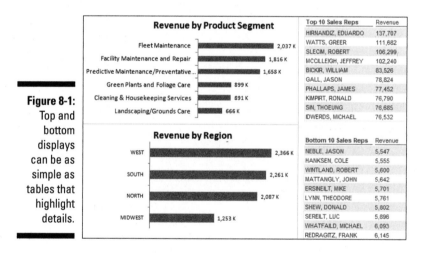

Figure 8-1:
Top and bottom displays can be as simple as tables that highlight details.

To get a little fancier, you can supplement your top and bottom displays with some ranking information, some in-cell bar charts, or some conditional formatting. (See Figure 8-2.)

You can create the in-cell bar charts with the REPT function, which I cover in Chapter 6. The arrows are simple conditional formatting rules that are evaluated against the variance in current and last months' ranks.

This gallery shows you some of the components you will find within the black and white pages of this book. Here you'll see them in full **Technicolor!** Ooooh! I've also included a few sample dashboards you may be able to use as inspiration for your next project. Enjoy!

Top 10 Sales Reps	Sales		Rank	Last Month	vs Last Month
HIRNANDIZ, EDUARDO	$137,707		1	1	⇨ 0
WATTS, GREER	$111,682		2	3	⇧ 1
SLECIM, ROBERT	$106,299		3	5	⇧ 2
MCCILLEIGH, JEFFREY	$102,240		4	2	⇩ -2
BICKIR, WILLIAM	$83,526		5	3	⇩ -2
GALL, JASON	$78,824		6	12	⇧ 6
PHALLAPS, JAMES	$77,452		7	7	⇨ 0
KIMPIRT, RONALD	$76,790		8	9	⇧ 1
SIN, THOEUNG	$76,685		9	8	⇨ -1
IDWERDS, MICHAEL	$76,532		10	4	⇩ -6

In Chapter 8, I talk about the benefits of including top and bottom views in your dashboard. This figure shows how you can supplement your top and bottom displays with some ranking information, some in-cell bar charts, and conditional formatting. These kinds of tables are typically placed to the right of a dashboard to highlight detailed data for top and bottom groups.

Bottom 10 Sales Reps	Sales		Rank	Last Month	vs Last Month
NEBLE, JASON	$5,547		244	244	⇨ 0
CELIMAN, WILLIAM	$9,779		243	241	⇩ -2
KRIZILL, ADAM	$11,454		242	235	⇩ -7
MIDANA, FRANK	$15,044		241	221	⇩ -20
GRANGIR, DAVID	$16,129		240	240	⇨ 0
DALLEARE, ANDRE	$16,265		239	239	⇨ 0
HICKLIBIRRY, JERRY	$16,670		238	225	⇩ -13
VAN HUILE, KENNETH	$18,821		237	242	⇧ 5
RACHERDSEN, KENNETH	$19,675		236	237	⇧ 1
STIGALL, DAVID	$20,092		235	243	⇧ 8

This technique, pulled from Chapter 7, shows how it can be far more effective to chart trend data side-by-side as opposed to jamming three lines on top of each other. Yes, this is all one chart!

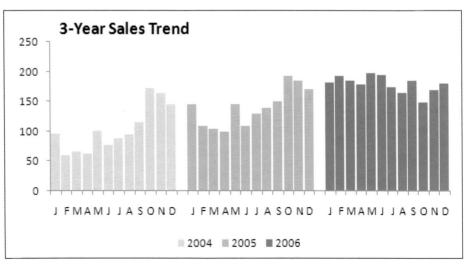

3-Year Sales Trend

J F M A M J J A S O N D   J F M A M J J A S O N D   J F M A M J J A S O N D

■ 2004   ■ 2005   ■ 2006

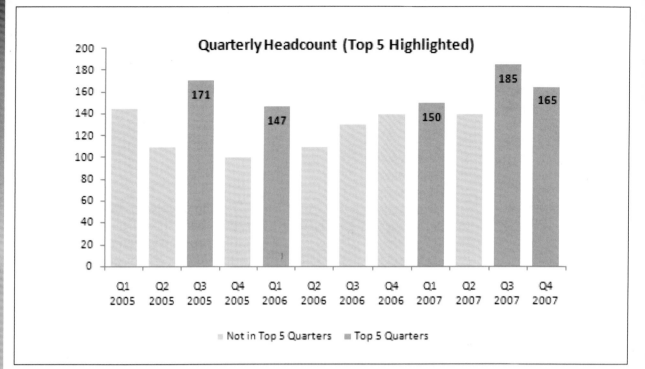

This chart purposely highlights the top five quarters based on headcount. No, the formatting and labeling was not done by hand. Excel actually calculates which quarters are in the top five and formats them automatically. You can find out how in Chapter 8.

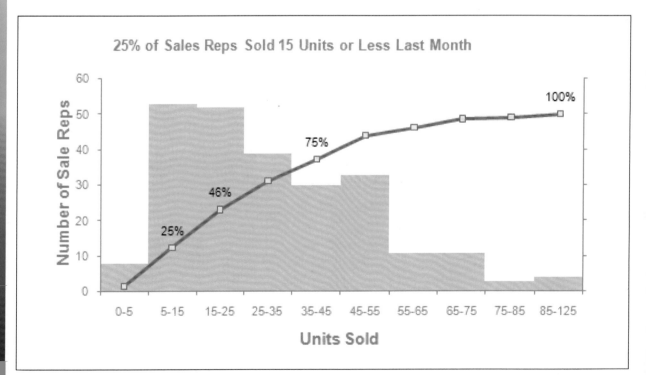

Histograms are awesome grouping components, helping you see the general distribution of a particular category or event. In Chapter 8, I show you how to create histograms from a pivot table!

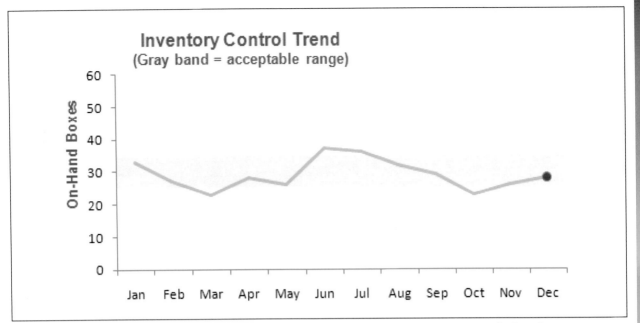

In some situations, you'll need to track performance against a target range instead of against a single target value. In this chart, monthly on-hand inventory is compared to an acceptable range. The cool thing about this component is that the target range can be adjusted by simply editing two cells. Check out Chapter 9 to see how this works.

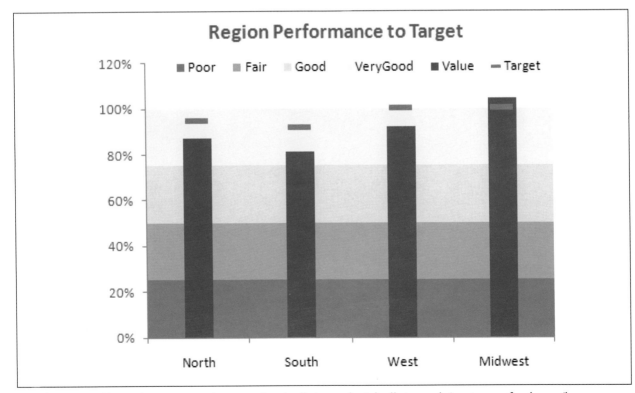

In Chapter 9, I introduce you to the amazing bullet graph. A bullet graph is a type of column/bar graph developed by visualization expert Stephen Few to display multiple perspectives in an incredibly compact space.

Foreign Exchange Dashboard - latest 24 months

November 1, 2007

Value of the US Dollar

Euro per USD		30-day Change	6-month Change	1-year Change
Latest	0.683	-4%	-8%	-13%
High	0.857	11/17/2005		
Low	0.683	11/8/2007		
Average	0.776			

Australian $ per USD		30-day Change	6-month Change	1-year Change
Latest	1.070	-4%	-10%	-18%
High	1.420	3/30/2006		
Low	1.070	11/8/2007		
Average	1.278			

British Pound per USD		30-day Change	6-month Change	1-year Change
Latest	0.477	-3%	-5%	-9%
High	0.584	11/30/2005		
Low	0.477	11/8/2007		
Average	0.528			

Canadian $ per USD		30-day Change	6-month Change	1-year Change
Latest	0.915	-7%	-14%	-19%
High	1.194	11/15/2005		
Low	0.915	11/8/2007		
Average	1.118			

Value of the Euro

USD per Euro		30-day Change	6-month Change	1-year Change
Latest	1.463	4%	9%	15%
High	1.463	11/8/2007		
Low	1.167	11/17/2005		
Average	1.293			

Australian $ per Euro		30-day Change	6-month Change	1-year Change
Latest	1.566	0%	-2%	-6%
High	1.729	6/8/2006		
Low	1.556	7/27/2007		
Average	1.647			

British Pounds per Euro		30-day Change	6-month Change	1-year Change
Latest	0.698	1%	3%	4%
High	0.702	10/28/2007		
Low	0.655	1/24/2007		
Average	0.681			

Canadian $ per Euro		30-day Change	6-month Change	1-year Change
Latest	1.338	-4%	-6%	-7%
High	1.567	3/19/2007		
Low	1.338	11/8/2007		
Average	1.442			

Interactive National Park Comparison Report

Interactive National Park Attendance Comparison Report

Select 2 parks to compare:

1 | Big Bend NP | ▶

2 | Hawaii Volcanoes NP | ▶

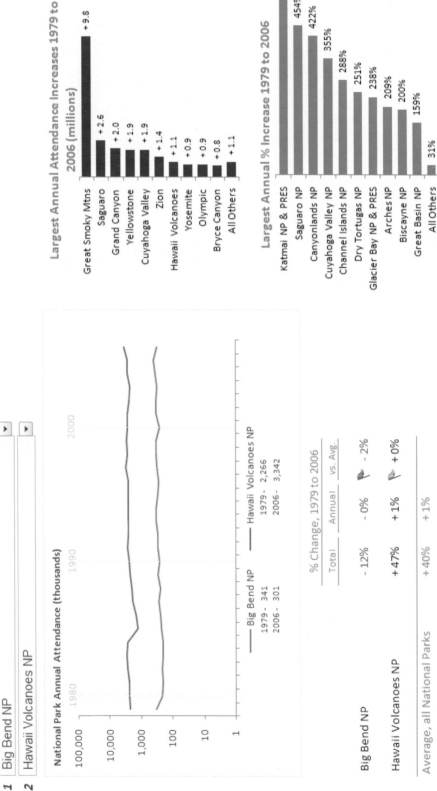

National Park Annual Attendance (thousands)

— Big Bend NP
1979 - 341
2006 - 301

— Hawaii Volcanoes NP
1979 - 2,266
2006 - 3,342

% Change, 1979 to 2006

	Total	Annual	vs. Avg.
Big Bend NP	- 12%	- 0%	- 2%
Hawaii Volcanoes NP	+ 47%	+ 1%	+ 0%
Average, all National Parks	+ 40%	+ 1%	

Largest Annual Attendance Increases 1979 to 2006 (millions)

Great Smoky Mtns	+ 9.8
Saguaro	+ 2.6
Grand Canyon	+ 2.0
Yellowstone	+ 1.9
Cuyahoga Valley	+ 1.9
Zion	+ 1.4
Hawaii Volcanoes	+ 1.1
Yosemite	+ 0.9
Olympic	+ 0.9
Bryce Canyon	+ 0.8
All Others	+ 1.1

Largest Annual % Increase 1979 to 2006

Park	% Increase
Katmai NP & PRES	544%
Saguaro NP	454%
Canyonlands NP	422%
Cuyahoga Valley NP	355%
Channel Islands NP	288%
Dry Tortugas NP	251%
Glacier Bay NP & PRES	238%
Arches NP	209%
Biscayne NP	200%
Great Basin NP	159%
All Others	31%

Division Sales Summary

Div Sales Summary

Sales

		Month			Year-to-Date	
		Sep 07	vs. Last Month		Sep 07	vs. Last Year
Div 1	$	78,653	+1.2%	$	692,159	+2.4%
Div 2	$	10,293	-0.6%	$	92,982	+2.1%
Div 3	$	29,541	+0.1%	$	266,343	-1.8%
Div 4	$	35,551	+2.0%	$	313,965	+1.7%
Div 5	$	7,565	-0.7%	$	67,084	+2.2%
Div 6	$	17,461	-0.5%	$	157,879	-1.1%
Div 7	$	25,027	+1.1%	$	219,650	+8.6%
Total	$	204,091	+0.9%	$	1,810,062	+2.0%

Gross Margin

		Month			Year-to-Date	
		Sep 07	vs. Last Month		Sep 07	vs. Last Year
Div 1	$	13,450	+6.2%	$	113,376	+4.9%
Div 2	$	2,810	-2.0%	$	25,719	+8.6%
Div 3	$	5,554	+11.3%	$	45,518	+2.9%
Div 4	$	6,257	+1.4%	$	55,540	+5.9%
Div 5	$	840	+16.0%	$	6,480	+23.4%
Div 6	$	4,086	+1.3%	$	36,375	+7.5%
Div 7	$	14,240	-2.5%	$	129,132	+4.7%
Total	$	47,236	+2.6%	$	412,141	+5.4%

Average Monthly Sales Trend — Total Company

2004	2005	2006	Last 6 Months	Last 3 Months	Last Month	Current Month
175 K	187 K	197 K	202 K	203 K	202 K	204 K

Margin Comparison-Sep 07

	Cost of Sales	Gross Margin
Div 1	65 K	13 K
Div 2	7 K	3 K
Div 3	24 K	6 K
Div 4	29 K	6 K
Div 5	7 K	1 K
Div 6	13 K	4 K
Div 7	11 K	14 K

Margin Comparison-YTD

	Cost of Sales	Gross Margin
Div 1	579 K	113 K
Div 2	67 K	26 K
Div 3	221 K	46 K
Div 4	258 K	56 K
Div 5	61 K	6 K
Div 6	122 K	36 K
Div 7	91 K	129 K

Airline Route Analysis

Airline Route Analysis

Top 10 Domestic Routes by Revenue

From	To	Revenue (000's)	% Domestic Revenue		Margin (000's)	% Domestic Margin		Revenue per Passenger	Margin per Passenger
New York	Detroit	12,180	11%		2,408	11%		177	35
New York	Washington	6,355	6%		1,230	6%		186	36
Chicago	New York	4,674	4%		337	2%		222	16 ✕
Atlanta	New York	3,602	3%		956	5%		245	65
New York	Philadelphia	3,583	3%		(717)	-3% loss		125	-25 ✕
New York	San Francisco	3,221	3%		1,856	9%		590	340
New York	Phoenix	2,847	3%		1,436	7%		555	280
New York	Toronto	2,800	3%		1,089	5%		450	175
New York	Seattle	2,792	3%		467	2%		448	75
Columbus (Ohio)	New York	2,483	2%		1,537	7%		202	125
Total Domestic routes		**108,891**			**21,049**	**19%**		**272**	**53**

Legend ✕ <10% Margin

Top 10 International Routes by Revenue

From	To	Revenue (000's)	% Domestic Revenue		Margin (000's)	% Domestic Margin		Revenue per Passenger	Margin per Passenger
New York	London	22,326	25%		11,163	23%		1,811	906
Detroit	Sao Paolo	5,648	6%		1,977	4%		1,765	618
Atlanta	Lima	3,609	4%		2,346	5%		2,123	1,380
Detroit	Frankfurt	3,584	4%		2,330	5%		2,560	1,664
Phoenix	Sydney	2,504	3%		626	1%		1,565	391
New York	Adelaide	2,042	2%		817	2%		2,722	1,089
New York	Mexico City	1,784	2%		268	1%		555	83 ✕
New York	Lima	1,500	2%		390	1%		1,250	325
New York	Veracruz	1,174	1%		141	0%		485	58 ✕
Denver	Bogota	956	1%		210	0%		956	210
Total International Routes		**89,092**			**49,115**	**55%**		**1,324**	**730**

Legend ✕ <20% Margin

Cancellations & Delays - Worst 10 Routes (last 3 months)

From	To	Cancelation %		Delays %	
Detroit	Orlando	5.1%		31.4%	
Chicago	Dallas	4.6%		26.3%	
Minneapolis	Denver	4.2%		29.7%	
Houston	Orlando	4.1%		21.7%	
Chicago	Orlando	3.9%		25.6%	
Memphis	Detroit	3.2%		15.8%	
Salt Lake City	Boston	2.8%		19.7%	
Oakland	Orlando	1.9%		14.9%	
Dallas	Houston	1.1%		16.7%	
Oakland	Seattle	0.9%		14.3%	
Total Domestic routes		**0.3%**		**9.8%**	

Cancellations - Causes (last 30 days)

Weather	6
Missing/Late Flight Crew	2
Mechanical	1
Missing/Late Ground Crew	1
Gate Handling	0
Other	2

Delays - Causes (last 30 days)

Weather	76
Missing/Late Flight Crew	17
Mechanical	15
Missing/Late Ground Crew	4
Gate Handling	2
Other	3

Compact KPI Summary (created using Bonavista's Microcharts® Excel add-in)

Compact KPI Summary

Sparklines and mini-charts created with BonaVista's Microcharts® Excel add-in

		Nov 05	Last 3 Mo Avg	Last 12 mo Avg	12 Month Trend	Targets	% of Target
Finance	$ Revenues	$18,134 K	$17,985 K	$17,728 K		$18,000 K	101%
	$ Expenses	$11,358 K	$11,186 K	$11,580 K		$12,600 K	90%
Metrics	$ Profits	$6,776 K	$6,799 K	$6,147 K		$5,400 K	125%
	% Market Share	44%	46%	45%		52%	85%
	Flights	446	447	449		500	89%
	Passengers	63 K	62 K	61 K		65 K	97%
	Miles	346 K	347 K	349 K		395 K	88%
	Pssng. Miles	31,206 K	31,376 K	31,510 K		36,000 K	87%
Flight	Cancelled Flights	9	9	10		15	60%
Metircs	Late Arrivals	63	71	64		45	141%
	Minutes Late	1,302	1,472	1,337		1,000	130%
	$ Fuel Costs	$1,293 K	$1,332 K	$1,326 K		$1,080 K	120%
	Customer Satisfaction	4.52	4.5	4.5		4.80	94%
	Flight Utilization	92%	91%	91%		94%	98%
Ratios	Revenue / Pssng. Mile	$0.58	$0.57	$0.56		$0.50	116%
	Profit / Mile	$19.56	$19.59	$17.61		$15.00	130%
	Revenue / Mile	$52.34	$51.82	$50.80		$50.00	105%
	Fuel Costs / Mile	$3.73	$3.84	$3.80		$3.00	124%
	Profit / Pssng. Mile	$0.22	$0.22	$0.20		$0.15	145%
	Revenue / Passenger	304	297	294		277	110%

Top 10 Sales Reps	Sales	Rank	Last Month	vs Last Month	
HIRNANDIZ, EDUARDO	$137,707	1	1	⇨	0
WATTS, GREER	$111,682	2	3	⇧	1
SLECIM, ROBERT	$106,299	3	5	⇧	2
MCCILLEIGH, JEFFREY	$102,240	4	2	⇩	-2
BICKIR, WILLIAM	$83,526	5	3	⇩	-2
GALL, JASON	$78,824	6	12	⇧	6
PHALLAPS, JAMES	$77,452	7	7	⇨	0
KIMPIRT, RONALD	$76,790	8	9	⇧	1
SIN, THOEUNG	$76,685	9	8	⇩	-1
IDWERDS, MICHAEL	$76,532	10	4	⇩	-6

Bottom 10 Sales Reps	Sales	Rank	Last Month	vs Last Month	
NEBLE, JASON	$5,547	244	244	⇨	0
CELIMAN, WILLIAM	$9,779	243	241	⇩	-2
KRIZILL, ADAM	$11,454	242	235	⇩	-7
MIDANA, FRANK	$15,044	241	221	⇩	-20
GRANGIR, DAVID	$16,129	240	240	⇨	0
DALLEARE, ANDRE	$16,265	239	239	⇨	0
HICKLIBIRRY, JERRY	$16,670	238	225	⇩	-13
VAN HUILE, KENNETH	$18,821	237	242	⇧	5
RACHERDSEN, KENNETH	$19,675	236	237	⇧	1
STIGALL, DAVID	$20,092	235	243	⇧	8

Figure 8-2: You can use the REPT function and some conditional formatting to add visual components to your top and bottom displays.

Using pivot tables to create interactive top and bottom views

If you read Chapter 3, you know that a pivot table is an amazing tool that can help create interactive reporting. Take a moment to walk through an example of how pivot tables can help you build interactive top and bottom displays. You can open the `Chapter 8 Sample File.xlsx` file, found on this book's companion Web site, to follow along. Follow these steps to build a display with a pivot table:

1. **Start with a pivot table that shows the data you want to display with your top and bottom views.**

   In this case, the pivot table shows Sales Rep and Sales_Amount. (See Figure 8-3.)

	A	B
1	Region	(All)
2	Market	(All)
3		
4	Sales Rep	Sales_Amount
5	ABERRA, CHRISTOPHER	$28,370
6	ADEMO, DANIEL	$20,259
7	ADEMS, KYLE	$21,500
8	ADEMS, TAIWAN	$27,593
9	ALCERO, ROBERT	$42,697
10	ANDIRSEN, DORAN	$47,857
11	ASHEM, CHRIS	$23,283
12	ATKANS, TERRY	$24,297
13	BEALIY, CHRISTOPHER	$38,132
14	BECHMAN, JOHN	$20,310
15	BECKMAN, ADRIAN	$9,236
16	[illegible]	[illegible]

Figure 8-3: Start with a pivot table that contains the data you want to filter.

2. Right-click any Sales Rep name in the table, choose Filter, and then choose Top 10, as demonstrated in Figure 8-4.

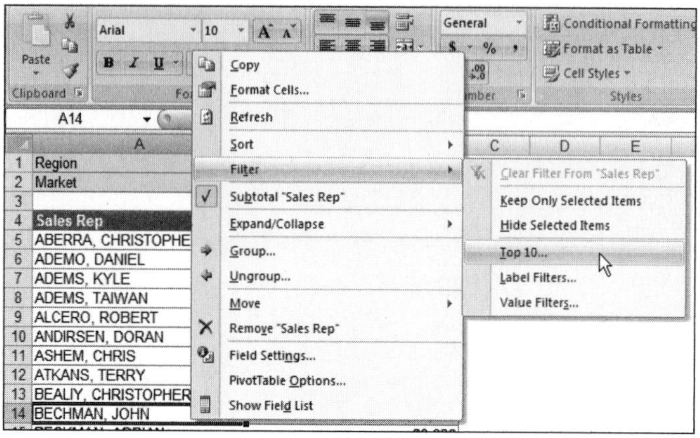

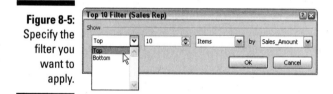

Figure 8-4: Select the Top 10 filter option.

The Top 10 Filter (Sales Rep) dialog box appears. (See Figure 8-5.)

Figure 8-5: Specify the filter you want to apply.

3. In the Top 10 Filter (Sales Rep) dialog box, define the view you're looking for.

In this example, you want the Top 10 Items (Sales Reps) as defined by the Sales_Amount field.

Note that the drop-down box in Figure 8-5 contains options for Top and Bottom. You can use the same dialog box to get the bottom ten items.

4. Click OK to apply the filter.

At this point, your pivot table is filtered to show you the top ten sales reps for the selected Region and Market. You can change the Market filter to Charlotte and get the top ten sales reps for Charlotte only. (See Figure 8-6.)

Figure 8-6:
You can
interactively
filter your
pivot table
report to
instantly
show the
top ten
sales reps
for any
Region and
Market.

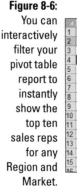

	A	B
1	Region	(All)
2	Market	CHARLOTTE
3		
4	**Sales Rep**	**Sales Amount**
5	MCCILLEIGH, JEFFREY	$98,090
6	CERDWILL, TIMOTHY	$54,883
7	BRADFERD, JAMES	$49,435
8	DIDLIY, CHARLES	$47,220
9	SWANGIR, ADAM	$46,608
10	SKILTEN, JAMES	$43,569
11	PIORSEN, HEYWARD	$41,005
12	CRIOMIR, TIMOTHY	$34,169
13	PERSENS, GREGORY	$33,026
14	BIOCH, RONALD	$30,168
15	**Grand Total**	**$478,172**

5. To create the bottom ten Sales Rep list, copy the entire pivot table and paste it next to the existing one.

There's no need to create another pivot table from scratch. You can copy and paste any pivot table to create various views using the same data source. The best part is that when you copy and paste a pivot table, you don't add to your file's memory or file size because you're using the same data cache.

6. Repeat Steps 2–4 in the newly-copied pivot table except this time choose to filter on the *bottom* ten items as defined by the Sales_Amount field.

If all went well, you now have two pivot tables similar to Figure 8-7: one that shows the top ten sales reps, and one that shows the bottom ten. You can link back to these two pivot tables using formulas. This way, when the data is refreshed, your top and bottom displays are updated.

Figure 8-7:
You now
have two
pivot tables
that show
top and
bottom
displays.

	A	B	C	D	E
1	**Top Sales Reps**			**Bottom Sales Reps**	
2	Region	(All)		Region	(All)
3	Market	CHARLOTTE		Market	CHARLOTTE
4					
5	**Sales Rep**	**Sales Amount**		**Sales Rep**	**Sales Amount**
6	MCCILLEIGH, JEFFREY	$98,090		MEERE, RUSSELL	$6,635
7	CERDWILL, TIMOTHY	$54,883		GERRUIS, ROBERT	$7,786
8	BRADFERD, JAMES	$49,435		BECKMAN, ADRIAN	$9,236
9	DIDLIY, CHARLES	$47,220		REBIRTS, ADAMS	$13,237
10	SWANGIR, ADAM	$46,608		HELT, CHRISTOPHER	$15,147
11	SKILTEN, JAMES	$43,569		HERVIY, CHRISTOPHER	$15,260
12	PIORSEN, HEYWARD	$41,005		WALLAEMS, SHAUN	$15,477
13	CRIOMIR, TIMOTHY	$34,169		CRAVIY, ANTHONY	$22,761
14	PERSENS, GREGORY	$33,026		BRAGHT, THOMAS	$25,005
15	BIOCH, RONALD	$30,168		MEERE, TERRY	$27,149
16	**Grand Total**	**$478,172**		**Grand Total**	**$157,693**
17					

If there's a tie for any rank in the top or bottom values, Excel shows you all the tied records. This means you may get more than the number you filtered for. In other words, if you filtered for the top 10 sales reps and there's a tie for number the number 5 rank, Excel shows you 11 sales reps (both reps ranked at number 5 will be shown).

Using Histograms to Track Relationships and Frequency

A *histogram* is essentially a graph that plots frequency distribution. What's a frequency distribution, you ask? A *frequency distribution* shows how often an event or category of data occurs. With a histogram, you can visually see the general distribution of a certain attribute.

To see what I mean, take a look at the histogram shown in Figure 8-8. This histogram represents the distribution of units sold in one month among your sales reps. As you can see, most reps sell somewhere between 5 and 25 units a month. As a manager, you want the hump in the chart to move to the right — more people selling a higher number of units per month. So you set a goal to have a majority of your sales reps sell between 15 and 25 units within the next three months. With this histogram, you can visually track the progress toward that goal.

Figure 8-8: A histogram showing the distribution of units sold per month among your sales force.

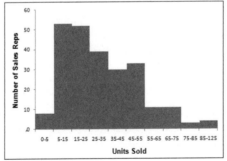

Before you get started creating your first histogram, it's important to note the several ways to do this in Excel. In this chapter, I show you how to create a histogram using formulas and pivot tables. The techniques I cover here fit nicely in reporting data models where there is a separation of data, analysis, and presentation. In addition, these techniques allow for a level of automation and interactivity that come in handy when refreshing reports each month.

Creating formula-driven histograms

First, you need a table that contains your raw data. The raw data should ideally consist of records that represent unique counts for the data you want to group. For instance, the raw data table in Figure 8-9 contains unique sales reps and the number of units each has sold. Follow these steps to create a formula-driven histogram:

1. **Before you create your histogram, you need to create a Bin table.**

   The Bin table dictates the grouping parameters that are used to break your raw dataset into the frequency groups. The Bin table in Figure 8-9 tells Excel to cluster all sales reps selling less than 5 units into the first frequency group, any sales reps selling 5 to 14 units in the second frequency group, and so on.

Figure 8-9:
Start with
your raw
data table
and a Bin
table.

	A	B	C	D
1	Sales Rep	Units Sold		
2	ERSINEILT, MIKE	5		Bins
3	HANKSEN, COLE	5		0
4	LYNN, THEODORE	5		5
5	MATTANGLY, JOHN	5		15
6	NEBLE, JASON	5		25
7	SEREILT, LUC	5		35
8	SHEW, DONALD	5		45
9	WINTLAND, ROBERT	5		55
10	BLANCHIT, DANNY	6		65
11	BLEKE JR, SAMUEL	6		75
12	ETEVAC, ROBERT	6		85
13	KNEIR, ANTHONY	6		125
14	MEERE, RUSSELL	6		
15	PHALLADS, SEAN	5		

You can freely set your own grouping parameters when you build your Bin table. However, it's generally a good idea to keep your parameters as equally spaced as possible. I typically end my Bin tables with the largest number in my dataset. This allows me to have clean groupings that end in a finite number — not in an open-ended *greater than* designation.

2. **After your raw data and Bin tables are ready, you must create a new column that holds the FREQUENCY formulas. Name the new column Frequency Formulas as seen in Figure 8-10.**

   Excel's FREQUENCY function counts how often values occur within the ranges you specify in a Bin table.

3. **Highlight a number of cells equal to the cells in your Bin table.**

4. **Type the FREQUENCY formula you see in Figure 8-10 and then press Ctrl+Shift+Enter on your keyboard.**

The FREQUENCY function does have a quirk that often confuses first-time users. The FREQUENCY function is an *array formula* — that is, it's a formula that returns many values at one time. In order for this formula to work properly, you have to press Ctrl+Shift+Enter on your keyboard after typing the formula. If you simply hit the Enter key, you won't get the results you need.

	A	B	C	D	E
1	Sales Rep	Units Sold			
2	ERSINEILT, MIKE	5		Bins	Frequency Formulas
3	HANKSEN, COLE	5		0	=FREQUENCY(B2:B245,D3:D13)
4	LYNN, THEODORE	5		5	
5	MATTANGLY, JOHN	5		15	
6	NEBLE, JASON	5		25	
7	SEREILT, LUC	5		35	
8	SHEW, DONALD	5		45	
9	WINTLAND, ROBERT	5		55	
10	BLANCHIT, DANNY	6		65	
11	BLEKE JR, SAMUEL	6		75	
12	ETEVAC, ROBERT	6		85	
13	KNEIR, ANTHONY	6		125	
14	MEEDE, RUSSELL	6			

Figure 8-10: Enter the FREQUENCY formula you see here.

At this point, you should have a table that shows the number of sales reps that fall into each of your Bins. You could chart this table, but the data labels would come out wonky. For the best results, build a simple chart feeder table that creates appropriate labels for each Bin. You do this in the next step.

5. Create a new table that feeds the charts a bit more cleanly (see Figure 8-11).

Use a simple formula that concatenates Bins into appropriate labels. Use another formula to bring in the results of your FREQUENCY calculations.

In Figure 8-11, I made the formulas in the first record of the chart feeder table visible. These formulas are essentially copied down to create a table appropriate for charting.

Figure 8-11: Build a simple chart feeder table that creates appropriate labels for each Bin.

	C	D	E	F	G	H
1		Frequency Formulas			Chart Feeder	
2		Bins	Frequency Formulas		Units Sold	Count of Sales Reps
3		0	0		=D3& "-" &D4	=E4
4		5	8		5-15	53
5		15	53		15-25	52
6		25	52		25-35	39
7		35	39		35-45	30
8		45	30		45-55	33
9		55	33		55-65	11
10		65	11		65-75	11
11		75	11		75-85	3
12		85	3		85-125	4
13		125	4			

6. **Use your newly-created chart feeder table to plot the data into a column chart.**

   Figure 8-12 illustrates the resulting chart.

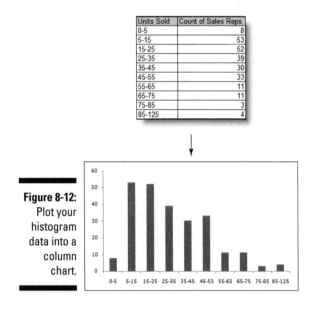

Figure 8-12: Plot your histogram data into a column chart.

Units Sold	Count of Sales Reps
0-5	8
5-15	53
15-25	52
25-35	39
35-45	30
45-55	33
55-65	11
65-75	11
75-85	3
85-125	4

   You can very well use the initial column chart as your histogram. If you like your histograms to have spaces between the data points, you're done.

   If you like the continuous blocked look you get with no gaps between the data points, follow the next few steps.

7. **Right-click any of the columns in the chart and choose Format Data Series.**

   The Format Data Series dialog box appears.

8. **In the dialog box, select the Series Options button and adjust the Gap Width property to 0%. (See Figure 8-13.)**

Adding a cumulative percent to your histogram

A nice feature to add to your histograms is a cumulative percent series. With a cumulative percent series, you can show the percent distribution of the data points to the left of the point of interest.

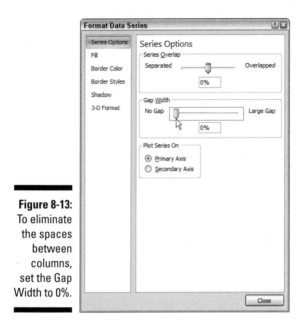

Figure 8-13:
To eliminate the spaces between columns, set the Gap Width to 0%.

Figure 8-14 shows an example of a cumulative percent series. At each data point in the histogram, the cumulative percent series tells you the percent of the population that fills all the Bins up to that point. For instance, you can see that 25% of the sales reps represented sold 15 units or less. In other words, 75% of the sales reps sold more than 15 units.

Take another look at the chart in Figure 8-14 and find the point where you see 75% on the cumulative series. At 75%, look at the label for that Bin range (you see 35–45). The 75% mark tells you that 75% of sales reps sold between 0 and 45 units. This means that only 25% of sales reps sold more than 45 units.

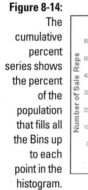

Figure 8-14:
The cumulative percent series shows the percent of the population that fills all the Bins up to each point in the histogram.

To create a cumulative percent series for your histogram, follow these steps:

1. **After you perform Steps 1 through 5 of creating a histogram (which I outline in the earlier section, "Creating formula-driven histograms"), add a column to your chart feeder table that calculates the percent of total sales reps for the first Bin (See Figure 8-15).**

   Note the dollar symbols ($) used in the formula to lock the references while you copy the formula down.

2. **Copy the formula down for all the Bins in the table.**

3. **Use the chart feeder table to plot the data into a line chart.**

   As you can see in Figure 8-16, the resulting chart needs some additional formatting.

Figure 8-15:
In a new column, create a formula that calculates the percent of total sales reps for the first Bin.

	F	G	H	I
1		Chart Feeder		
2		Units Sold	Count of Sales Reps	Cumulative %
3		0-5	8	=SUM($H$3:H3)/SUM($H$3:$H$12)
4		5-15	53	
5		15-25	52	
6		25-35	39	
7		35-45	30	
8		45-55	33	
9		55-65	11	
10		65-75	11	
11		75-85	3	
12		85-125	4	

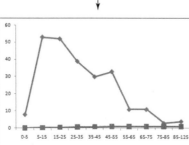

Units Sold	Count of Sales Reps	Cumaltive %
0-5	8	3%
5-15	53	25%
15-25	52	46%
25-35	39	62%
35-45	30	75%
45-55	33	88%
55-65	11	93%
65-75	11	97%
75-85	3	98%
85-125	4	100%

Figure 8-16:
Just a little formatting fixes this chart.

4. **Right-click the series that makes up your histogram (Count of Sales Rep), select Change Chart Type, and then change the chart type to a column chart.**

5. **Right-click any of the columns in the chart and choose Format Data Series.**

6. **Select the Series Options button and adjust the Gap Width property to 0%, as illustrated in Figure 8-13.**

7. **Right-click Cumulative Percent series and choose Format Data Series.**

8. **In the Format Data Series dialog box, select the Series Options button. Change the Plot Series On option to Secondary Axis.**

9. **Right-click Cumulative Percent series and choose Add Data Labels.**

At this point, your base chart is complete. It should look similar to the one shown at the beginning of this section in Figure 8-14. When you get to this point, you can adjust the colors, labels, and other formatting.

Creating a histogram with a pivot table

Did you know you can use a pivot table as the source for a histogram? That's right. With a little-known trick, you can create a histogram that is as interactive as a pivot chart!

As in the formula-driven histogram, the first step in creating a histogram with a pivot table is to create a frequency distribution. Here's how you do it:

1. **Create a pivot table and plot the data values in the row area (not the data area).**

   As you can see in Figure 8-17, the SumOfSales Amount field is placed in the row area. Place the Sales Rep field in the data area as a Count.

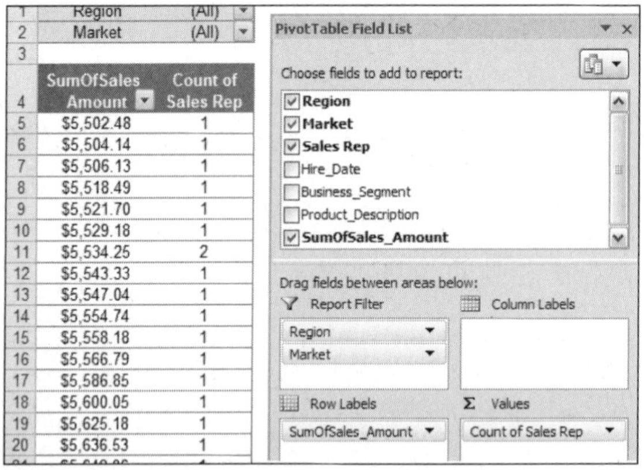

Figure 8-17: Place your data values in the row area and the Sales Rep field in the data area as a Count.

2. **Right-click any value in the row area and choose Group.**

   The Grouping dialog box appears. (See Figure 8-18.)

Figure 8-18:
The
Grouping
dialog box.

Grouping

Auto

☐ Starting at: 5000

☐ Ending at: 100000

By: 1000

OK   Cancel

3. **In the dialog box, set the start and end values and then set the intervals.**

   This essentially creates your frequency distribution. In Figure 8-19, the distribution is set to start at 5,000 and to create groups in increments of 1,000 until it ends at 100,000.

   After you click OK, the pivot table calculates the number of sales reps for each defined increment, just as in a frequency distribution. (See Figure 8-19.) You can now leverage this result to create a histogram!

Figure 8-19:
The
resulting of
grouping the
values in the
Row area is
a frequency
distribution
that can be
charted into
a histogram.

	A	B
1	Region	(All)
2	Market	(All)
3		
4	SumOfSales_Amount	Count of Sales Rep
5	5000-6000	69
6	6000-7000	78
7	7000-8000	58
8	8000-9000	66
9	9000-10000	41
10	10000-11000	45
11	11000-12000	39
12	12000-13000	33
13	13000-14000	25
14	14000-15000	25
15	15000-16000	22

The obvious benefit to this technique is that after you have a frequency distribution and a histogram, you can interactively filter the data based on other dimensions, like Region and Market. For instance, you can see the histogram for the Canada market and then quickly switch to see the histogram for the California market.

As far as your humble author can tell, you can't add cumulative percentages to a histogram based on a pivot table.

Highlighting Top Values in Charts

Sometimes a chart is indeed the best way to display a set of data, but you still would like to call attention to the top values in that chart. In these cases, you can use a technique that *actually* highlights the top values in your charts. That is to say, you can use Excel to figure out which values in your data series are in the top *n*th value and then apply special formatting to them. Figure 8-20 illustrates an example where the top five quarters are highlighted and given a label.

The secret to this technique lies in Excel's obscure LARGE function. The LARGE function returns the *n*th largest number from a dataset. In other words, you tell it where to look and the number rank you want.

To find the largest number in the dataset, you'd enter the formula LARGE (Data_Range, 1). To find the fifth largest number in the dataset, you'd use LARGE(Data_Range, 5). Figure 8-21 illustrates how the LARGE function works.

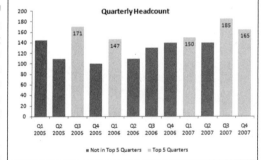

Figure 8-20:
This chart highlights the top five quarters with different font and labeling.

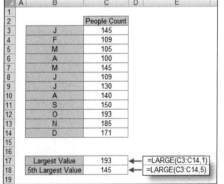

Figure 8-21:
Using the LARGE function returns the *n*th largest number from a dataset.

The idea is fairly simple. In order to identify the top five values in a dataset, you first need to identify the fifth largest number (LARGE function to the rescue) and then test each value in the dataset to see if it's bigger than the fifth largest number. Here's what you do:

1. **Build a chart feeder that consists of formulas that link back to your raw data.**

   The feeder should have two columns: one to hold data that isn't in the top five, and one to hold data that is in the top five. (See Figure 8-22.)

2. **In the first row of the chart feeder, enter the formulas shown in Figure 8-22.**

   The formula for the first column (F4) checks to see if the value in cell C4 is less than the number returned by the LARGE formula (the fifth largest value). If it is, the value in Cell C4 is returned. Otherwise, NA is used. The formula for the second column works in the same way except the IF statement is reversed: If the value in cell C4 is less than the number returned by the LARGE formula, NA is used; otherwise the value is returned.

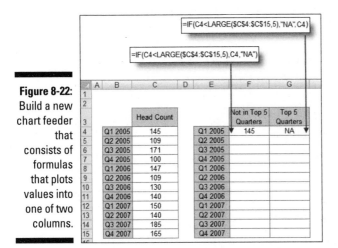

Figure 8-22: Build a new chart feeder that consists of formulas that plots values into one of two columns.

3. **Copy the formulas down to fill the table.**

4. **Use the chart feeder table to plot the data into a stacked column chart.**

   You immediately see a chart that displays two data series: one for data points not in the top five, and one for data points in the top five. (See Figure 8-23.)

5. **Right-click the top five data series and choose Add Data Label.**

   Notice in Figure 8-23 that the chart shows some rogue zeros. You can fix the chart so that the zeros don't display by performing the next few steps.

Figure 8-23:
After adding data labels to the top five data series and doing a bit of formatting, your chart should look similar to the one shown here.

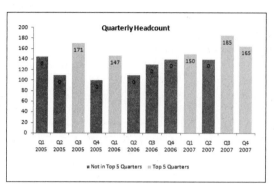

6. **Right-click any of the data labels for the top five series and choose Format Data Labels.**

7. **In the Format Data Labels dialog box, select the Numbers button and select Custom in the Category list.**

8. **Enter** #,##0;; **as the custom number format, as demonstrated in Figure 8-24.**

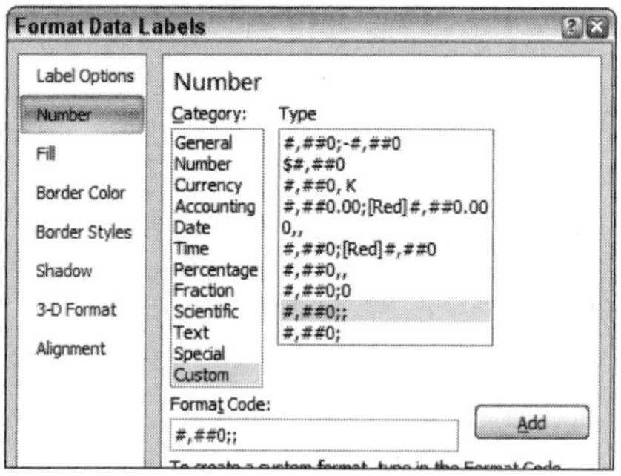

Figure 8-24:
Entering #,##0;; as the custom format for a data label renders all zeros in that data series hidden.

9. **Click the Add button and then click Close.**

When you go back to your chart, you see that the rogue zeros are now hidden and your chart is ready for colors, labels, and other formatting you want to apply.

You can apply the same technique to highlight the bottom five values in your data set. The only difference is that instead of using the LARGE function, you use the SMALL function. Whereas the LARGE function returns the largest *n*th value from a range, the SMALL function returns the smallest *n*th value.

Figure 8-25 illustrates the formulas you'd use to apply the same technique outlined here for the bottom five values.

The formula for the first column (F4) checks to see if the value in cell C4 is greater than the number returned by the SMALL formula (the fifth smallest value). If it is, the value in Cell C4 is returned. Otherwise, NA is used. The formula for the second column works in the same way except the IF statement is reversed: If the value in cell C4 is greater than the number returned by the SMALL formula, NA is used; otherwise the value is returned.

Figure 8-25:
Use the
SMALL
function to
highlight the
bottom
values in a
chart.

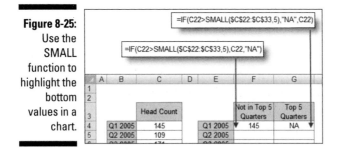

Chapter 9

Components That Display Performance against a Target

*H*opefully, this is an easy one to grasp. Someone sets a target, and someone else tries to reach that target. The target could be anything from a certain amount of revenue to a number of boxes shipped or to phone calls made. The business world is full of targets and goals. Your job is to find effective ways to represent performance against those targets.

What do I mean by "performance against a target"? Imagine your goal is to break the land speed record, which is currently 763 miles per hour. That makes your target 764 miles per hour, which will break the record. After you jump into your car and go as fast as you can, you will have a final speed of some number. That number is your performance against the target.

In this chapter, I explore some new and interesting ways to create components that show performance against a target.

Showing Performance with Variances

The standard way of displaying performance against a target is to plot the target and then plot the performance. This is usually done with a line chart or a combination chart, such as the one shown in Figure 9-1.

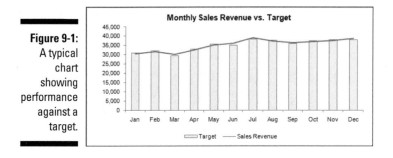

Figure 9-1:
A typical
chart
showing
performance
against a
target.

Although this chart allows you to visually pick the points where performance exceeded or fell below targets, it gives you a rather one-dimensional view and provides minimal information. Even if this chart offered labels that showed the actual percent of revenue versus target, you'd still get only a mildly informative view.

I've always thought that a more impactful and informative way of displaying performance against a goal is to plot the variances between the target and the performance. Figure 9-2 shows the same performance data you see in Figure 9-1, but includes the variances (sales revenue minus target). This way, you not only see where performance exceeded or fell below targets, but you get an extra layer of information showing the dollar impact of each rise and fall.

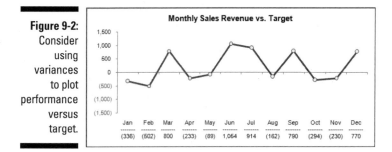

Figure 9-2:
Consider
using
variances
to plot
performance
versus
target.

Showing Performance against Organizational Trends

The target you use to measure performance doesn't necessarily have to be one that is specifically set by management or organizational policy. In fact, some of the things you measure may never have a target or goal set for them. In situations where you don't have a target to measure against, it's often helpful to measure performance against some organizational statistic.

For example, the component in Figure 9-3 measures the sales performance for each division against the median sales for all the divisions. You can see that divisions 1, 3, and 6 fall well below the median for the group.

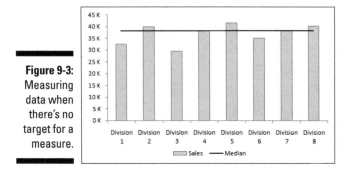

Figure 9-3: Measuring data when there's no target for a measure.

Here's how you'd create a median line similar to the one you see in Figure 9-3:

1. **Start a new column next to your data and enter a simple MEDIAN formula, as shown in Figure 9-4.**

   Note that this formula can be any mathematical or statistical operation that works with the data you are representing. Just ensure that the values returned are the same for the entire column. This gives you a straight line.

2. **Copy the formula down to fill the table.**

   Again, all the numbers in the newly-created column should be the same.

3. **Plot the table into a column chart.**

4. **Right-click the Median data series and choose Change Chart Type.**

5. **Change the chart type to a line chart.**

	A	B	C
1		Sales	Median
2	Division 1	32,526	=MEDIAN($B$2:$B$9)
3	Division 2	39,939	
4	Division 3	29,542	
5	Division 4	38,312	
6	Division 5	41,595	
7	Division 6	35,089	
8	Division 7	38,270	
9	Division 8	40,022	
10			

Figure 9-4: Start a new column and enter a formula.

Using Thermometer-Style Charts to Display Performance

A *thermometer-style chart* offers a unique way to view performance against a goal. As the name implies, the data points shown in this type of chart resemble a thermometer. Each performance value and its corresponding target are stacked on top of one another, giving an appearance similar to that of mercury rising in a thermometer. In Figure 9-5, you see an example of a thermometer-style chart.

Figure 9-5:
Thermom-
eter-style
charts offer
a unique
way to show
performance
against a
goal.

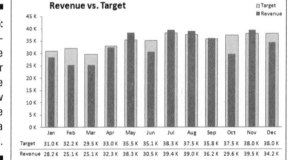

To create this type of chart, follow these steps:

1. **Starting with a table that contains revenue and target data, plot the data into a new column chart.**

2. **Right-click the Revenue data series and choose Format Data Series.**

   The Format Data Series dialog box appears.

3. **In the dialog box, select the Series Options button and click Secondary Axis.**

4. **Go back to your chart and delete the new axis that was added; it's the vertical axis to the right of the chart.**

5. **Right-click the Target series and choose Format Data Series.**

   The Format Data Series dialog box appears again.

6. **In the dialog box, select the Series Options button and adjust the Gap Width property so that the Target series is slightly wider than the Revenue series — between 45% and 55% is typically fine.**

An Introduction to the Bullet Graph

A *bullet graph* is a type of column/bar graph developed by visualization expert Stephen Few to serve as a replacement for dashboard gauges and meters. He developed bullet graphs to allow for the clear display of multiple layers of information without occupying a lot of space on a dashboard. A bullet graph, as illustrated in Figure 9-6, contains a single performance measure (such as YTD [year-to-date] revenue), compares that measure to a target, and displays it in the context of qualitative ranges, such as `Poor`, `Fair`, `Good`, and `Very Good`.

Figure 9-7 breaks down the three main parts of a bullet graph. The *performance bar* represents the performance measure. The *target marker* represents the comparative measure. And the *background fills* represent the qualitative range.

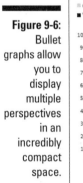

Figure 9-6:
Bullet graphs allow you to display multiple perspectives in an incredibly compact space.

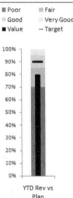

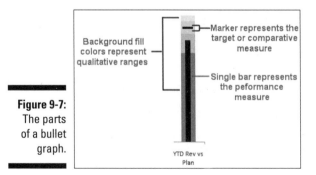

Figure 9-7:
The parts of a bullet graph.

Creating your first bullet graph

Creating a bullet graph in Excel isn't necessarily difficult, but it can be a bit tricky. Don't let "tricky" scare you, though. Follow these steps to create your first bullet graph:

1. **Start with a data table that gives you all the data points you need to create the three main parts of the bullet graph.**

   Figure 9-8 illustrates what that data table looks like. The first four values in the data set (`Poor`, `Fair`, `Good`, and `Very Good`) make up the qualitative range. You don't have to have four values — you can have as many or as few as you need. In this scenario, I want my qualitative range to span from 0 to 100%. Therefore, the percentages (75%, 15%, 10%, and 5%) must add up to 100%. Again, this can be adjusted to suit your needs.

   The fifth value in Figure 9-8 (`Value`) creates the performance bar. The sixth value (`Target`) makes the target marker.

2. **Highlight the entire table and plot the data on a stacked column chart.**

   The chart that's created is initially plotted in the wrong direction.

3. **To fix this, click the chart and select the Switch Row/Column button, as shown in Figure 9-9.**

4. **Right-click the Target series and choose Change Chart Type. Change the chart type to a line chart (with markers).**

5. **Right-click the Target series again and choose Format Data Series.**

   The Format Data Series dialog box appears.

6. **In the dialog box, click the Series Options button and click Secondary Axis.**

7. **Still in the Format Data Series dialog box, click the Marker Options button and adjust the marker to look like a dash, as demonstrated in Figure 9-10.**

8. **Still in the Format Data Series dialog box, click the Marker Fill button and select the Solid Fill property to set the color of the marker to black.**

9. **Still in the Format Data Series dialog box, click the Line Color button and select the No Line option.**

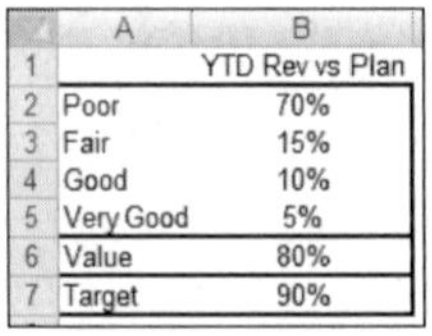

Figure 9-8:
Start with a dataset that contains the data points for the main parts of the bullet graph.

	A	B
1		YTD Rev vs Plan
2	Poor	70%
3	Fair	15%
4	Good	10%
5	Very Good	5%
6	Value	80%
7	Target	90%

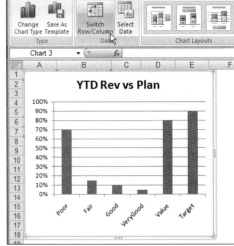

Figure 9-9:
Switch the orientation of the chart to read from columns.

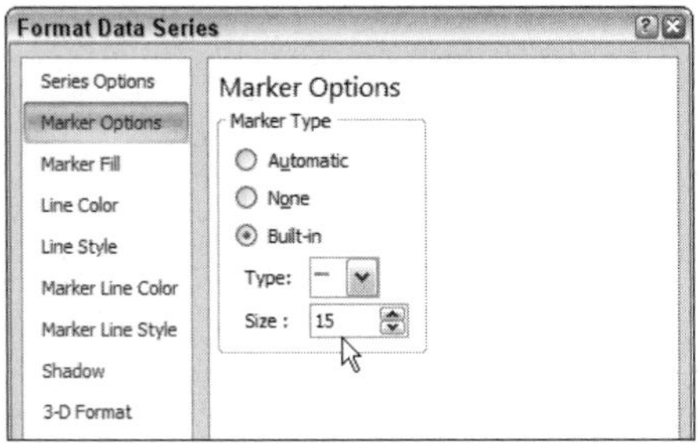

Figure 9-10:
Adjust the marker to a dash.

10. **Go back to your chart and delete the new secondary axis that was added to the right of your chart. (See Figure 9-11.)**

    This is an important step to ensure that the scale of the chart is correct for all data points.

11. **Right-click the Value series and choose Format Data Series.**

    The Format Data Series dialog box appears again.

12. **In the Format Data Series dialog box, click the Series Options button and click Secondary Axis.**

13. **Still in the Format Data Series dialog box under Series Options, adjust the Gap Width property so that the Value series is slightly narrower than the other columns in the chart — between 205% and 225% is typically okay.**

14. **Still in the Format Data Series dialog box, click the Fill button and select the Solid Fill property to set the color of the Value series to black.**

15. **You're almost done! All that's left to do is change the color for each qualitative range to incrementally lighter hues.**

At this point, your bullet graph is essentially done! You can apply whatever minor formatting adjustments to size and shape of the chart to make it look the way you want.

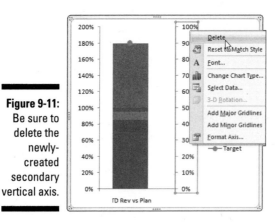

Figure 9-11: Be sure to delete the newly-created secondary vertical axis.

Adding data to your bullet graph

Now, here's the cool part. After you've built your chart for the first performance measure, you can simply use the same chart for any additional
measures. Take a look at Figure 9-12 to see what I mean.

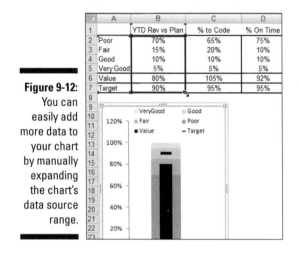

Figure 9-12:
You can
easily add
more data to
your chart
by manually
expanding
the chart's
data source
range.

As you can see in Figure 9-12, you've already created this bullet graph with
the first performance measure. Imagine you add two more measures and you
want to graph those. Here's the easy way to do it:

1. **Click the chart so that the blue outline appears around the original
   data set.**

2. **Hover your mouse over the blue dot in the lower-right corner of the
   blue box.**

   Your cursor turns into a diagonal double arrow, as demonstrated in
   Figure 9-12.

3. **Click and drag the blue dot to the last column in your expanded
   data set.**

Figure 9-13 illustrates how the new data points are added without one ounce
of extra work!

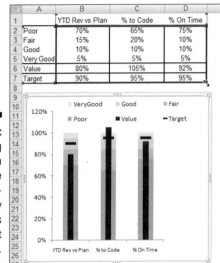

Figure 9-13:
Expanding
the data
source
automati-
cally
creates
new bullet
graphs.

Final thoughts on formatting bullet graphs

Before wrapping up this introduction to bullet graphs, I want to cover two
final thoughts I have on formatting:

- ✔ **Creating qualitative bands**
- ✔ **Creating horizontal bullet graphs**

These are discussed in the next two sections.

Creating qualitative bands

First, if the qualitative ranges are the same for all the performance measures
in your bullet graphs, you can format the qualitative range series to have no
gaps between them. For instance, Figure 9-14 shows a set of bullet graphs
where the qualitative ranges have been set to 0 Gap Width. This creates the
clever effect of qualitative bands.

1. **Right-click any one of the qualitative series and choose Format Data
   Series.**

   The Format Data Series dialog box appears.

2. **In the dialog box, select Series Options and adjust the Gap Width
   property to 0%.**

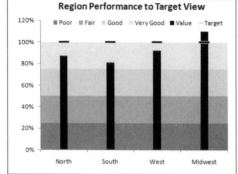

Figure 9-14:
Try setting gap widths to zero to create clean-looking qualitative bands.

Creating horizontal bullet graphs

For those of you who are waiting on the section about horizontal bullet graphs, I have good and bad news. The bad news is that creating a horizontal bullet graph from scratch in Excel is a much more complex endeavor than creating a vertical bullet graph — one that doesn't warrant the time and effort it takes to create them.

The good news is that your clever author has come up with a way get a horizontal bullet graph from a vertical one — and in three steps, no less. Here's how you do it:

1. **Create a vertical bullet graph.**

   See the section, "An Introduction to the Bullet Graph," earlier in this chapter, for more on creating bullet graphs.

2. **Change the alignment for the axis and other labels on the bullet graph so that they're rotated 270 degrees. (See Figure 9-15.)**

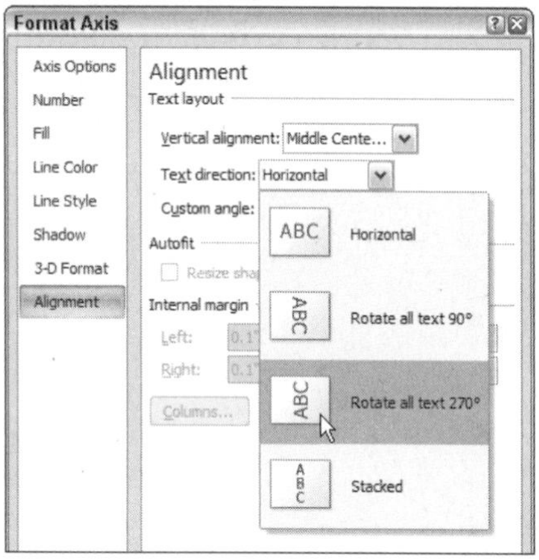

Figure 9-15:
Rotate all labels so that they're on their sides.

3. Use Excel's Camera tool to take a picture of the bullet graph.

When you have a picture, you can rotate it to be horizontal! Figure 9-16 illustrates a horizontal bullet graph.

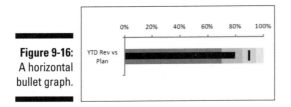

Figure 9-16:
A horizontal
bullet graph.

The nifty thing about this trick is that because the picture is taken with the Camera tool, the picture automatically updates when the source table changes.

Never heard of the Camera tool? Check out Chapter 6 for a detailed look at Camera tool.

Showing Performance against a Target Range

In some businesses, a target isn't one value — it's a range of values. That is to say, the goal is to stay within a defined target range. Imagine you manage a small business selling boxes of meat. Part of your job is to keep your inventory stocked between 25 and 35 boxes in a month. If you have too many boxes of meat, the meat will go bad. If you have too few boxes, you'll lose money.

To track how well you do at keeping your inventory of meat between 25 and 35 boxes, you need a performance component that displays on-hand boxes against a target range.

Figure 9-17 illustrates a component you can build to track performance against a target range. The gray band represents the target range you must stay within each month. The line represents the trend of on-hand meat.

Figure 9-17:
You can
create a
component
that plots
performance
against a
target range.

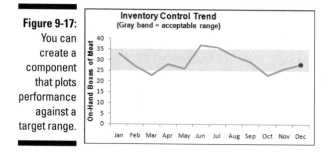

Obviously, the trick to this type of component is to set up the band that represents the target range. Here's how you do it:

1. **First, set up a *limit table* where you can define and adjust the upper and lower limits of your target range.**

   Cells B2 and B3 in Figure 9-18 serve as the place to define the limits for the range.

2. **Build a chart feeder that's used to plot the data points for the target range.**

   This feeder consists of the formulas revealed in cells B8 and B9 in Figure 9-18.

   The idea is to copy these formulas across the entire dataset. The values you see for Feb, Mar, and Apr are the results of these formulas.

Figure 9-18:
Create a
chart feeder
that
contains
formulas
that define
the data
points for
the target
range.

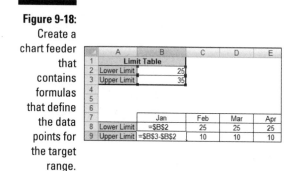

	A	B	C	D	E
1	Limit Table				
2	Lower Limit	25			
3	Upper Limit	35			
4					
5					
6					
7		Jan	Feb	Mar	Apr
8	Lower Limit	=$B$2	25	25	25
9	Upper Limit	=$B$3-$B$2	10	10	10

3. **Add a row for the actual performance values. (See Figure 9-19.)**

    These data points create the performance trend line.

	A	B	C	D	E	F
1	Limit Table					
2	Lower Limit	25				
3	Upper Limit	35				
4						
5						
6						
7		Jan	Feb	Mar	Apr	Ma
8	Lower Limit	25	25	25	25	2
9	Upper Limit	10	10	10	10	1
10	Values	33	27	23	28	2

4. **Highlight the entire chart feeder table and plot the data on a stacked area chart.**

5. **Right-click the Values series and choose Change Chart Type. Change the chart type to a line chart (no markers).**

6. **Right-click the Values data series again and choose Format Data Series.**

    The Format Data Series dialog box appears.

7. **In the dialog box, click the Series Options button and click Secondary Axis.**

8. **Go back to your chart and delete the new axis that was added; it's the vertical axis to the right of the chart.**

9. **Right-click the Lower Limit data series and choose Format Data Series.**

    The Format Data Series dialog box appears again.

10. **In the dialog box, click the Fill button and select the No Fill option.**

That's it. All that's left to do is apply the minor formatting adjusts to colors, labels, and other formatting.

Part IV
Advanced Reporting Techniques

The 5th Wave
By Rich Tennant

"I started running 'what if' scenarios on my spreadsheet, like, 'What if I were sick of this dirtwad job and funneled some of the company's money into an off-shore account?'"

In this part . . .

This section focuses on techniques that help you automate your reporting processes and gives your users an interactive user interface. Chapter 10 provides a clear understanding of how macros can be leveraged to supercharge and automate your reporting systems. Chapter 11 illustrates how you can provide your clients with a simple interface, allowing them to easily navigate through and interact with their reporting systems.

Chapter 10

Macro-Charged Reporting

· ·

· ·

A *macro* is essentially a set of instructions or code that you create to tell Excel to execute any number of actions. In Excel, macros can be written or recorded. The key word here is *recorded*.

The analogy I often use is that recording a macro is like programming a phone number into your cell phone. You first manually dial and save a number. Then when you want, you can redial those numbers with the touch of a button. Just as on a cell phone, you can record your actions in Excel while you perform them. While you record, Excel gets busy in the background, translating your keystrokes and mouse clicks to written code (also known as *VBA; Visual Basic for Applications*). After a macro is recorded, you can play back those actions anytime you wish.

In this chapter, I explore macros and reveal how you can use macros to automate your recurring processes to simplify your life.

Why Use a Macro?

The first step in using macros is admitting you have a problem. Actually, you have several problems:

> ✔ **Problem 1: You're making donuts:** You do the same tasks over and over again. As each new month rolls around, you have to *make the donuts* (that is, crank out those reports). You have to import that data. You have to refresh those pivot tables. You have to delete those columns, jump up, turn around, and do the hokey pokey. Who needs it? Wouldn't it be nice if you could fire up a macro and have those more redundant parts of your reporting processes done automatically?

✔ **Problem 2: You're making mistakes:** Admit it, your hand-to-hand combat style of using Excel leaves room for mistakes. When you're repeatedly applying formulas, sorting, and moving things around manually, there's always that risk of catastrophe. Add to that the looming deadlines and constant change requests, and your error rate goes up.

Why not calmly record a macro, ensure that everything is running correctly, and then forget it? The macro is sure to perform every action the same way every time you run it; reducing the chance of errors.

✔ **Problem 3: You're making people mad:** Remember that you're creating these dashboards and reports for an audience that probably has a limited knowledge of Excel. If your reports are a bit too difficult to use and navigate, you'll find that you'll slowly lose support for your cause.

It's always helpful to make your reports a bit more user-friendly. Here are some ideas for macros that make things easier for everyone:

✔ A macro to format and print a worksheet or range of worksheets at the touch of a button

✔ Macros that navigate a multi-sheet worksheet with a navigation page or with a *go to* button for each sheet in your workbook

✔ A macro that saves the open document in a specified location and then closes the application at the touch of a button

Obviously, each of the preceding examples can be performed in Excel without the aid of a macro. However, your audience will appreciate these little touches that help make perusal of your report a bit more pleasant.

Introducing the Macro Recorder

If you tried to skip ahead and create your own macro before reading this chapter, you may have found it difficult to pinpoint the *Macro Recorder* (the mechanism that lets you record macros). This is because the macro functionality is on the Developer tab, which is initially hidden in Excel 2007. By hidden, I mean you don't see a tab called Developer when you first open Excel 2007. You have to explicitly tell Excel to make it visible.

To enable the Developer tab, follow these steps:

1. **Select the Office icon (in the upper-left corner of Excel).**

2. **Click the Excel Options button.**

   The Excel Options dialog box appears.

3. **Make sure the Popular options are showing and ensure that the Show Developer Tab in the Ribbon option has a check beside it. (See Figure 10-1.)**

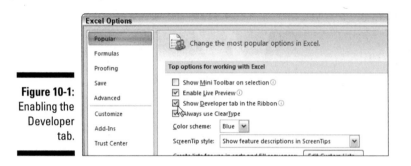

Figure 10-1:
Enabling the
Developer
tab.

The Macro Recorder user interface

Now that you have the Developer tab showing in the Excel Ribbon, you can
fire up the Macro Recorder and examine other critical macro options. Start
up the Macro Recorder by selecting Record Macro from the Developer tab.
This activates the Record Macro dialog box, as shown in Figure 10-2.

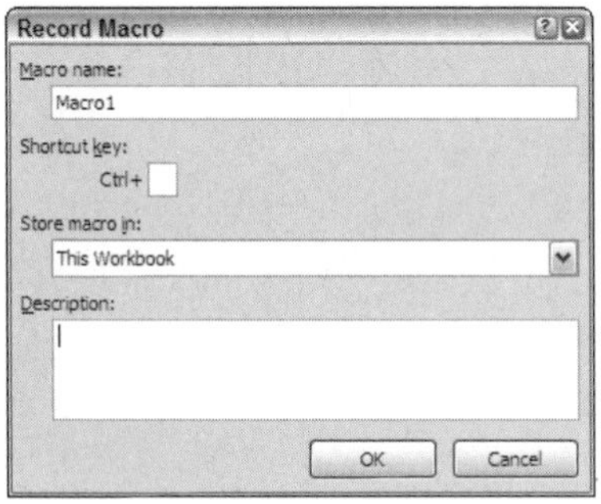

Figure 10-2:
The Record
Macro
dialog box.

Here are the four parts of the Record Macro dialog box:

- **At the top is a space for your macro name.** This should be self-
explanatory. Excel gives a default name to your macro, such as Macro1,
but I find it's best practice to give your macro a name more descriptive
of what it actually does. For example, you might name a macro that
formats a generic table as FormatTable.

- **Below the macro name field is the Shortcut Key field.** Every macro
or piece of code needs an *event,* or something to happen, for it to run.
This event can be a button press, a workbook opening, or in this case,
a keystroke combination. When you assign a shortcut key to your macro,
entering that combination of keys triggers your macro to run. This is an
optional field. You need not enter a shortcut key to run your macro.

✔ **Next, you find the Store Macro In field.** This Workbook is the default option. Storing your macro in This Workbook simply means that the macro is stored along with the active Excel file. The next time you open that particular workbook, the macro will be available to run. Similarly, if you send the workbook to another user, that user can run the macro as well (provided the macro security is properly set by your user — but more on that later).

✔ **Last, you see an option to enter a description for your macro.** This is an optional field, but it can come in handy if you have numerous macros in a spreadsheet or if you need to give a user a more detailed description about what the macro does.

Recording macros with absolute references

Now that you've read about the basics of the Macro Recorder interface, it's time to go deeper and begin recording macros. The first thing you need to understand before you begin is that Excel has two modes for recording — absolute reference and relative reference.

Excel's default recording mode is in absolute reference. As you may know, the term *absolute reference* is often used in the context of cell references found in formulas. When a cell reference in a formula is an absolute reference, it does not automatically adjust when the formula is pasted to a new location.

The best way to understand how this concept applies to macros is to try it out. Open the Chapter 10 SampleFile.xlsx file and record a macro that counts the rows in the Branchlist worksheet. (See Figure 10-3.)

	A	B	C	D	E	F	G	H	I
1		Region	Market	Branch			Region	Market	Branch
2		NORTH	BUFFALO	601419			SOUTH	CHARLOTTE	173901
3		NORTH	BUFFALO	701407			SOUTH	CHARLOTTE	301301
4		NORTH	BUFFALO	802202			SOUTH	CHARLOTTE	302301
5		NORTH	CANADA	910181			SOUTH	CHARLOTTE	601306
6		NORTH	CANADA	920681			SOUTH	DALLAS	202600
7		NORTH	MICHIGAN	101419			SOUTH	DALLAS	490260
8		NORTH	MICHIGAN	501405			SOUTH	DALLAS	490360
9		NORTH	MICHIGAN	503405			SOUTH	DALLAS	490460
10		NORTH	MICHIGAN	590140			SOUTH	FLORIDA	301316
11		NORTH	NEWYORK	801211			SOUTH	FLORIDA	701309
12		NORTH	NEWYORK	802211			SOUTH	FLORIDA	702309
13		NORTH	NEWYORK	804211			SOUTH	NEWORLEANS	601310
14		NORTH	NEWYORK	805211			SOUTH	NEWORLEANS	602310
15		NORTH	NEWYORK	806211			SOUTH	NEWORLEANS	801607

Figure 10-3: Your pre-totaled worksheet containing two tables.

The sample dataset used in this chapter can be found on this book's companion Web site.

Follow these steps to record the macro:

1. **Before recording, make sure cell A1 is selected.**

2. **Select Record Macro from the Developer tab.**

3. **Name the macro AddTotal.**

4. **Choose This Workbook for the save location.**

5. **Click OK to start recording.**

   At this point, Excel is recording your actions. While Excel is recording, perform the following steps:

6. **Select cell A16 and type** Total **in the cell.**

7. **Select the first empty cell in Column D (D16) and type** = COUNTA(D2:D15).

   This gives a count of branch numbers at the bottom of column D. You need to use the COUNTA function because the branch numbers are stored as text.

8. **Press Stop Recording from the Developer tab to end recording the macro.**

The formatted worksheet should look like something like the one in Figure 10-4.

	A	B	C	D	E	F	G	H	I	J
1		Region	Market	Branch			Region	Market	Branch	
2		NORTH	BUFFALO	601419			SOUTH	CHARLOTTE	173901	
3		NORTH	BUFFALO	701407			SOUTH	CHARLOTTE	301301	
4		NORTH	BUFFALO	802202			SOUTH	CHARLOTTE	302301	
5		NORTH	CANADA	910181			SOUTH	CHARLOTTE	601306	
6		NORTH	CANADA	920681			SOUTH	DALLAS	202600	
7		NORTH	MICHIGAN	101419			SOUTH	DALLAS	490260	
8		NORTH	MICHIGAN	501405			SOUTH	DALLAS	490360	
9		NORTH	MICHIGAN	503405			SOUTH	DALLAS	490460	
10		NORTH	MICHIGAN	590140			SOUTH	FLORIDA	301316	
11		NORTH	NEWYORK	801211			SOUTH	FLORIDA	701309	
12		NORTH	NEWYORK	802211			SOUTH	FLORIDA	702309	
13		NORTH	NEWYORK	804211			SOUTH	NEWORLEANS	601310	
14		NORTH	NEWYORK	805211			SOUTH	NEWORLEANS	602310	
15		NORTH	NEWYORK	806211			SOUTH	NEWORLEANS	801607	
16	Total			14						
17										
18										

Figure 10-4: Your post-totaled worksheet.

There you have it; you've recorded your first macro!

To see your macro in action, delete the total row you just added and play back your macro by following these steps:

1. **Select Macros from the Developer tab.**

2. **Find and select the AddTotal macro you just recorded.**

3. **Click the Run button.**

Pretty cool huh? The macro played back your actions to a T and gave your table a total.

Now here's the thing. No matter how hard you try, you can't make the AddTotal macro work on the second table. Why? Because you recorded it as an absolute macro.

To understand what this means, examine the underlying code. Don't run for the hills just yet; it's not as scary as it seems.

To examine the code, select Macros from the Developer tab to get the Macro dialog box you see in Figure 10-5.

Figure 10-5:
The Excel
Macro
dialog box.

Select the AddTotal macro and click the Edit button. This opens the Visual Basic Editor to show you the code that was written when you recorded your macro:

Sub AddTotal()

  Range("A16").Select

  ActiveCell.FormulaR1C1 = "Total"

  Range("D16").Select

  ActiveCell.FormulaR1C1 = "=COUNTA(R[-14]C:R[-1]C)"

End Sub

Pay particular attention to lines two and four of the macro. When you asked Excel to select cell range A16 and then D16, those cells are exactly what it selected. Because the macro was recorded in absolute reference mode, Excel interpreted your range selection as absolute. In other words, if you select cell A16, that cell is what Excel gives you. In the next section, you take a look at what the same macro looks like when recorded in relative reference mode.

Recording macros with relative references

In the context of Excel macros, *relative* means relative to the currently active cell. So you should use caution with your active cell choice — both when you record the relative reference macro and when you run it.

First, make sure the Chapter 10 SampleFile.xlsx file is open. (This file is available on this book's companion Web site.) Then, use the following steps to record a relative-reference macro:

1. **Select the Use Relative References option from the Developer tab, as demonstrated in Figure 10-6.**

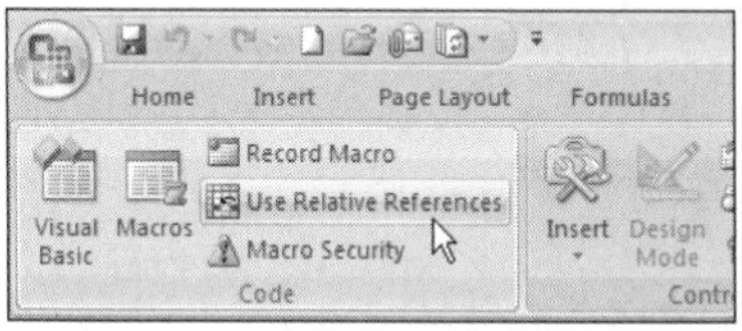

Figure 10-6: Select relative reference macro recording.

2. **Before recording, make sure cell A1 is selected.**

3. **Select Record Macro from the Developer tab.**

4. **Name the macro AddTotalRelative.**

5. **Choose This Workbook for the save location.**

6. **Click OK to start recording.**

7. **Select cell A16 and type** Total **in the cell.**

8. **Select the first empty cell in Column D (D16) and type** = COUNTA(D2:D15).

9. **Press Stop Recording from the Developer tab to end recording the macro.**

At this point, you have two macros recorded. Take a moment to examine the code for your newly-created macro.

Select Macros from the Developer tab to get the Macro dialog box. Here, choose the AddTotalRelative macro and click Edit.

Again, this opens the Visual Basic Editor to show you the code that was written when you recorded your macro. This time, your code looks something like the following:

```
Sub AddTotalRelative()

  ActiveCell.Offset(15, 0).Range("A1").Select

  ActiveCell.FormulaR1C1 = "Total"

  ActiveCell.Offset(0, 3).Range("A1").Select

  ActiveCell.FormulaR1C1 = "=COUNTA(R[-14]C:R[-1]C)"

End Sub
```

Do you notice anything different about code lines two and four? There are no references to any specific cell ranges at all! Of course you see "A1", but that's just the starting point. How does this code define where to *make* the changes? Well, without getting too technical, let's take a quick look at what the relevant parts of this VBA code really mean.

Notice that in line 2, Excel uses the Offset property of the active cell. This property tells the cursor to move a certain number of cells up or down and a certain number of cells left or right.

The Offset property code tells Excel to move 15 rows down and 0 columns across from the active cell (in this case, A1). So there's no need for Excel to explicitly select a cell as it did when recording an absolute reference macro.

To see this macro in action, delete the total row for both tables and do the following.

1. **Select cell Al.**
2. **Select Macros from the Developer tab.**
3. **Find and select the AddTotalRelative macro.**
4. **Click the Run button.**
5. **Select cell F1.**
6. **Select Macros from the Developer tab.**
7. **Find and select the AddTotalRelative macro.**
8. **Click the Run button.**

Notice that this macro, unlike your previous macro, works on both sets of data! Because the macro applies the totals *relative* to the currently active cell, the totals are applied correctly.

For this macro to work, you simply need to ensure that

✔ You've selected the correct starting cell before running the macro.

✔ The block of data has the same number of rows and columns as the data on which you recorded the macro.

Hopefully this simple example has given you a firm grasp of macro recording with both absolute and relative references.

Assigning a macro to a button

When you create macros, you want to give your audience a clear and easy way to run each macro. A basic button, used directly in the dashboard or report, can provide a simple but effective user interface.

As luck would have it, Excel offers a set of controls — *Form controls* — designed specifically for creating user interfaces directly on spreadsheets. There are several different types of Form controls, from buttons (the most-commonly-used control) to scrollbars.

The idea behind using a Form control is simple. You place a Form control on a spreadsheet and then assign a macro to it — that is, a macro you've already recorded. When a macro is assigned to the control, that macro is executed, or *played,* when the control is clicked.

Take a moment to create a button for the AddTotalRelative macro you created earlier. Here's how:

1. **Click the Insert drop-down list under the Developer tab. (See Figure 10-7.)**

2. **Select the Button Form Control.**

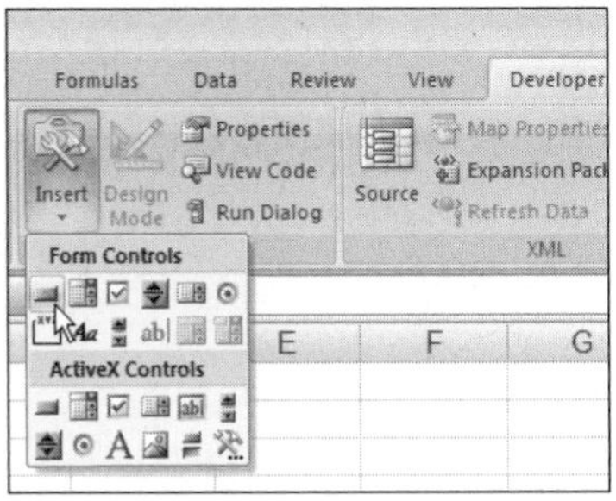

Figure 10-7: You can find the Form controls in the Developer tab.

Form controls versus ActiveX controls

Notice the Form controls and ActiveX controls in Figure 10-7. Although they look similar, they're quite different. Form controls are designed specifically for use on a spreadsheet, and ActiveX controls are typically used on Excel Userforms. As a general rule, you always want to use Form controls when working on a spreadsheet. Why? Form controls need less overhead, so they perform better, and configuring Form controls is far easier than configuring their ActiveX counterparts.

3. **Click the location you want to place your button.**

   When you drop the button control onto your spreadsheet, the Assign Macro dialog box, as shown in Figure 10-8, activates and asks you to assign a macro to this button.

4. **Select the macro you want to assign to the button and then click OK.**

At this point, you have a button that runs your macro when you click it! Keep in mind that all the controls in the Forms toolbar work in the same way as the command button, in that you assign a macro to run when the control is selected.

The buttons you create come with a default name, such as Button3. To rename your button, right-click the button and then click the existing name. Then you can delete the existing name and replace it with a name of your choosing.

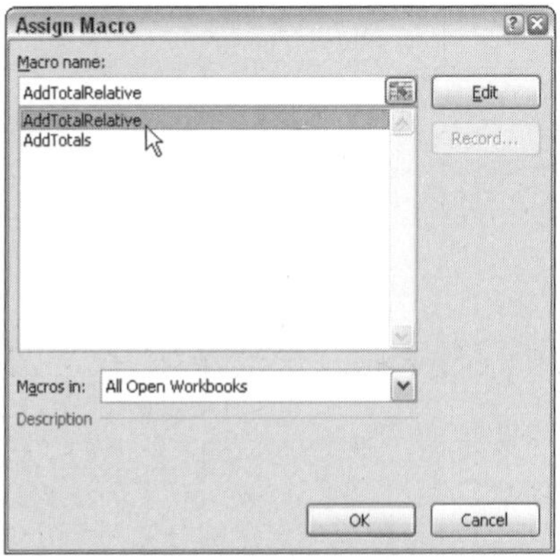

Figure 10-8:
Assign a
macro to
the newly-
added
button.

Macro Security in Excel 2007

For better or worse, Microsoft has introduced some significant security changes for Office 2007. It's important to understand the impact of these changes so that you can help your audience use your macros without crashing and burning.

One of the most significant changes for Excel 2007 is that macros are disabled by default under certain circumstances. For example, if you create the Excel macro file and use it on your computer, your macros work fine. However, when another user tries to use macros in a file you've created, the macros are disabled.

With earlier versions of Excel, you'd often see a pop-up box informing you that the file contains macros. Depending on your Excel security settings, you'd have the option to enable or disable macros in the file. This is no longer the case for 2007.

If users open one of your Excel 2007 file, they get a small message under the Ribbon stating that Macros Have Been Disabled. The message looks like Figure 10-9.

As noble as the aim of these security features are, I have to admit it's a little annoying. There are actually two ways to overcome this security block. That is, there's a short-term solution and a long-term solution. These are discussed in the next two sections.

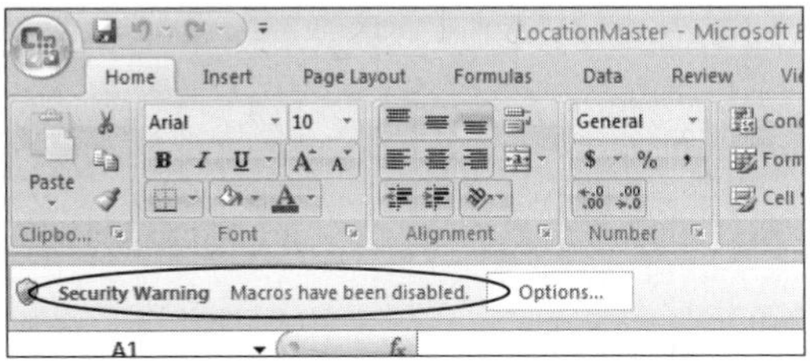

Figure 10-9:
Security
warning
when
macros are
present.

The short-term solution to disabled macros

The short-term solution is to temporarily enable the macro content in the current workbook. This allows you to use the macros during the current session, but Excel blocks the macros each time the workbook is opened.

To temporarily enable the content, simply click the Options button beside the warning message to activate the Microsoft Office Security Options dialog box, as shown in Figure 10-10.

Here, they can select the Enable This Content option to activate the use of macros for this session.

The long-term solution to disabled macros

The long-term solution is to set up a trusted location for your files. A t*rusted location* is a directory that is deemed a safe zone where only trusted workbooks are placed. A trusted location allows you and your clients to run a macro-enabled workbook with no security restrictions as long as the workbook is in that location.

To set up a trusted location, follow these steps:

1. **Select the Macro Security button on the Developer tab.**

   This activates the Trust Center dialog box.

2. **Select the Trusted Locations button.**

   This opens the Trusted Locations menu (see Figure 10-11), which shows you all the directories that are considered trusted.

3. **Click the Add New Location button.**

4. **Click Browse to find and specify the directory that will be considered a trusted location.**

After you specify a trusted location, any Excel file that's opened from this location will have macros automatically enabled. The idea is to have your clients specify a trusted location and use your Excel files from there.

The new macro-enabled file extensions

As another security feature, Microsoft has created a separate file extension for workbooks that contain macros. By default, Excel 2007 workbooks have the file extension .xlsx. Well, standard Excel 2007 .xlsx files can't contain macros. If your workbook contains macros and you then save that workbook as an .xlsx file, your macros are removed automatically. Of course, Excel warns you that macro content will be disabled when saving a workbook with macros as an .xlsx file.

If you want to retain the macros, you must save your file as an *Excel Macro-Enabled Workbook*. This gives your file an .xlsm extension. The idea is that all workbooks with an .xlsx file extension are automatically known to be safe whereas you can recognize .xlsm files as a potential threat.

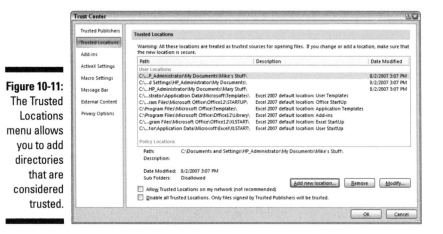

Figure 10-11:
The Trusted Locations menu allows you to add directories that are considered trusted.

Excel Macro Examples

Covering the fundamentals of building and using macros is one thing. Coming up with good ways to incorporate them into your reporting processes is another. Take a moment to review a few examples of how you can implement macros in your dashboards and reports. Open the Chapter 10 SampleFile.xlsx file found on this book's companion Web site to follow along in the next section.

Building navigation buttons

The most common use of macros is navigation. Workbooks that have many worksheets or tabs can be frustrating to navigate. To help your audience, you can create some sort of a switchboard, like the one shown in Figure 10-12. When a user clicks the Example 1 button, he's taken to the Example 1 sheet.

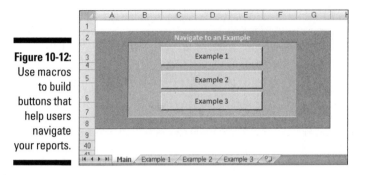

Figure 10-12:
Use macros
to build
buttons that
help users
navigate
your reports.

Creating a macro to navigate to a sheet is quite simple. You start at the sheet that will become your switchboard or starting point and then start recording a macro. While recording, click the destination sheet (the sheet this macro will navigate to). After you click the destination sheet, stop recording the macro. It's as easy as that.

It's useful to know that Excel has a built-in Hyperlink feature, allowing you to convert the contents of a cell into a hyperlink that links to another location. That location can be a separate Excel workbook, a Web site, or even another tab in the current workbook. Although using a hyperlink may be easier than setting up a macro, you can't apply a hyperlink to Form controls (like buttons). Instead of a button, you'd use text to let users know where they'll go when they click the link.

Dynamically rearranging pivot table data

In the example illustrated in Figure 10-13, macros allow a user to change the perspective of the chart simply by selecting any one of the buttons shown.

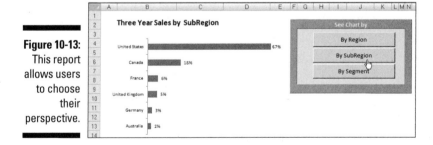

Figure 10-13:
This report
allows users
to choose
their
perspective.

Figure 10-14 reveals that the chart is actually a pivot chart tied to a pivot table. The recorded macros assigned to each button are doing nothing more than rearranging the pivot table to slice the data using various pivot fields.

To create this type of setup, you first create a pivot table and a pivot chart. Next, start recording a macro. While recording, move a pivot field from one area of the pivot table to the other. When you're done, stop recording the macro. Record another macro to move the data field back to its original position. After both macros are set up, you can fire them in turn to see your pivot field dynamically move back and forth.

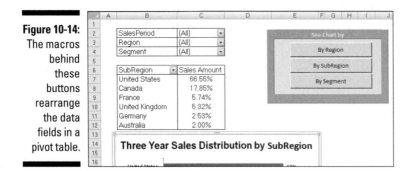

Figure 10-14: The macros behind these buttons rearrange the data fields in a pivot table.

Offering one-touch reporting options

The last two examples demonstrate that you can record any action that you find of value. That is, if you think users would appreciate a certain feature being automated for them, why not record a macro to do so?

In Figure 10-15, notice that you can filter the pivot table for top or bottom 20 customers. Because I pre-recorded the steps to filter a pivot table for the top and bottom 20, my users don't have to. This not only saves them time and effort, but it also allows users that don't know how to take these actions to benefit from them.

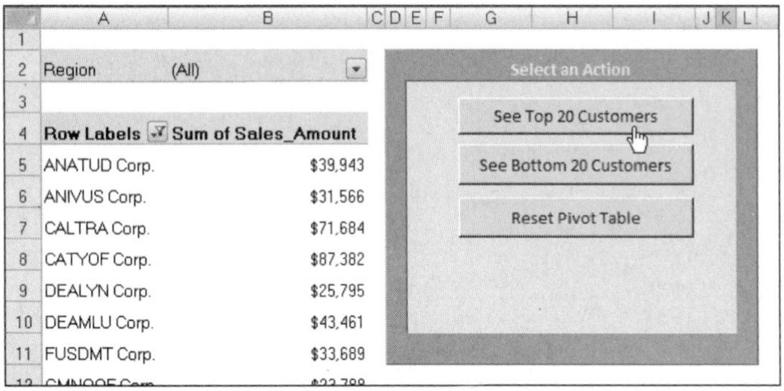

Figure 10-15: Help your audience save time and effort by offering pre-recorded views.

Feel free to visit Chapter 3 for a refresher on how create the top and bottom reports you see in Figure 10-15.

Figure 10-16 demonstrates how you can give your audience a quick and easy way to see the same data on different charts. Don't laugh too quickly at the uselessness of this example. I actually worked for a guy who wanted to see two different charts with the same data. Instead of taking up real estate, I just recorded a macro that changed the Chart Type of his chart. He could switch views to his heart's content.

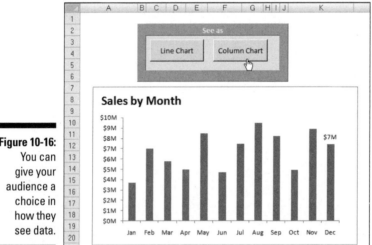

Figure 10-16:
You can give your audience a choice in how they see data.

Chapter 11

Giving Users an Interactive Interface

* *

In This Chapter

▶ Introducing, adding, and configuring Form controls

▶ Using Check Box controls

▶ Using Option Buttons

▶ Offering choices with Combo Boxes and List Boxes

* *

A h, life was so much simpler in the days of one-view reports and static dashboards. Remember the good old days when a static report was enough to have managers carrying you on their shoulders?

Today, managers increasingly want to be *empowered* to switch from one view of data to another with a simple selection from a menu of choices. For those of us who build dashboards and reports, this *empowerment* comes with migraines and acid reflux. How do you handle a manager that wants to see multiple views for multiple regions or markets?

Fortunately, Excel does offer a handful of tools that enable you to add interactivity into your reports. With these tools and a bit of creative data modeling, you can give your managers the choices they crave with relative ease.

In this chapter, I show you how to incorporate menus, options, and selectors into your reporting mechanisms and offer a few useful examples you can implement into your processes.

Introducing Form Controls

Excel offers a set of controls called *Form controls,* designed specifically for creating user interfaces directly on a spreadsheet. The idea behind using a Form control is simple. You place a Form control on a spreadsheet and then configure it to give it a specific task.

Excel's Form controls can be found on the Developer tab, which is initially hidden in Excel 2007. By hidden, I mean you don't see a tab called Developer when you first open Excel 2007. You have to explicitly tell Excel to make it visible. To enable the Developer tab, follow these steps:

1. **Select the Office icon (in the upper-left corner of Excel).**

2. **Click the Excel Options button.**

   The Excel Options dialog box appears.

3. **Make sure the Popular options are showing and ensure that the Show Developer Tab in the Ribbon option has a check beside it. (See Figure 11-1.)**

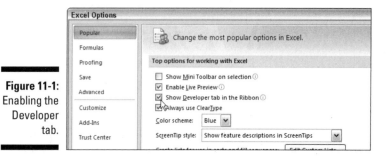

Figure 11-1: Enabling the Developer tab.

When the Developer tab is visible, click it and select the Insert Icon button, as shown in Figure 11-2. Here you find two sets of controls: Form controls and ActiveX controls. Form controls are designed specifically for use on a spreadsheet whereas ActiveX Controls are typically used on Excel Userforms. Because Form controls need less overhead and can be configured far easier than their ActiveX counterparts, you generally want to use Form controls.

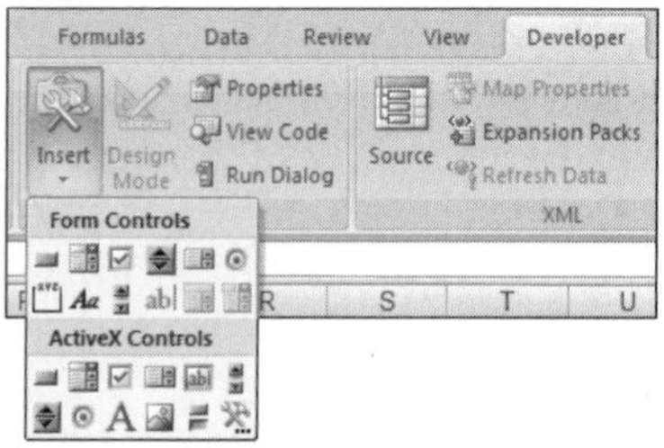

Figure 11-2: Form controls and ActiveX controls

Here are the nine form controls you can use directly on a spreadsheet (see Figure 11-3). They are as follows:

- ✔ **Button:** Provides users with a button that, when clicked, executes an assigned macro.

- ✔ **Combo Box:** Gives users an expandable list of options from which to choose.

- ✔ **Check Box:** Provides a mechanism for a select/unselect scenario. When the Check Box is selected, it returns a value of `True`. When it isn't selected, `False` is returned.

- ✔ **Spin Button:** Enables users to easily increment or decrement a value by clicking the arrow buttons provided.

- ✔ **List Box:** Gives users a list of options from which to choose.

- ✔ **Option Button:** Enables users to toggle through several options one at a time. The idea is to have two or more Option Buttons in a group. Then selecting one Option Button automatically deselects the others.

- ✔ **Scroll Bar:** Provides users a mechanism to scroll to a value or position using a sliding scale that can be moved by clicking and dragging the mouse.

- ✔ **Label:** True to its name, this control allows you to add text labels to your spreadsheet. You can also assign a macro to the label, effectively using it as a button of sorts.

- ✔ **Group Box:** Typically used for cosmetic purposes, this control serves as a container for groups of controls.

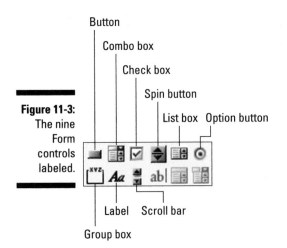

Figure 11-3: The nine Form controls labeled.

Adding and Configuring Controls

To add a control onto the spreadsheet, simply click the control you require and click the spreadsheet in the approximate location you want the control placed. You can easily move and resize the control just as you would a chart or shape.

After you add a control, you want to configure it to define its look, behavior, and utility. Each control has its own set of configuration options that allow you to customize it for your purposes. To get to these options, right-click the control and select Format Control, as demonstrated in Figure 11-4. This opens the Format Control dialog box with all the configuration options for that control.

Figure 11-4: Right-clicking and selecting Format Control opens a dialog box with the configuration options.

You'll notice in Figure 11-4 that there are five tabs listed in the Format Control dialog box: Size, Protection, Properties, Web, and Control.

All but two controls have the Size, Protection, Properties, Web, and Control tabs in their configuration options (the Button and label controls don't have the Control tab). These tabs work the same way for each control. A handful of controls do have additional formatting-oriented tabs used to configure formatting options.

These tabs are as follows:

- ✔ **The Size tab:** Gives you options for detailed sizing and scaling of controls.

- ✔ **The Protection tab:** Allows you to specify how the control will behave when the worksheet is in a protected state. Here you can choose to disable or enable the control when the worksheet is protected.

- ✔ **The Properties tab:** Lets you control how the control is positioned in relation to the cells and columns in your spreadsheet. Here, you can specify whether you want the control to be resized or re-positioned when the worksheet cells are adjusted. You can also specify whether you want the control to be printed.

✔ **The Web tab:** Expose some options that determine how the control will behave when the worksheet is saved as an HTML Web page.

✔ **The Control tab:** This tab, which is different for each control, is where the meat of the configuration lies. Here, you find the variables and settings that need to be defined in order for the control to function.

Now that I've covered the administrative aspects of how Form controls work, you're ready for the rest of this chapter. Throughout, I offer some examples of how to use the most practical controls, demonstrating how each one works. Plus, I walk you through a scenario for each control, showing how the control can enhance your reporting mechanisms.

Using the Button Control

The Button control gives your audience a clear and easy way to execute the macros you've recorded. To insert and configure a Button control, follow these steps:

1. **Click the Insert drop-down list under the Developer tab.**

2. **Select the Button Form control.**

3. **Click the location in your spreadsheet where you want to place your button.**

   The Assign Macro dialog box appears and asks you to assign a macro to this button. (See Figure 11-5.)

4. **Select the macro you want to assign to the button and then click OK.**

Figure 11-5: Assign a macro to the newly-added button.

5. **Edit the text shown on the button by right-clicking the button, highlighting the existing text, and then overwriting it with your own.**

To assign a different macro to the button, simply right-click and select Assign Macro to reactivate the Assign Macro dialog box, as shown in Figure 11-5.

Using the Check Box Control

The Check Box control provides a mechanism for selecting/deselecting options. When a Check Box is selected, it returns a value of `True`. When it isn't selected, `False` is returned. To add and configure a Check Box control, follow these steps:

1. **Click the Insert drop-down list under the Developer tab.**

2. **Select the Check Box Form control.**

3. **Click the location in your spreadsheet where you want to place your Check Box.**

4. **After you drop the Check Box control onto your spreadsheet, right-click the control and select Format Control.**

5. **Click the Control tab to see the configuration options, as shown in Figure 11-6.**

6. **First, select the state in which the Check Box control should open.**

   The default selection (Unchecked) typically works for most scenarios, so it's rare you have to update this selection.

7. **Next, in the Cell Link box, enter the cell to which you want the Check Box to output its value.**

   By default, a Check Box control outputs either `True` or `False`, depending on whether it's checked. Notice in Figure 11-6 that this particular Check Box outputs to cell A5.

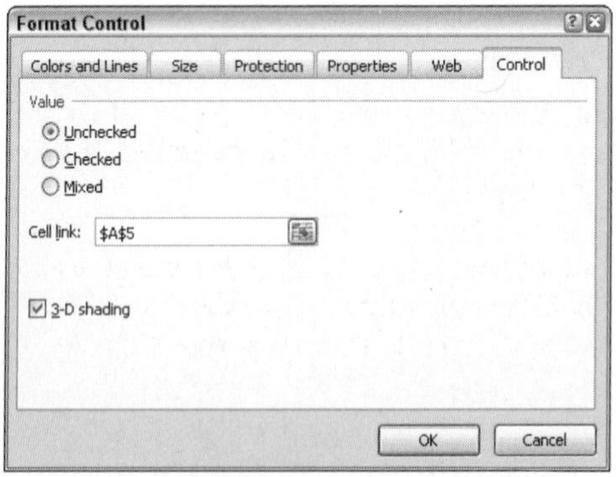

Figure 11-6:
Formatting
the Check
Box Control.

8. **(Optional) You can check the 3D property if you want the control to have a three-dimensional appearance.**

9. **Click OK to apply your changes.**

To rename the Check Box control, right-click the control, select Edit Text, and then overwrite the existing text with your own.

As Figure 11-7 illustrates, the Check Box outputs its value to the specified cell. If the Check Box is selected, a value of `TrueTrue` is output. If the Check Box isn't selected, a value of `FalseFalse` is output.

If you're having a hard time figuring out how this could be useful, fear not. I have an example that illustrates how a Check Box can be used to toggle a chart series on and off!

Figure 11-7:
The two states of the Check Box.

Check Box Example: Toggling a Chart Series On and Off

Figure 11-8 shows the same chart twice. Notice that the top chart contains only one series, with a Check Box offering to Show 2004 Trend data. The bottom chart shows the same chart with the Check Box selected. The on/off nature of the Check Box control is ideal for when interactivity calls for a visible/not visible state.

To see all the examples in this chapter live, open the `Chapter 11 Sample File` available on this book's companion Web site.

To create this example, I start with raw data that contains both 2004 and 2005 data (see Figure 11-9). Next to the raw data, I reserve a cell where the Check Box control will output its value (Cell A12 in this example). This cell will either contain `TrueTrue` or `False`.

I then create a shadow dataset that consists of all formulas, as shown here in Figure 11-10. The idea is that the chart actually reads from this data, not the raw data. This way, I can control what the chart sees.

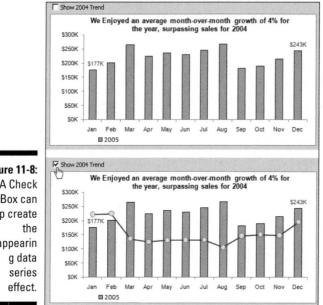

Figure 11-8:
A Check Box can help create the disappearing data series effect.

Figure 11-9:
Start with raw data and a cell where a Check Box can output its value.

	A	B	C	D	E	F	G
10			Raw Data				
11	Toggle for 2004 Data		Jan	Feb	Mar	Apr	May
12	TRUE	2004	$222,389	$224,524	$136,104	$125,260	$130,791	$1
13		2005	$176,648	$201,000	$265,720	$225,461	$235,494	$2

Figure 11-10:
Create a shadow dataset that will feed the chart. The values of this dataset are all formulas.

4						
5			Jan	Feb	Mar	
6		2004	=IF($A12=TRUE,C12,NA())	=IF($A12=TRUE,D12,NA())	=IF($A12=TRUE,E12,NA())	=IF
7		2005	=C13	=D13	=E13	=F
8						
9						
10			Raw Data			
11	Toggle for 2004 Data		Jan	Feb	Mar	
12	TRUE	2004	222389	224524	136104	12
13		2005	176648	201000	265720	22

As you can see in Figure 11-10, the formulas for the 2005 row simply reference the cells in the raw data for each respective month. I do that because I want the 2005 data to show at all times.

For the 2004 row, I test the value of Cell A12 (the cell that contains the output from the Check Box). If A12 reads `True`, I reference the respective 2004 cell in the raw data. If A12 doesn't read `True`, the formula uses Excel's `NA()` function to return an #N/A error. Excel charts can't read any cell with the #N/A error. Therefore, they simply don't show the data series for any cell that contains #N/A. This is ideal when you don't want a data series to be shown at all.

Notice that the formula shown in Figure 11-10 uses an absolute reference with cell A12. That is, the reference to cell A12 in the formula is prefixed with a $ sign ($A12). This ensures that the column references in the formulas don't shift when they're copied across.

Figure 11-11 illustrates the two scenarios in action. In the scenario shown at the top of Figure 11-11, Cell A12 is `True`, so the shadow dataset actually brings in 2004 data. In the scenario shown at the bottom of Figure 11-11, Cell A12 is `False`, so the shadow dataset returns #N/A for 2004.

After this setup is created, all that's left to do is create the chart using the shadow data. As you can see, the combination of clever data modeling and a Check Box control can produce some pretty cool effects.

Figure 11-11: When Cell A12 reads True, 2004 data is displayed; when it reads False, the 2004 row shows only #N/A errors.

		Jan	Feb	Mar	Apr	May	J
5							
6	2004	$222,389	$224,524	$136,104	$125,260	$130,791	$1
7	2005	$176,648	$201,000	$265,720	$225,461	$235,494	$2
8							
10		Raw Data					
11 Toggle for 2004 Data		Jan	Feb	Mar	Apr	May	J
12 TRUE	2004	$222,389	$224,524	$136,104	$125,260	$130,791	$13
13	2005	$176,648	$201,000	$265,720	$225,461	$235,494	$22

		Jan	Feb	Mar	Apr	May	J
5							
6	2004	#N/A	#N/A	#N/A	#N/A	#N/A	#1
7	2005	$176,648	$201,000	$265,720	$225,461	$235,494	$2
8							
10		Raw Data					
11 Toggle for 2004 Data		Jan	Feb	Mar	Apr	May	J
12 FALSE	2004	$222,389	$224,524	$136,104	$125,260	$130,791	$13
13	2005	$176,648	$201,000	$265,720	$225,461	$235,494	$22

Using Option Button Controls

Option Buttons allow users to toggle through several options one at a time. The idea is to have two or more Option Buttons in a group. Then selecting one Option Button automatically deselects the others. To add Option Buttons to your worksheet, follow these steps:

1. **Click the Insert drop-down list under the Developer tab.**

2. **Select the Option Button Form control.**

3. **Click the location in your spreadsheet where you want to place your Option Button.**

4. **After you drop the control onto your spreadsheet, right-click the control and select Format Control.**

5. **Click the Control tab to see the configuration options, as shown in Figure 11-12.**

6. **First, select the state in which the Option Button should open.**

   The default selection (Unchecked) typically works for most scenarios, so it's rare you have to update this selection.

7. **Next, in the Cell Link box, enter the cell to which you want the Option Button to output its value.**

   By default, an Option Button control outputs a number that corresponds to the order it was put onto the worksheet. For instance, the first Option Button you place on your worksheet outputs a number 1; the second outputs a number 2; the third outputs a number 3; and so on. Notice in Figure 11-12 that this particular control outputs to cell A1.

8. **(Optional) You can check the 3D property if you want the control to have a three-dimensional appearance.**

9. **Click OK to apply your changes.**

10. **To add another Option Button, simply copy the button you created and paste as many Option Buttons as you need.**

    The cool thing about copying and pasting is that all the configurations you made to the original persist in all the copies.

To give your Option Button a meaningful label, right-click the control, select Edit Text, and then overwrite the existing text with your own.

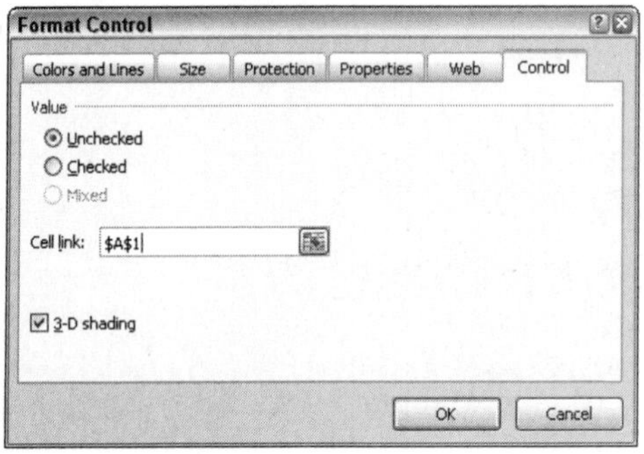

Figure 11-12:
Formatting
the Option
Button
control.

Option Button Example: Showing Many Views through One Chart

One of the ways you can use Option Buttons is to feed a single chart with different data, based on the option selected. Figure 11-13 illustrates an example of this. When each category is selected, the single chart is updated to show the data for that selection.

Now, you could create three separate charts and show them all on your dashboard at the same time. However, using this technique as an alternative saves on valuable real estate by not having to show three separate charts. Plus, it's much easier to troubleshoot, format, and maintain one chart than it is three.

To create this example, I start with three raw datasets (as shown in Figure 11-14) that contain three categories of data: Income, Expense, and Net. Near the raw data, I reserve a cell where the Option Buttons output their values (Cell A8 in this example). This cell contains the ID of the option selected: 1, 2, or 3.

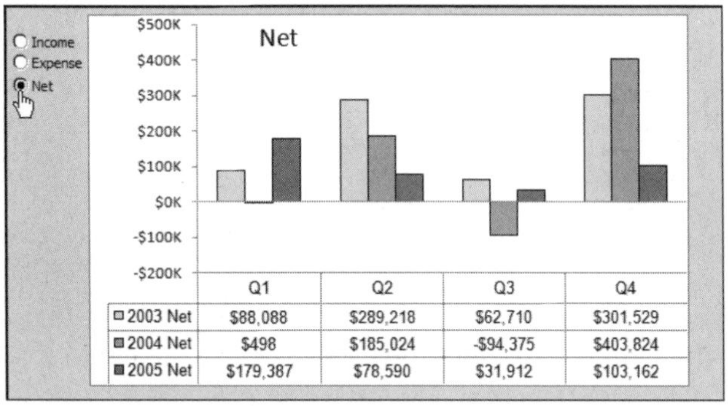

Figure 11-13: This chart is dynamically fed different data based on the selected Option Button.

	Q1	Q2	Q3	Q4
□ 2003 Net	$88,088	$289,218	$62,710	$301,529
▩ 2004 Net	$498	$185,024	-$94,375	$403,824
■ 2005 Net	$179,387	$78,590	$31,912	$103,162

Figure 11-14: Start with the raw datasets and a cell where the Option Buttons can output their values.

	A	B	C	D	E	F
7	Option Button Trigger					
8	1		Q1	Q2	Q3	Q4
9		2005 Income	$399,354	$573,662	$244,661	$790,906
10		2004 Income	$219,967	$495,072	$212,749	$687,744
11		2003 Income	$159,832	$289,825	$181,961	$456,016
12						
13		2005 Expense	$219,967	$495,072	$212,749	$687,744
14		2004 Expense	$219,468	$310,048	$307,124	$283,920
15		2003 Expense	$71,744	$607	$119,251	$154,487
16						
17		2005 Net	$179,387	$78,590	$31,912	$103,162
18		2004 Net	$498	$185,024	-$94,375	$403,824
19		2003 Net	$88,088	$289,218	$62,710	$301,529

I then create a shadow dataset that consists of all formulas, as shown in Figure 11-15. The idea is that the chart reads from this shadow dataset, allowing you to control what the chart sees. The first cell of the shadow dataset contains the following formula:

```
=IF($A$8=1,B9,IF($A$8=2,B13,B17))
```

This formula tells Excel to check the value of cell A8 (the cell where the Option Buttons output their values). If the value of cell A8 is 1, which represents the value of the Income option, the formula returns the value in the Income dataset (cell B9). If the value of cell A8 is 2, which represents the value of the Expense option, the formula returns the value in the Expense dataset (cell B13). If the value of cell B1 is not 1 or 2, the value in cell B17 is returned.

Notice that the formula shown in Figure 11-15 uses absolute references with cell A8. That is, the reference to cell A8 in the formula is prefixed with $ signs ($A$8). This ensures that the cell references in the formulas don't shift when they're copied down and across.

To test that the formula is working fine, you could change the value of cell A8 manually, from 1 to 3. When the formula works, you'd simply copy the formula across and down to fill the rest of the shadow dataset.

When the setup is created, all that's left to do is create the chart using the shadow data. Again, the major benefits you get from this type of setup is that any formatting changes can be made to one chart, and it's easy add another dataset by adding another Option Button and editing your formulas.

	A	B	C	
1				
2			Q1	
3		=IF($A$8=1,B9,IF($A$8=2,B13,B17))		
4				
5				
7	Option Button Trigger			
8	1		Q1	
9		2005 Income	399353.9	57
10		2004 Income	219966.6	49
11		2003 Income	159831.87	28
13		2005 Expense	219966.6	49
14		2004 Expense	219468.16	31
15		2003 Expense	71743.63	60
17		2005 Net	179387.3	78
18		2004 Net	498.440000000002	18
19		2003 Net	88088.24	28
20				

Figure 11-15: Create a shadow dataset and enter this formula in the first cell.

Using the Combo Box Control

The Combo Box control allows users to select from a list of predefined options from a drop-down list. The idea is that when an item from the Combo

Box control is selected, some action is taken with that selection. To add a Combo Box to your worksheet, follow these steps:

1. **Click the Insert drop-down list under the Developer tab.**

2. **Select the Combo Box Form control.**

3. **Click the location in your spreadsheet where you want to place your Combo Box.**

4. **After you drop the control onto your spreadsheet, right-click the control and select Format Control.**

5. **Click the Control tab to see the configuration options, as shown in Figure 11-16.**

6. **In the Input Range setting, identify the range that holds the predefined items you want to present as choices in the Combo Box.**

   As you can see in Figure 11-16, this Combo Box is filled with months.

7. **Next, in the Cell Link box, enter the cell to which you want the Combo Box to output its value.**

   By default, a Combo Box control outputs the index number of the selected item. This means if the second item on the list was selected, the number 2 would be output. If the fifth item on the list was selected, the number 5 would be output. Notice in Figure 11-16 that this particular control outputs to cell E15.

8. **In the Drop Down Lines box, enter the number of items you want shown at one time.**

   As you can see in Figure 11-6, this control is formatted to show 12 items at one time. This means when the Combo Box is expanded, the user sees 12 items.

9. **(Optional) You can check the 3D property if you want the control to have a three-dimensional appearance.**

10. **Click OK to apply your changes.**

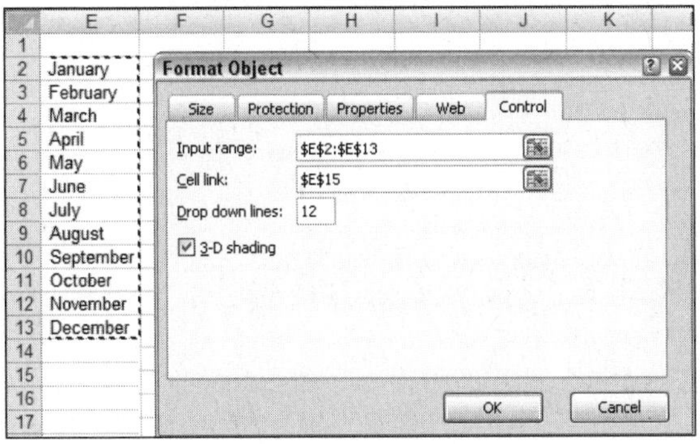

Figure 11-16: Formatting the Combo Box control.

Combo Box Example: Controlling Multiple Pivot Tables with One Combo Box

Here's the deal. The report in Figure 11-17 contains two pivot tables — one showing revenue for the selected market and one showing volume. Note that each pivot table has its own Filter field, allowing for the selection of a Market. The problem is that each time a market is selected from the Filter field in one pivot table, the same market from the Filter field in the other pivot table must be selected to ensure the correct Volume versus Revenue.

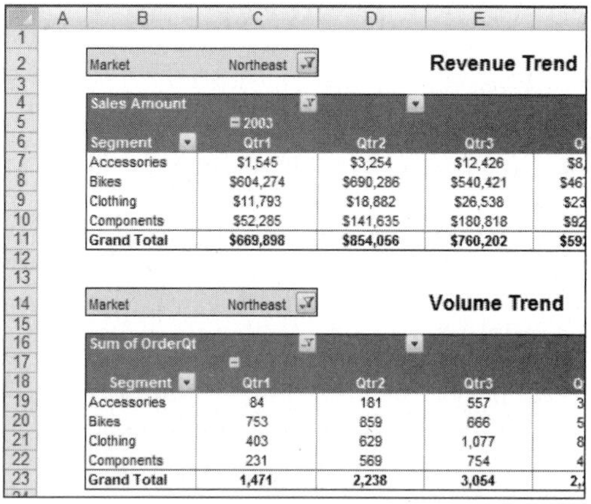

Market: Northeast — Revenue Trend

Sales Amount, 2003

Segment	Qtr1	Qtr2	Qtr3	Q
Accessories	$1,545	$3,254	$12,426	$8,
Bikes	$604,274	$690,286	$540,421	$46
Clothing	$11,793	$18,882	$26,538	$23
Components	$52,285	$141,635	$180,818	$92
Grand Total	$669,898	$854,056	$760,202	$59

Market: Northeast — Volume Trend

Sum of OrderQt

Segment	Qtr1	Qtr2	Qtr3	Q
Accessories	84	181	557	3
Bikes	753	859	666	5
Clothing	403	629	1,077	8
Components	231	569	754	4
Grand Total	1,471	2,238	3,054	2,

Figure 11-17: You must synchronize multiple pivot table reports to get the correct analysis.

Not only is it annoying to have to synchronize both pivot tables each time you want to analyze a new market's data, but there's a chance you, or your audience, may forget to do so.

A Combo Box control can help in this situation. The idea is to record a macro that automatically selects a market from the Market field of both tables. Then alter the macro to filter both pivot tables, using the value selected from a Combo Box control.

Using the `Chapter 11 Sample File` that appears on this book's companion Web site, take a moment to walk through this example with me. For this example, use the pivot tables found in the Using Combo Box Controls tab of the sample file.

1. **Create a new macro and call it SwitchMarkets. When recording starts, select the Southwest market from the Market field in both pivot tables and then stop recording.**

TIP

Feel free to review Chapter 10 for a refresher on how to record macros.

2. **Place a Combo Box onto your spreadsheet.**

3. **Right-click your Combo Box and select Format Control.**

   The Format Control dialog box appears.

4. **Specify an Input Range for the list you're using to fill your Combo Box.**

   In this case, reference the list of markets already created in column Q.

5. **Next, specify a Cell Link.**

   This is the cell that shows the index number of the item you select (cell O2 is the cell link in this example). When you've configured your Combo Box, your dialog box should look similar to Figure 11-18.

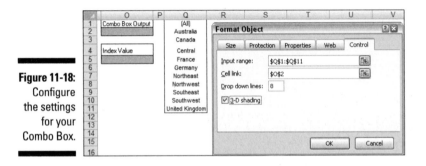

Figure 11-18:
Configure
the settings
for your
Combo Box.

At this point, you can now select a market from your Combo Box and see the associated index number in cell O2. In order to make use of this index number, you have to pass it through the INDEX function. The INDEX function converts an index number to a value that can be recognized.

An INDEX function requires two arguments in order to work properly. The first argument is the range of the list you're working with. In most cases, use the same range that's feeding your Combo Box. The second argument is the index number. If the index number is in a cell (like in cell O2), you can simply reference the cell.

6. **In cell O5, enter an INDEX function that converts the index number in cell O2 to a value.**

   As you can see in Figure 11-19, the formula used is =INDEX(Q1:Q11,O2).

   The trick now is to edit the SwitchMarkets macro you recorded earlier to use the value in cell O5, instead of a hard-coded value. This calls for editing the macro-generated code via the Visual Basic Editor. Don't worry, it won't get too crazy.

7. Click the Macros button on the Developer tab.

This activates the Macro dialog box, as shown in Figure 11-20. From here, you can select the SwitchMarkets macro and then click the Edit button.

Remember that when you recorded your macro, you selected the Southwest market from the Market field in both pivot tables. As you can see in Figure 11-21, the text `"Southwest"` is indeed hard-coded in the macro-generated code.

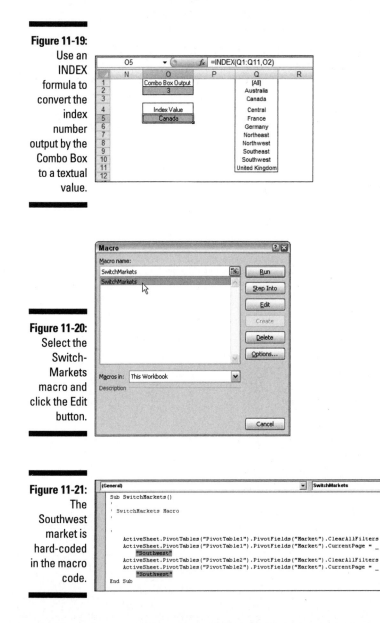

Figure 11-19:
Use an INDEX formula to convert the index number output by the Combo Box to a textual value.

Figure 11-20:
Select the Switch-Markets macro and click the Edit button.

Figure 11-21:
The Southwest market is hard-coded in the macro code.

8. **Replace "Southwest" with `ActiveSheet.Range("O5").Value` as demonstrated in Figure 11-22.**

    This tells the macro to get the market name from cell O5. After you've edited the macro, close the Visual Basic Editor to get back to the spreadsheet.

    The final step is to ensure the macro plays each time you select a market from the Combo Box.

9. **Right-click the Combo Box and select Assign Macro. Select the SwitchMarkets macro and then click OK.**

10. **(Optional) You can clean up the formatting on your newly-created report by hiding the rows and columns that hold the Filter fields in your pivot tables, plus any lists or formulas you don't want your audience to see.**

    As you can see in Figure 11-23, this setup provides an easy and reliable way to navigate pivot tables using one control.

Figure 11-22:
Replace "Southwest" with ActiveSheet. Range("O5"). Value.

Figure 11-23:
You can now navigate two pivot tables with just one Combo Box!

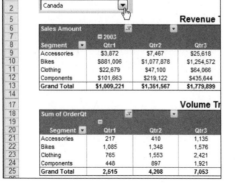

You may notice your pivot table automatically adjusts the columns to fit the data each time you select a new market. This default behavior can be bothersome to someone using your pivot table reports. You can suppress this behavior by right-clicking each pivot table and selecting Table Options. This activates the PivotTable Options dialog box, where you can deselect the Autofit Column Widths On Update selection. Remember, you have to do this for each pivot table individually.

Using the List Box Control

The List Box control allows users to select from a list of predefined choices. The idea is that when an item from the List Box control is selected, some action is taken with that selection. To add a List Box to your worksheet, follow these steps:

1. **Click the Insert drop-down list under the Developer tab.**

2. **Select the List Box Form control.**

3. **Click the location in your spreadsheet where you want to place your List Box.**

4. **After you drop the control onto your spreadsheet, right-click the control and select Format Control.**

5. **Click the Control tab to see the configuration options, as shown in Figure 11-24.**

6. **In the Input Range setting, identify the range that holds the predefined items you want to present as choices in the combo box.**

   As you can see in Figure 11-24, this List Box is filled with region selections.

7. **Next, in the Cell Link box, enter the cell where you want the List Box to output its value.**

   By default, a List Box control outputs the index number of the selected item. This means if the second item on the list was selected, the number 2 would be output. If the fifth item on the list was selected, the number 5 would be output. Notice in Figure 11-24 that this particular control outputs to cell P2.

   The Selection Type setting allows users to choose more than one selection in the List Box. The choices here are Single, Multi, and Extended.

   Always leave this setting on Single, as Multi and Extended work only in the VBA (Visual Basic for Applications) environment.

8. **(Optional) You can check the 3D property if you want the control to have a three-dimensional appearance.**

9. **Click OK to apply your changes.**

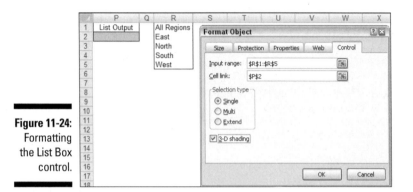

Figure 11-24:
Formatting
the List Box
control.

List Box Example: Controlling Multiple Charts with One Selector

One of the more useful ways to use a List Box is to control multiple charts with one selector. Figure 11-25 illustrates an example of this. As a region selection is made in the List Box, all three charts are fed the data for that region, adjusting the charts to correspond with the selection made. Happily, all this is done without VBA code, just a handful of formulas and a List Box.

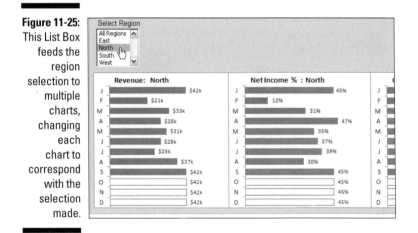

Figure 11-25:
This List Box
feeds the
region
selection to
multiple
charts,
changing
each
chart to
correspond
with the
selection
made.

To create this example, I start with three raw datasets (as shown in Figure 11-26) that contain three categories of data; Revenues, Net Income %, and Gross Margin. Each dataset contains a separate line for each region.

I then add a List Box that outputs the index number of the selected item to cell P2. (See Figure 11-27.)

I then create a shadow dataset that will consist of all formulas. In this shadow dataset, I use the Excel's CHOOSE function to select the correct value from the raw data tables based on the selected region.

TIP

In Excel, the ~~CHOOSE~~ function returns a value from a specified list of values based on a specified position number. For instance, the formula CHOOSE(3,"Red", "Yellow", "Green", "Blue") returns Green because Green is the third item in the list of values. The formula CHOOSE(1, "Red", "Yellow", "Green", "Blue") returns Red.

See Chapter 14 to get a detailed look at the CHOOSE function.

As you can see in Figure 11-28, the CHOOSE formula retrieves the target position number from Cell P2 (the cell where the List Box outputs the index number of the selected item) and then matches that position number to the list of cell references given. The cell references come directly from the raw data table.

In the example shown in Figure 11-28, the data that would be returned with this CHOOSE formula would be 98741. Why? Because cell P2 contains the number 1, and the first cell reference within the CHOOSE formula is cell B7.

I entered the same type of CHOOSE formula into the Jan column and then copied it across. (See Figure 11-29.)

To test that your formulas are working, change the value of cell P2 manually, entering **1**, **2**, **3**, **4**, or **5**. When the formulas work, all that's left to do is create the charts using the shadow data.

Figure 11-26:
Start with
the raw
datasets
that contain
one line per
region.

	A	B	C	D	E	F	G
5							
6	Revenues	Jan	Feb	Mar	Apr	May	Ju
7	All Regions	98,741	54,621	96,555	109,625	87,936	84,
8	East	27,474	22,674	35,472	36,292	31,491	27,
9	North	41,767	20,806	32,633	28,023	31,090	27,
10	South	18,911	1,125	17,020	34,196	12,989	18,
11	West	10,590	10,016	11,430	11,115	12,367	10,
12							
13	Net Income %	Jan	Feb	Mar	Apr	May	Ju
14	All Regions	49.9%	50.6%	48.7%	47.8%	41.4%	
15	East	63.1%	53.6%	55.8%	47.4%	41.5%	
16	North	45.3%	11.8%	31.0%	47.5%	35.2%	
17	South	31.2%	61.7%	41.8%	30.9%	9.0%	
18	West	60.1%	75.4%	66.1%	65.2%	79.8%	
19							
20	Gross Margin	Jan	Feb	Mar	Apr	May	Ju
21	All Regions	48,508	22,850	44,586	48,340	35,056	37,
22	East	17,326	12,154	19,799	17,206	13,079	11,
23	North	18,914	2,455	10,115	13,299	10,938	10,
24	South	5,904	694	7,115	10,582	1,171	7,
25	West	6,364	7,547	7,557	7,253	9,867	8,

Figure 11-27:
Add a List
Box and
note the cell
where the
output value
will be
placed.

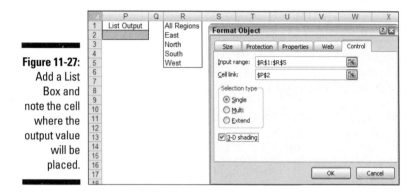

	P	Q	R	S	T	U	V	W	X
1	List Output		All Regions						
2			East						
3			North						
4			South						
5			West						

Format Object

| Size | Protection | Properties | Web | Control |

Input range: $R$1:$R$5

Cell link: $P$2

Selection type
- ⦿ Single
- ○ Multi
- ○ Extend

☑ 3-D shading

OK   Cancel

Figure 11-28:
Use the
CHOOSE
function to
capture the
correct data
correspond-
ing to the
selected
region.

	A	B	C		P
1		Jan	Feb		List Output
2	Revenues	=CHOOSE($P$2,B7,B8,B9,B10,B11)			1
3	Net Income %				
4	Gross Margin				
5					
6	Revenues	Jan	Feb		
7	All Regions	98741	54,621		
8	East	27474	22,674		
9	North	41767	20,806		
10	South	18911	1,125		
11	West	10590	10,016		

Figure 11-29:
Create
similar
CHOOSE
formulas for
each row/
category of
data and
then copy
the choose
formulas
across
months.

	A	B	C
1		Jan	Feb
2	Revenues	=CHOOSE($P$2,B7,B8,B9,B10,B11)	=CHOOSE($P$2,C7,C8,C9,C10,C11)
3	Net Income %	=CHOOSE($P$2,B14,B15,B16,B17,B18)	=CHOOSE($P$2,C14,C15,C16,C17,C18)
4	Gross Margin	=CHOOSE($P$2,B21,B22,B23,B24,B25)	=CHOOSE($P$2,C21,C22,C23,C24,C25)

Part V
Working with the Outside World

"I've used several spreadsheet programs, but this is the best one for designing quilt patterns."

In this part . . .

The theme of this section is importing and exporting information to and from Excel. Chapter 12 explores some of the ways to incorporate data that doesn't originate in Excel. In that chapter, I show you how to import data from external sources as well as how to create systems that allow for the dynamic refreshing of external data sources. Chapter 13 wraps up this look on Excel dashboards and reports by showing you the various ways to distribute and present your work.

Chapter 12

Using External Data for Your Dashboards and Reports

· ·

· ·

*W*ouldn't it be wonderful if every dataset you came across were neatly packed in one easy-to-use Excel table? Unfortunately, there are people (and you know who they are) who insist on using platforms other than Excel. Imagine the gall.

Of course, I'm being cheeky. The reality is that you will undoubtedly encounter situations when the data you need comes from external data sources. External data is exactly what it sounds like; data that isn't located in the Excel workbook in which you're operating. Some examples of external data sources are text files, Access tables, SQL Server tables, and even other Excel workbooks.

Throughout this book, I advocate the separation of data and presentation. When dealing with small datasets that are developed and maintained in Excel, you have to make a conscious effort to make that separation. However, in complex models where large volumes of data come from Access or SQL, the effort on your part is eliminated. That data is already separated, baby. The worry in these situations is how to efficiently move that data from over there to over here. This chapter explores the most efficient ways to get external data into Excel.

Before jumping in, however, there are a couple of disclaimers your humble author would like to throw out there. First, the focus of this chapter is on getting data from Access and SQL Server databases; mainly because the data for a typical Excel user resides in Access or SQL Server. Second, there are numerous ways to get data into Excel. In fact, between the functionality found in the user interface and the VBA/code techniques, there are too many to focus on in one chapter. For this adventure, I focus on two techniques: using the Get External Data group and using MS Query. Why these two techniques? Both of these techniques are easy to grasp, can be implemented in most situations, and don't come with a lot of pitfalls and gotchas. Now that you can't sue me anymore, let's get started.

Using the Get External Data Group

Although the option to import external data was available in earlier versions of Excel, this functionality was buried several layers deep. In Excel 2007 however, Microsoft made importing Access data from the Excel user interface very simple — it's right on the Ribbon! Click the Data tab on the Ribbon to expose the Get External Data group, as shown in Figure 12-1.

Clicking any one of the data source types (each represented by an icon) activates an easy-to-use wizard that walks you through a process unique to that type. In this section, I walk through the process of importing both Access and SQL Server data using the Get External Data group.

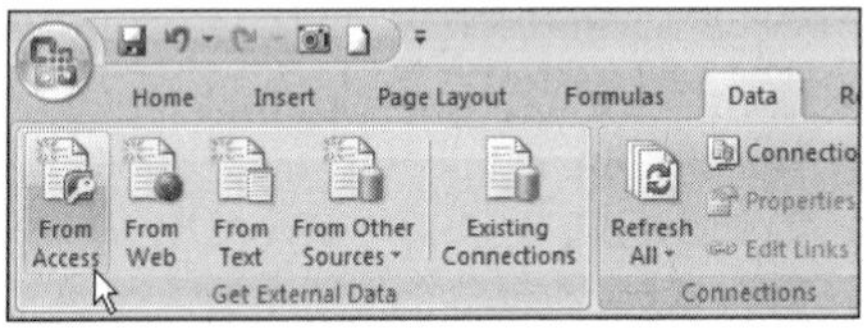

Figure 12-1:
The Get External Data group contains the icons for various external data sources.

Importing Access data with the Get External Data Group

The process of importing Access data is unbelievably simple in Excel 2007. Here's what you do:

1. **Select the Data tab from the Ribbon and select the From Access icon.**

   The first step is to browse for our Access database. If the database from which you wish to import is local, simply browse to the file location and open it. If you have an Access database on a network drive at your employer, you may also select that database as well — provided you have the proper authorization and access.

2. **Select the Access database from which you want to import and select Open. (See Figure 12-2.)**

Figure 12-2: Select the target Access database.

Note that you can import the older Access `.mdb` file formats as well as Access 2007 `.accdb` databases.

The Select Table dialog box appears. (See Figure 12-3.)

3. **Choose an existing Access Table or Query.**

Note that both tables and queries are available for you to choose.

Figure 12-3: Select the needed table or query.

Name	Description	Modified	Created
Employee_Master		12/29/2006 8:12:35 AM	5/5/2005 12:54:32
LocationMaster		7/29/2007 12:58:15 AM	5/5/2005 11:57:22
PriceMaster		12/10/2006 7:56:28 AM	5/18/2005 3:11:28
ProductMaster		12/10/2006 7:56:28 AM	5/5/2005 12:25:12
PvTblFeed		7/23/2005 3:05:40 PM	7/22/2005 4:53:24
SalesByRegion		12/10/2006 2:35:10 PM	12/10/2006 2:32:07
TransactionMaster		7/29/2007 12:58:15 AM	7/29/2007 12:51:19

4. **Choose the location and format for data that's to be imported.**

In the example in Figure 12-4, Table is chosen.

5. **Click OK to start the import process.**

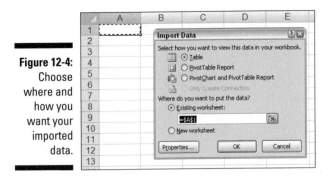

Figure 12-4:
Choose
where and
how you
want your
imported
data.

If you choose the Table option in the step shown in Figure 12-4, the raw data is written directly onto your spreadsheet. If you choose the PivotTable or PivotChart options, the data is saved to a pivot cache without writing the actual data to the spreadsheet. This allows your pivot table to function as normal without having to import potentially hundreds of thousands of data rows twice (once for the pivot cache and once for the spreadsheet). Feel free to review Chapter 3 for a quick explanation of pivot caches.

The incredibly powerful thing about data that has been imported this way is that it's refreshable! That's right. If you import data from Access using this technique, Excel creates a table that can be refreshed by right-clicking and selecting Refresh, as demonstrated in Figure 12-5. When you refresh your imported data, Excel goes out to the external data source and re-imports the data, overwriting the old table or pivot table.

Figure 12-5:
Refresh your
imported
table by
right-
clicking
inside the
table.

Think about what this means in terms of building a reporting process. You can create a dashboard or report based on external data that can be refreshed when you need. When your data is refreshed, any charts, matrixes, conditional formatting, or pivot tables that are built on top of this data are automatically updated with the latest data. It's a beautiful thing.

Importing SQL Server data with the Get External Data menu

Although a few more steps are involved with importing SQL Server data in Excel, it's just as easy as importing Access data. Just follow these steps:

1. **Select the Data tab from the Ribbon and click From Other Sources. Choose the From SQL Server option from drop-down list, as shown in Figure 12-6.**

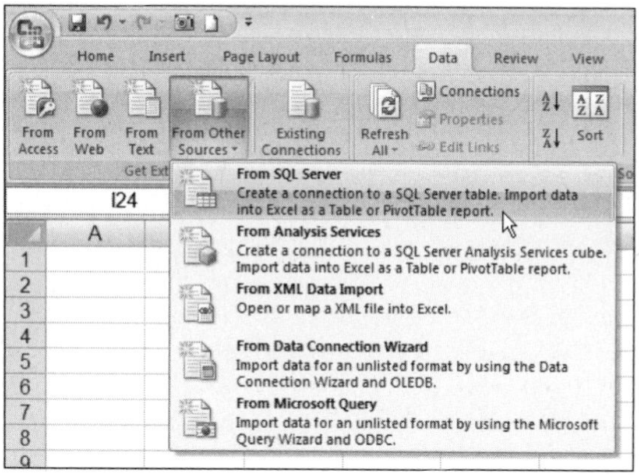

Figure 12-6: Select the From SQL Server option.

Selecting this option activates the Data Connection Wizard, as shown in Figure 12-7. The idea is to configure your connection settings from Excel to the server.

2. **Enter the name of your server as well as your username and password.**

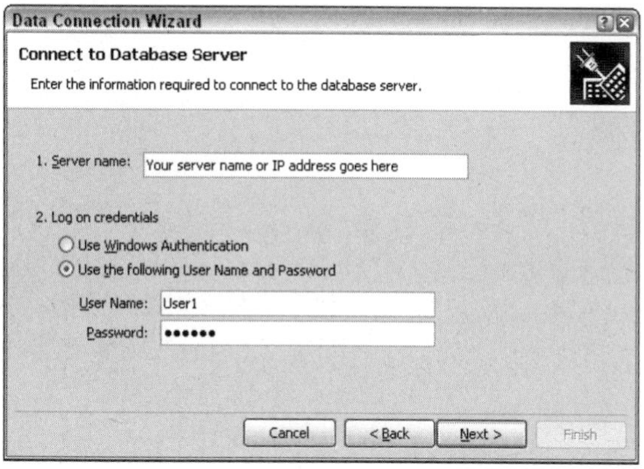

Figure 12-7: Step 1 of the Data Connection Wizard is to enter some authentication information.

TIP

If you're typically authenticated via Windows authentication, simply select the Use Windows Authentication option.

3. **Select the database from which you want to import data.**

As you can see in Figure 12-8, the Facility_Svcs_Database database has been selected.

After the database is selected, all tables and views in that database are displayed in the list of objects below the drop-down list.

4. **Choose the table or view you want to analyze and then click the Next button.**

Figure 12-8:
Specify the database you're using and then choose the table or view you need to import.

Data Connection Wizard						
Select Database and Table						
Select the Database and Table/Cube which contains the data you want.						

Select the database that contains the data you want:

Facility_Svcs_Database

☑ Connect to a specific table:

Name	Owner	Description	Modified	Created	Type
CustomerMaster	dbo			6/18/2006 4:12:19 AM	TABLE
Employee_Master	dbo			6/18/2006 4:12:19 AM	TABLE
LocationMaster	dbo			6/18/2006 4:12:19 AM	TABLE
PriceMaster	dbo			6/18/2006 4:12:19 AM	TABLE
ProductMaster	dbo			6/18/2006 4:12:35 AM	TABLE
Sales_By_Employees	dbo			6/18/2006 4:12:35 AM	TABLE
TransactionMaster	dbo			6/18/2006 4:12:35 AM	TABLE

Cancel | < Back | Next > | Finish

5. **In the next screen in the wizard, shown in Figure 12-9, you can enter some descriptive information about the connection you've just created.**

6. **When you're satisfied with your descriptive edits, click the Finish button to finalize your connection settings.**

Note that all the fields in the screen shown in Figure 12-9 are optional. That is, if you bypass this screen without editing anything, your data imports just fine. The fields that are most often used on this screen are

- *File Name:* In the File Name input box, you can change the filename of the .odc (Office Data Connection) file generated to store the configuration information for the link you just created.

- *Save Password in File:* Under the File Name input box, you can save the password for your external data in the file itself (via the Save Password in File check box). Placing a check in this check box actually enters your password in the file. Keep in mind that this password isn't encrypted, so anyone interested enough could potentially get the password for your data source simply by viewing your file with a text editor.

- *Description:* In the Description field, you can enter a plain description of what this particular data connection does.

- *Friendly Name:* The Friendly Name field allows you to specify your own name for the external source. You typically enter a name that's descriptive and easy to read.

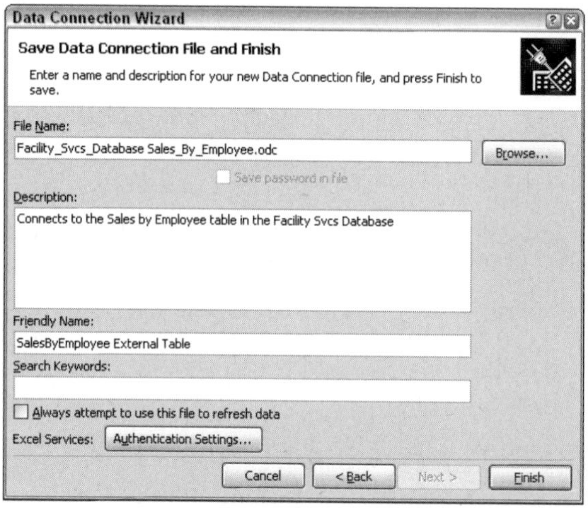

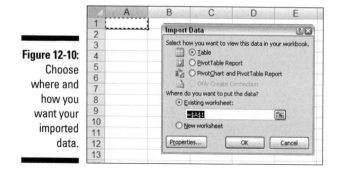

Figure 12-9:
Add some
descriptive
information
for your
connection.

7. **Choose the location and format for data that's to be imported. (See Figure 12-10.)**

8. **Click OK to start the import process.**

Figure 12-10:
Choose
where and
how you
want your
imported
data.

Using the MS Query Wizard

Microsoft Query (affectionately known as MS Query) is a standalone program that, like the Get External Data option, establishes a refreshable data connection through the Excel user interface. The advantage in using MS Query is that you can manipulate the data you want to import. You can select records from Access objects subject to your own criteria or even user supplied criteria!

MS Query may or may not be installed on your system, based on how you performed your Office installation. Keep in mind that if you don't have the MS Query program installed on your system, you can't link to external data sources in Excel. To install MS Query, you need your Microsoft Office installation disk. Start the Microsoft Office Setup and choose to customize your installation. While you're customizing your installation, look for Office Tools. Find the Microsoft Query under Office Tools entry. Make sure you set it to Run from My Computer and then complete the installation.

You can find the MS Query option under the From Other Sources drop-down list, as shown in Figure 12-11. To import data using the MS Query Wizard, follow these steps:

1. **Select the From Microsoft Query option.**

   After MS Query fires up, you see the Choose Data Source dialog box, as shown in Figure 12-12.

   In this walkthrough, source some data from the `ZalexCorp.accdb` Access database. This file can be found on this book's companion Web site.

2. **Choose <New Data Source> from the Databases tab and click OK.**

   The Create New Data Source dialog box appears.

Figure 12-11: Start the MS Query Wizard.

3. **Type a name for your data source at the top of the dialog box.**

   As you can see in Figure 12-13, I call it ZalexCorp.

4. **Choose a type of driver for the database to which you wish to connect.**

   In this walkthrough, I select Microsoft Access Driver (*.mdb, *.accdb), as shown in Figure 12-14.

5. **Click the Connect button to activate the ODBC Microsoft Access Setup dialog box.**

Figure 12-12:
The MS
Query
Wizard
starts by
asking you
to choose
your data
source.

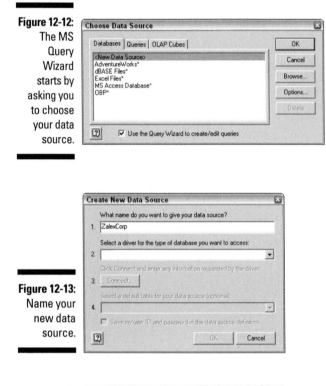

Figure 12-13:
Name your
new data
source.

Figure 12-14:
Choose the
Access
database
driver.

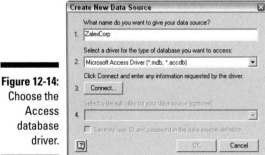

6. **Click the Select button.**

   The Select Database dialog box appears.

7. **Navigate to the Access database (see Figure 12-15), select it, and click OK.**

8. **After you select your database, continue to press OK until you come back to the Choose Data Source dialog box.**

   As Figure 12-16 illustrates, your newly-linked ZalexCorp database is now displayed in list of data sources. After a database appears in the data sources list, you no longer have to perform Steps 2–8 to access it. You can simply click the name (in this case ZalexCorp) and connect directly. This is somewhat like setting a bookmark to a Web site.

Figure 12-15:
Select the database to which you're connecting.

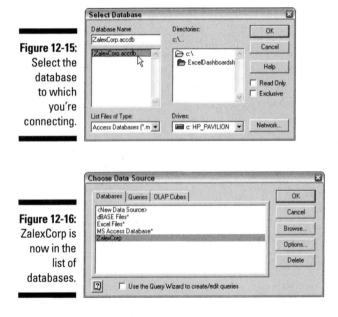

Figure 12-16:
ZalexCorp is now in the list of databases.

9. **Select ZalexCorp and click OK to display a list of tables and queries available within the ZalexCorp database.**

10. **Pull the fields you want into your query. To do this, click the expand icon to the left of your chosen table name (see Figure 12-17). Then select each field and click the right-facing arrow to move the field into the Columns in Your Query box.**

   A quick way to choose all the fields in a table is to select the table (without expanding it) and then click the arrow to move the fields in this table over to the Columns in Your Query box.

11. **If you wish to change field ordering after you select your fields, you can use the up and down arrows to the right of the Columns in Your Query box.**

In Figure 12-18, the Market field has been moved to be the first column of the query.

TIP

By default, the MS Query Wizard arranges the fields in the order in which you choose them. Changing the order of fields is something you can't do with the Get External Data functionality.

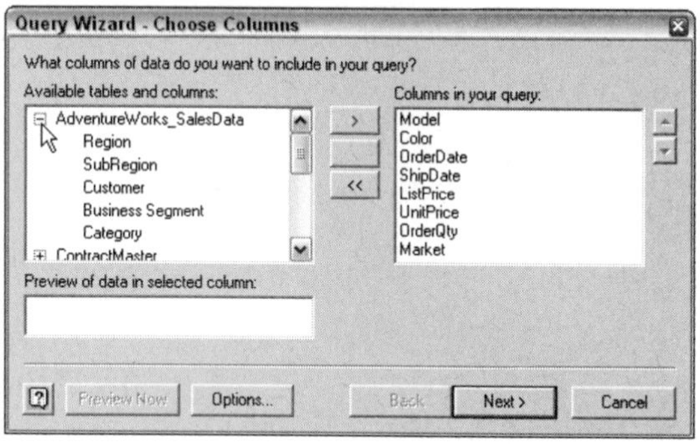

Figure 12-17: Select the fields you want in your query.

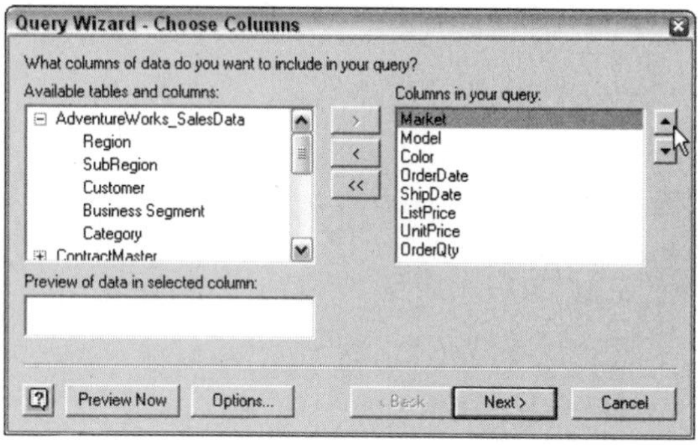

Figure 12-18: MS Query actually lets you reorder the fields you select.

The next pane of the MS Query Wizard gives you options to apply your own criteria to filter your data before importing. (See Figure 12-19.)

To activate a filter, select the field you wish to filter from the Column to Filter box on the left. Doing so activates the filter options on the right side of the wizard. The first field allows you to select a condition from a drop-down list (such as Equals, Does Not Equal, or Greater Than or Equal To). The second field allows you to specify criteria for this condition. This section of the wizard allows you to combine up to three filters with and/or logical operators. Again, applying filters on the fly is something you can't do with the Get External Data functionality.

12. **Apply a filter to include only those records that have a UnitPrice greater than 200 and then click Next.**

The next pane of the Query Wizard allows you to provide a custom sort to your data. In this pane, you can apply only three consecutive sorts. (See Figure 12-20.)

13. **Apply a sort on Market in Ascending order and then click Next.**

    You're almost done. The next pane asks whether you wish to return the data to Excel or further modify the query in MS Query. (See Figure 12-21.) Also note the Save Query button. With this button, you can save your query so you can access it from the Queries tab of the Choose Data Source dialog box. In this example, don't save your query and instead choose to view your data in Excel.

14. **Select the Return Data to Microsoft Office Excel option and then click Finish.**

15. **Choose the location and format for data that's to be imported (see Figure 12-22) and then click OK to start the import process.**

    As with tables created with the Get External Data functionality, data imported using MS Query is refreshable! You can refresh the data by right-clicking inside the table and selecting Refresh. When you refresh your imported data, Excel goes out to the external data source and re-imports the existing data.

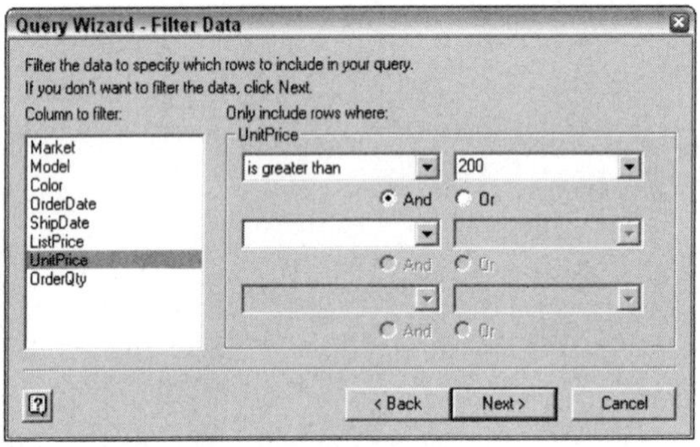

Figure 12-19:
MS Query lets you apply criteria to filter data before importing.

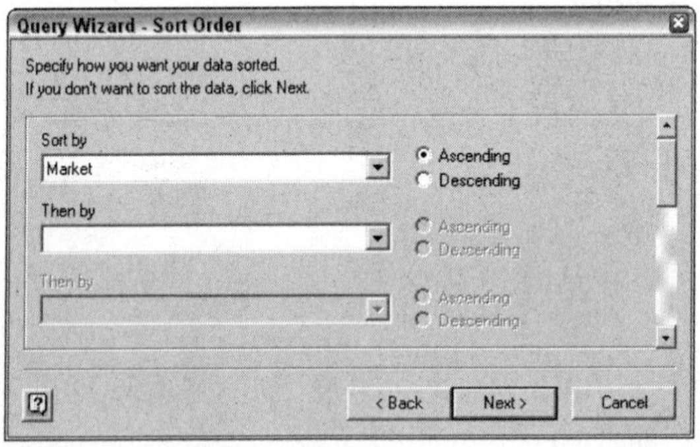

Figure 12-20:
Apply a custom sort order.

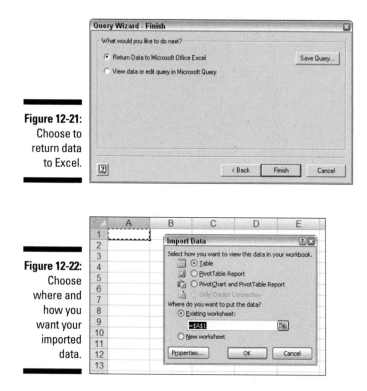

Figure 12-21:
Choose to
return data
to Excel.

Figure 12-22:
Choose
where and
how you
want your
imported
data.

Managing External Data Properties

External data tables have a few adjustable properties that are exposed via the Properties dialog box. You can get to the properties of a particular External data table by clicking the target table and selecting the Properties icon under the Data tab. (See Figure 12-23.)

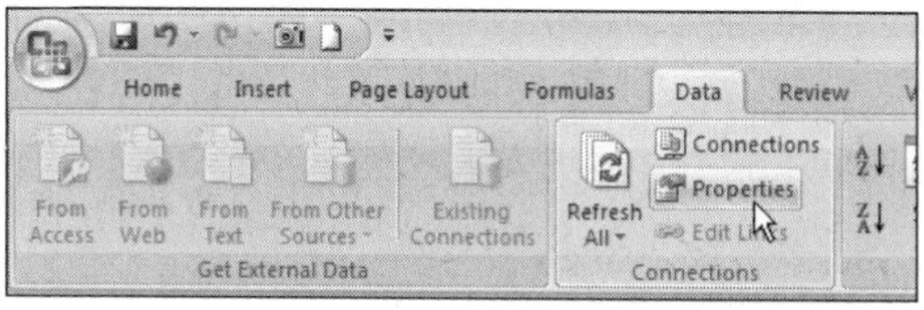

Figure 12-23:
Getting
to the
properties of
an external
data table.

Activating the properties of an external data table calls up the External Data Properties dialog box, as shown in Figure 12-24. Take a moment to understand what each of these properties does. They are as follows:

✔ **Include Row Numbers:** This property is unchecked by default. Checking this property creates a dummy column that contains row numbers. The first column of your dataset is this row number column upon refresh.

✔ **Adjust Column Width:** This property is checked by default, telling Excel to adjust the column widths each time the data is refreshed. Removing this check causes the column widths to remain the same.

✔ **Preserve Column/Sort/Filter/Layout:** If this is checked, the order of the columns and rows of the Excel range remains unchanged. This way, you can rearrange and sort the columns and rows of the external data in your spreadsheet without worrying about blowing away your formatting each time you refresh.

✔ **Preserve Cell Formatting:** This is checked by default, telling Excel to keep the applied cell formatting when you refresh.

✔ **Insert cells for New Data, Delete Unused Cells:** This is the default setting for data range changes. When data rows decrease, you may have errors in adjacent cells that reference your external range. The cells these formulas referenced are deleted, so when you reference them you get a #VALUE error in your formula cells.

✔ **Insert Rows for New Data, Clear Unused Cells:** This option ensures that unused cells are not deleted, but only cleared when refreshing your data source. This is handy when you have formulas that reference the cells within your query results. When the unused cells are cleared instead of deleted, formulas that reference those cells retain the their reference addresses instead of returning #Ref errors.

✔ **Overwrite Existing Cells with New Data, Clear Unused Cells:** The third option should be the same as option two when rows decrease as unused cells are cleared.

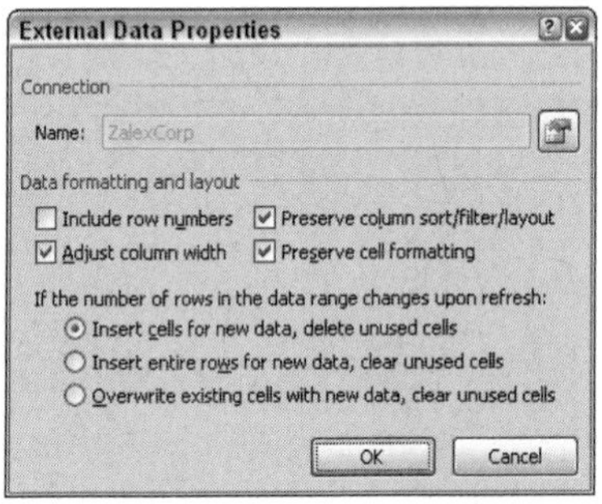

Figure 12-24:
The External
Data
Properties
dialog box.

Chapter 13

Sharing Your Work with the Outside World

*L*et's face it; you're not making these dashboards and reports for your amusement. At some point, you'll want to share your handiwork with others. The focus of this chapter is preparing your dashboards for life outside your PC. Here, explore the various methods of protecting your work from accidental and purposeful meddling and discover how you can distribute your dashboards via PowerPoint and PDF (Portable Document Format).

Protecting Your Dashboards and Reports

You've put in a ton of hours getting your dashboard and reports to work the way you want them to. The last thing you need is to have a clumsy client or an overzealous power-user botching up your Excel file.

Before distributing any Excel-based work, you should always consider protecting your file by using the protection capabilities native to Excel. Although none of Excel's protection methods are hacker-proof, they do serve to protect the formulas, data structures, and other objects that make your reporting mechanisms tick.

Securing the entire workbook using file protection options

Perhaps the best way to protect your Excel file is to employ Excel's file protection options. These options enable you to apply protection at the workbook level, requiring a password to view or make changes to the file. This method is by far the easiest to apply and manage. With this method, there's no need to protect each worksheet one at a time. You can simply apply a blanket protection to guard against unauthorized access and edits. Take a moment to review the File Sharing options, which are as follows:

- ✔ Forcing Read Only mode unless a password is given
- ✔ Requiring a password to open an Excel file
- ✔ Removing workbook level protection

The next few sections discuss these options in detail.

Forcing Read Only mode unless a password is given

You can force your workbook to go into Read Only mode unless the user has the appropriate password. This way you can keep your file safe from unauthorized changes, yet still allow authorized users to edit the file.

Here are the steps to force Read Only mode:

1. **Open an existing Excel file and click the Office icon in the upper-left corner.**

2. **Select Save As to activate the Save As dialog box.**

3. **In the Save As dialog box, click the Tools button and select General Options, as demonstrated in Figure 13-1.**

    The General Options dialog box appears.

4. **Enter an appropriate password in the Password to Modify input box (as illustrated in Figure 13-2) and click OK.**

    Note that Excel passwords are case-sensitive, so make sure Caps Lock on your keyboard is in the off position when entering your password.

5. **Excel asks you to reenter your password, so reenter your chosen password.**

6. **Save your file to a new name.**

    At this point, your file is password-protected from unauthorized changes. If you were to open your file, you'd see something similar to Figure 13-3. Failing to enter the correct password causes the file to go into Read Only mode.

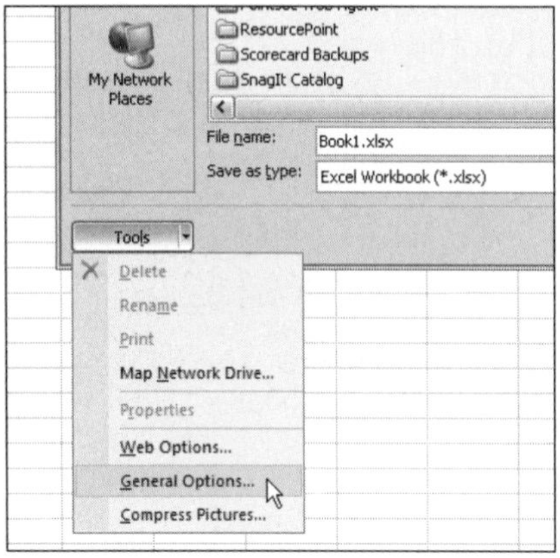

Figure 13-1:
The File Sharing options are well hidden in the Save As dialog box under General Options.

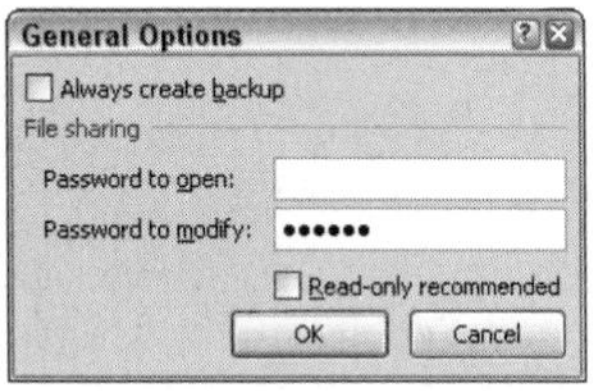

Figure 13-2:
Enter the password needed to modify the file.

Figure 13-3:
A password is now needed to make changes to the file.

Requiring a password to open an Excel file

You may have instances where your Excel dashboards are so sensitive only certain users are authorized to see them. In these cases, you can force your workbook to require a password to open. Here are the steps to employ a password to open the file.

1. **Open an existing Excel file and click the Office icon in the upper-left corner.**

2. **Select Save As to activate the Save As dialog box.**

3. **In the Save As dialog box, click the Tools button and select General Options. (Refer to Figure 13-1.)**

The General Options dialog box opens.

4. **Enter an appropriate password in the Password to Open input box (as illustrated in Figure 13-4) and click OK.**

5. **Excel asks you to reenter your password.**

6. **Save your file to a new name.**

At this point, your file is password-protected from unauthorized viewing.

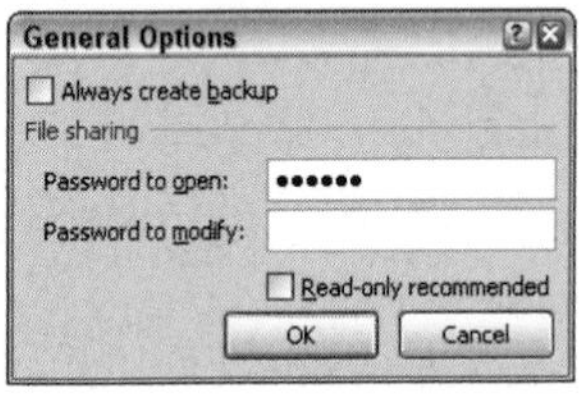

Figure 13-4:
Enter the
password
needed to
modify
the file.

General Options

☐ Always create backup
File sharing

Password to open: ●●●●●●
Password to modify:

☐ Read-only recommended

OK   Cancel

Removing workbook level protection

Removing workbook level protection is as easy as clearing the passwords from the General Options dialog box. Here's how you do it:

1. **Open an existing Excel file and click the Office icon in the upper-left corner.**

2. **Select Save As to activate the Save As dialog box.**

3. **In the Save As dialog box, click the Tools button and select General Options. (Refer to Figure 13-1.)**

The General Options dialog box opens.

4. **Clear the Password to Open input box as well as the Password to Modify input box and click OK.**

5. **Save your file.**

Notice the Read-Only Recommended check box in the General Options dialog box (refer to Figure 13-4). When you place a check in this check box, you get a cute but useless message recommending read-only mode upon opening the file. This message is only a recommendation and does not prevent anyone from opening the file as read/write.

Protecting worksheets

You may find that you need to apply protection to specific worksheets, preventing users from taking certain actions. For example, you may not want users to break your data model by inserting or deleting columns and rows. You can prevent this by applying protection to your worksheet.

Unlocking editable ranges

By default, all cells in a worksheet are set to be locked when you apply worksheet level protection. That is to say, after you protect a worksheet, the cells on that worksheet can't be altered in any way. That being said, you may find you need certain cells or ranges to be editable even in a locked state, like the example shown in Figure 13-5.

1. **Select the cells you need to unlock.**

2. **Right-click and choose Format Cells.**

3. **On the Protection tab, as shown in Figure 13-6, deselect the Locked property.**

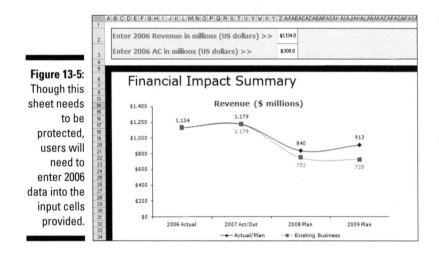

Figure 13-5: Though this sheet needs to be protected, users will need to enter 2006 data into the input cells provided.

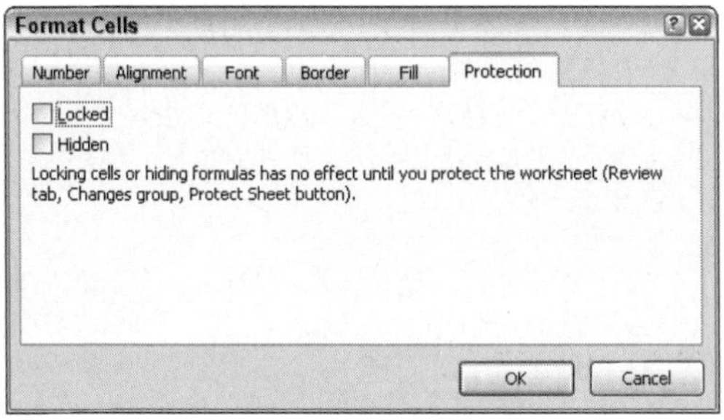

Figure 13-6: To ensure a cell remains unlocked when the worksheet is protected, deselect the Locked property.

4. Click OK to apply the change.

Applying worksheet protection

After you've selectively unlocked the necessary cells, you can commence to applying worksheet protection. Just follow these steps:

1. Click the Protect Sheet button on the Review tab of the Ribbon (see Figure 13-7) to activate the Protect Sheet dialog box.

Figure 13-7:
Click
Protect
Sheet in the
Review tab.

2. Enter a password in the given input box, as demonstrated in Figure 13-8, then click the OK button.

This is the password that removes worksheet protection. Note that specifying a password is optional, as you can apply and remove worksheet protection without one.

Figure 13-8:
Specify a
password
that
removes
worksheet
protection.

3. In the list below the password input (see Figure 13-8), specify which elements users are allowed to change when you protect the worksheet.

When a check box is cleared for a particular action, Excel prevents users from taking that action.

Take a moment to familiarize yourself with the some of the actions you can limit when protecting a worksheet. They are as follows:

• *Select Locked Cells:* Allows or prevents the selection of locked cells.

- *Select Unlocked Cells:* Allows or prevents the selection of unlocked cells.

- *Format Cells:* Allows or prevents the formatting of cells.

- *Format Columns:* Allows or prevents the use of column formatting commands, including changing column width or hiding columns.

- *Format Rows:* Allows or prevents the use of row formatting commands, including changing row height or hiding rows.

- *Insert Columns:* Allows or prevents the inserting of columns.

- *Insert Rows:* Allows or prevents the inserting of rows.

- *Insert Hyperlinks:* Allows or prevents the inserting of hyperlinks.

- *Delete Columns:* Allows or prevents the deleting of columns. Note that if Delete Columns is protected and Insert Columns is *not* protected, you can technically insert columns you can't delete.

- *Delete Rows:* Allows or prevents the deleting of rows. Note that if Delete Rows is protected and Insert Rows is *not* protected, you can technically insert columns you can't delete.

- *Sort:* Allows or prevents the use of Sort commands. Note that this doesn't apply to locked ranges. Users can't sort ranges that contain locked cells on a protected worksheet, regardless of this setting.

- *Use AutoFilter:* Allows or prevents use of Excel's AutoFilter functionality. Users can't create or remove AutoFiltered ranges on a protected worksheet, regardless of this setting.

- *Use PivotTable Reports:* Allows or prevents the modifying, refreshing, or formatting of pivot tables found on the protected sheet.

- *Edit Objects:* Allows or prevents the formatting and altering of shapes, charts, text boxes, controls, or other graphics objects.

- *Edit Scenario:* Allows or prevents the viewing of scenarios.

4. **If you provided a password, reenter the password.**

5. **Click OK to apply the worksheet protection.**

Removing worksheet protection

Just follow these steps to remove any worksheet protection you may have applied:

1. **Click the Unprotect Sheet button on the Review tab.**

2. **If you specified a password while protecting the worksheet, Excel asks you for that password (see Figure 13-9). Enter the password and click OK to immediately remove protection.**

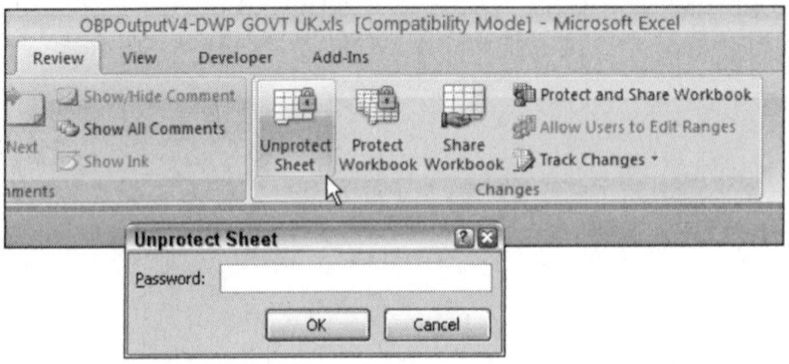

Figure 13-9:
The
Unprotect
Sheet
button
removes
worksheet
protection.

OBPOutputV4-DWP GOVT UK.xls [Compatibility Mode] - Microsoft Excel

Review   View   Developer   Add-Ins

Show/Hide Comment   Protect and Share Workbook
Show All Comments   Allow Users to Edit Ranges
Next   Show Ink   Unprotect   Protect   Share   Track Changes
Sheet   Workbook   Workbook
ments   Changes

Unprotect Sheet

Password:

OK   Cancel

Protecting the workbook structure

If you look under the Review tab in the Ribbon, you see the Protect Workbook button next to the Protect Sheet button. Protecting the workbook enables you to prevent users from taking any action that affects the structure of your workbook, such as adding/deleting worksheets, hiding/unhiding worksheets, and naming or moving worksheets. Just follow these steps to protect a workbook:

1. **Click the Protect Workbook button on the Review tab of the Ribbon to activate the Protect Structure and Windows dialog box, as shown in Figure 13-10.**

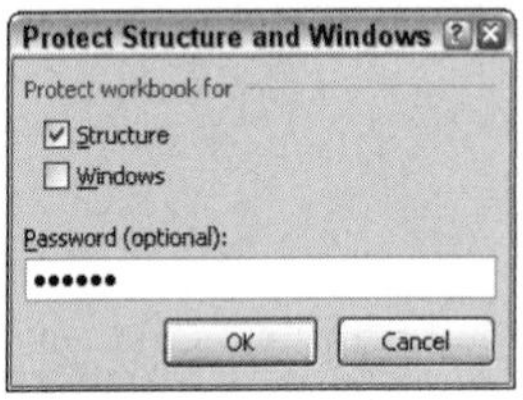

Figure 13-10:
The Protect
Structure
and
Windows
dialog box.

Protect Structure and Windows

Protect workbook for
☑ Structure
☐ Windows

Password (optional):
••••••

OK   Cancel

2. **Choose which elements you want to protect: workbook structure, windows, or both.**

   When a check box is cleared for a particular action, Excel prevents users from taking that action.

   Selecting Structure prevents users from

   - Viewing worksheets that you've hidden
   - Moving, deleting, hiding, or changing the names of worksheets
   - Inserting new worksheets or chart sheets
   - Moving or copying worksheets to another workbook

- Displaying the source data for a cell in a pivot table Data area or displaying pivot table Page field pages on separate worksheets

- Creating a scenario summary report

- Using any Analysis Toolpak utilities that require results to be placed on a new worksheet

- Recording new macros

Choosing Windows prevents users from changing, moving, or sizing the workbook windows while the workbook is opened.

3. **If you provided a password, reenter the password.**

4. **Click OK to apply the worksheet protection.**

Linking Your Excel Dashboards into PowerPoint

There are at least eight different methods to get Excel data into PowerPoint. For our purposes, I'll focus on the method that is most conducive to presenting frequently updated dashboards and reports in PowerPoint — creating a dynamic link. A *dynamic link* allows your PowerPoint presentation to automatically pick up changes you make to your Excel files.

Creating the link between Excel and PowerPoint

When you copy and paste a range of data, you're simply creating a picture of the range. However, when you create a link to a range, PowerPoint stores the location information to your source field and then displays a representation of the linked data. The net effect is that when the data in your source file changes, PowerPoint updates its representation of the data to reflect the changes.

To test this concept of linking to an Excel range, follow these steps:

1. **Open the `Chapter 13 Sample File.xlsx` file.**

   This file is available on this book's companion Web site.

2. **Click the chart once to select it and press Ctrl+C on your keyboard to copy the chart.**

If you're copying multiple charts, you don't have to copy one at a time. Simply select the range of cells that contain the charts and press Ctrl+C to copy. This way, you're copying everything in that range of cells — charts and all.

3. **Open a new PowerPoint document and place your cursor at the location you want the linked table to be displayed.**

4. **On the Home tab in PowerPoint, choose Paste⇨Paste Special, as demonstrated in Figure 13-11.**

   The Paste Special dialog box appears. (See Figure 13-12.)

5. **Select the Paste Link radio button and choose Microsoft Excel Chart Object from the list of document types.**

Figure 13-11:
Select Paste Special from the home tab in PowerPoint.

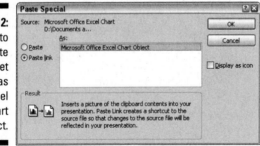

Figure 13-12:
Be sure to select Paste Link and set the link as an Excel Chart Object.

6. **Click OK to apply the link.**

   At this point, you have a chart on your PowerPoint presentation that's linked back to your Excel file. (See Figure 13-13.)

This technique of linking Excel charts to PowerPoint is ideal if you aren't proficient at building charts in PowerPoint. Build the chart in Excel and then simply create a link for the chart in PowerPoint.

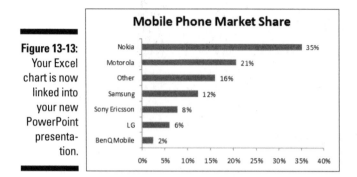

Manually refreshing links to capture updates

The wonderful thing about dynamic links is they can be refreshed, enabling you to capture any updates in your Excel files without recreating the links. To see how this works, follow these steps:

1. **Go back to your Excel file (from the example in the previous section) and change the values for Samsung and Nokia, as demonstrated in Figure 13-14.**

   Note the chart has changed.

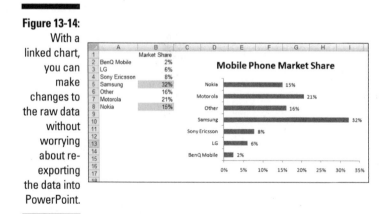

2. **Return to PowerPoint, right-click the chart link in your presentation and choose Update Link, as demonstrated in Figure 13-15.**

   You see that your linked chart automatically captures the changes.

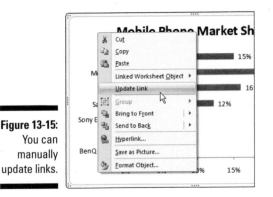

Figure 13-15:
You can
manually
update links.

3. **Save and close both your Excel file and your PowerPoint presentation, and then open only your newly-created PowerPoint presentation.**

   This time you see the message shown in Figure 13-16. Clicking the Update Links button refreshes all links in the PowerPoint presentation. Each time you open any PowerPoint presentation with links, it asks you whether you want to update the links.

Figure 13-16:
PowerPoint,
by default,
asks if you
want to
update all
links in the
presenta-
tion.

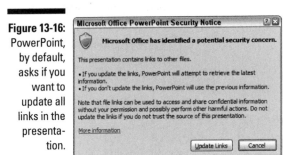

Automatically refreshing links to capture updates

Having PowerPoint ask you whether you want to update the links each and every time you open your presentation quickly gets annoying. You can avoid this message by specifying that PowerPoint automatically refresh your dynamic links upon opening the file. Here's how:

1. **In PowerPoint, click the Office icon in the upper-left corner.**

2. **Select the Prepare option and then click Edit Links to Files, as shown in Figure 13-17.**

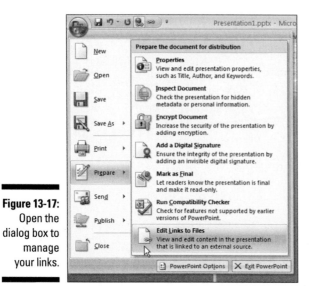

Figure 13-17:
Open the
dialog box to
manage
your links.

The Links dialog box appears. (See Figure 13-18.)

3. **Click each of your links and select the Automatic radio button.**

To select multiple links in the Links dialog box, hold down the Ctrl key
on your keyboard while you select your links.

Figure 13-18:
Setting the
selected
links to
update
automati-
cally.

When your links are set to update automatically, PowerPoint automatically synchronizes with your Excel file and ensures that all your updates
are displayed.

Distributing Your Dashboards via PDF

In Excel 2007, Microsoft has made it possible to convert your Excel Worksheets to PDF (Portable Document Format) or XPS (XML Paper Specification). *PDF* is the standard document sharing format developed by Adobe. *XPS* is Microsoft's own open-source competitor to Adobe's PDF file format. Distributing your reports and dashboards as PDF or XPS documents allows you to share your work without sharing your entire workbook.

Due to some legal complications, Microsoft was unable to include the "convert to PDF" functionally natively to Excel. That is, you won't find that option in Excel by default. You'll have to install Microsoft's free utility to convert your work to PDF.

To install this utility, follow these steps:

1. **Click on the Office icon in the upper-left corner of Excel**

2. **Select Save As, then choose Find Add-Ins for Other File Formats.**

   A Help file opens.

3. **In the Help file, select the Install and Use the Publish as PDF or XPS Add-in from Microsoft option.**

4. **Click on the link to go to the Web site for the Microsoft Save as PDF or XPS Add-in.**

5. **When asked for software validation and installation of the Genuine Advantage plug-in, click Continue.**

   This is Microsoft's piracy protection check.

6. **After the Genuine Advantage plug-in has done its check, click the Download button to download the Save as PDF or XPS Add-in. Keep a note of where the file is downloaded.**

7. **Double-click on the downloaded file, accept the user agreement that displays, and follow the installation steps.**

The reward for all your work is a new menu selection in Excel's Save As menu. After you have this selection, you can convert a worksheet to PDF or XPS by clicking on the Office Icon, selecting Save As, and then choosing PDF or XPS.

Part VI
The Part of Tens

The 5th Wave   By Rich Tennant

"Nifty chart, Frank, but not entirely necessary."

In this part . . .

*B*oth of the chapters found in this section offer approximately ten pearls of wisdom, delivered in bite-sized pieces. In Chapter 14, I share with you ten (or so) best practices for chart building, helping you to design more effective charts. In Chapter 15, I provide a checklist of questions you should ask yourself before sharing your Excel dashboards and reports.

Chapter 14

Ten Chart Design Principles

1'm the first to admit, I've created my share of poorly-designed charts — bar charts with every color known to man, line charts with ten or more lines slapped on top of each other, and pie charts with slices so thin they melded into a blob of black ink. When I look at these early disasters, my look of shame is similar to that of a baby boomer looking at pictures of himself in white bell-bottom jeans.

Excel makes charting so simple, it's often tempting to accept the charts it creates no matter how bad the default colors or settings are. But I'm here to implore you to turn away from the glitzy lure of the default settings. You can easily avoid charting fiascos by following a few basic design principles.

In this chapter, I share with you a few of these principles and help you avoid some of the mistakes I've made in the past. (No thanks needed.)

Avoid Fancy Formatting

One of Microsoft's major selling points of Excel 2007 is the new graphics engine that occupies the new Office suite. Excel 2007 makes it easy to apply effects that make everything look shiny, glittery, and oh-so-pretty. Now don't get me wrong, these new graphics are more-than-okay for charts created for sales and marketing presentations. However, when it comes to dashboards, you definitely want to stay away from them.

Remember that a *dashboard* is a platform to present your case with data. Why dress up your data with superfluous formatting when the data itself is the thing you want to get across? It's like making a speech in a Roman general's uniform. How well will you get your point across when your audience is thinking, "What's the deal with Tiberius?"

Take Figure 14-1, for instance. I created this chart (formatting and all) with just a few clicks. Excel makes it super easy to achieve these types of effects with its new Layout and Style features. The problem is that these effects subdue the very data you're trying to present. Furthermore, if you include this chart on a page with five to ten other charts with the same formatting, you get a blinding mess that's difficult to look at, much less read.

The key to communicating effectively with your charts is to present your data as simply as possible. I promise you, your data is interesting on its own. There's no need to wrap it in eye candy to make it more interesting.

Figure 14-2 shows the same data without the fancy formatting. I think you'll find that not only is the chart easier to read, but you can process the data more effectively from this chart.

Here are some simple tips to keep from overdoing the fancy factor:

- **Don't apply background colors to the Chart or Plot area.** Colors in general should be reserved for key data points in your chart.

- **Don't use 3D charts or 3D effects.** No one's going to give you an Oscar for special effects. Anything 3D doesn't belong on a dashboard.

- **Avoid applying fancy effects, such as gradients, pattern fills, shadows, glow, soft edges, and other formatting.** Again, the word of the day is *focus,* as in "focus on the data and not the shiny happy graphics."

- **Don't try to enhance your charts with clip art or pictures.** Not only do they do nothing to further data presentation, but they often just look tacky.

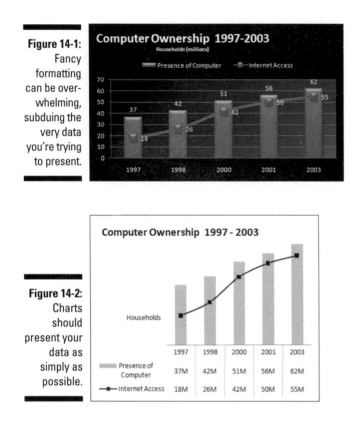

Figure 14-1: Fancy formatting can be overwhelming, subduing the very data you're trying to present.

Figure 14-2: Charts should present your data as simply as possible.

Skip the Unnecessary Chart Junk

Data visualization pioneer Edward Tufte introduced the notion of *data to ink ratio.* Tufte's basic idea is that a large percentage of the ink on your chart or dashboard should be dedicated to data. Very little ink should be used to present what he calls *chart junk:* borders, gridlines, trend lines, labels, backgrounds, and so on.

Figure 14-3 illustrates the impact chart junk can have on your ability to communicate your data. At first glance, the top chart in Figure 14-3 may look over-exaggerated in its ambition to show many chart elements at one time, but believe me, there are charts out there that look like this. Notice how convoluted and cramped the data looks.

The bottom chart presents the same information as the top chart. However, the bottom chart more effectively presents the core message that driver registrations in Texas rose from 10+ million to almost 17+ million (a message that was somehow diluted in the top chart). You can see from this simple example how a chart can be dramatically improved by simply removing the elements that don't directly contribute to the core message of the chart.

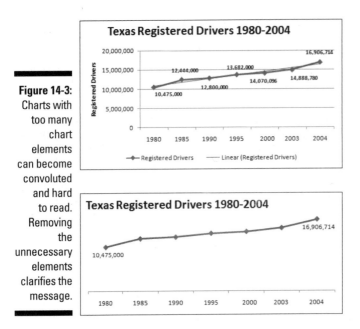

Figure 14-3:
Charts with
too many
chart
elements
can become
convoluted
and hard
to read.
Removing
the
unnecessary
elements
clarifies the
message.

Here are a few ways to avoid chart junk and ensure your charts clearly present your data:

✔ **Remove gridlines:** Gridlines (both vertical and horizontal) are almost always unnecessary. The implied reason for gridlines is that they help to visually gauge the value represented by each data point. The truth is, however, we typically gauge the value of a data point by comparing its position to the other data points in the chart. So gridlines become secondary reference points that simply take up ink.

✔ **Remove borders:** You'll find that eliminating borders and frames gives your charts a cleaner look and helps avoid the dizzying lines you get when placing many charts with borders on a single dashboard. Instead of borders, space your charts to make use of the white space between the charts as implied borders.

✔ **Skip the trend lines:** Seldom does a trend line provide insight that can't be gained with the already plotted data or a simple label. In fact, trend lines often state the obvious and sometimes confuse readers into thinking they're another data series. Why place a trend line on a line chart when the line chart is in and of itself a trend line of sorts? Why place a trend line on a bar chart when it's just as easy to look at the top of the bars? In lieu of trend lines, add a simple label that states what you're trying to say about the overall trend of the data.

✔ **Avoid data label overload:** Nothing says you need to show the data label for every value on your chart. It's okay to plot a data point but not display its value. You'll find that your charts have more impact when you show only numbers that are relevant to your message. For example, Figure 14-3 shows a trend that includes seven years of data. Although all the years are plotted to show the trend, only values of the first and last plotted years are shown. The first and last plotted year's data is enough to fulfill the purpose of this chart, which is to show the trend and ultimate growth of driver registrations.

✔ **Don't show a legend if you don't have to:** When you're plotting one data series, there's no need to display a space-taking chart legend. If you allow your chart title to identify the one data series in your chart, you can simply delete the legend.

✔ **Remove any axis that doesn't provide value:** The purpose of the *x*- and *y*-axes are to help a user visually gauge and position the values represented by each data point. However, if the nature and utility of the chart doesn't require a particular axis, you should remove it. In Figure 14-3, there's no real need for the *y*-axis because the two data points I'm trying to draw attention to are labeled already. Again, the goal here isn't to hack away at your chart. The goal is to only include those chart elements that directly contribute to the core message of your chart.

Format Large Numbers Where Possible

It's never fun to count the zeros in a large number, especially when you're staring at 8-pitch font. When plotting very large numbers on a chart, consider formatting the values so that they're truncated for easy reading.

For instance, in Figure 14-4, I've formatted the values to be displayed as `10M` and `17M` instead of the hard-to-read `10,475,000` and `16,906,714`.

You can easily format large numbers in Excel by using the Format Cells dialog box. Here, you can specify a custom number format by selecting Custom in the Category list and entering the desired number format code in the Type input box. If Figure 14-5, the code `"0,,"M"` ensures the numbers are formatted to millions with an `M` appendage.

Figure 14-4:
Formatting large numbers to millions or thousands makes for a clearer chart.

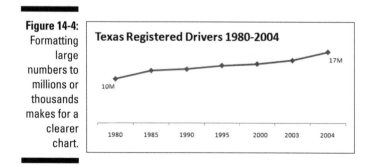

Texas Registered Drivers 1980-2004

17M

10M

1980   1985   1990   1995   2000   2003   2004

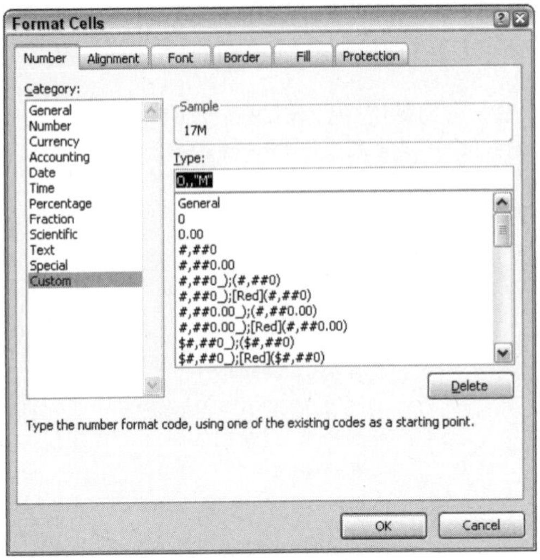

Figure 14-5:
Select
Custom
in the
Category list
and enter a
number
format code
in the Type
input box.

To get to the Format Cells dialog box, highlight the numbers you're formatting, right-click, and then choose Format Cells.

It's generally good practice to format the source data that feeds your chart as opposed to the data labels on your chart. This way, your formatting persists even as you add and remove data labels.

In Chapter 1, you will find a table under the section "A Quick Look at Dashboard Design Principles" which lists some common format codes and how they can affect your numbers.

Use Data Tables instead of Data Labels

There may be situations where it's valuable to show all the data values along with the plotted data points. However, you've already seen how data labels can inundate your users with chart junk.

Instead of using data labels, you can attach a data table to your Excel chart. A *data table* allows you to see the data values for each plotted data point, beneath the chart. Figure 14-6 illustrates a data table, showing the data values for two series. As you can see, a lot of information is shown here without overcrowding the chart itself.

Although it is true that data tables increase the space your charts take up on your dashboard, they respond well to formatting and can be made to meld nicely into your charts. Data tables come in particularly handy if your clients are constantly asking to see the detailed information behind your charts.

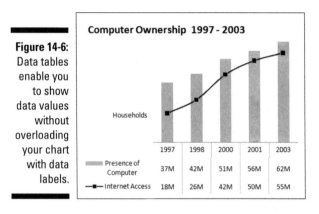

Figure 14-6:
Data tables
enable you
to show
data values
without
overloading
your chart
with data
labels.

Here are the steps you take to add a data table to your chart:

1. **Click your chart and select the Layout tab.**

2. **Click the Data Table icon and select Show Data Table with Legend Keys, as demonstrated in Figure 14-7.**

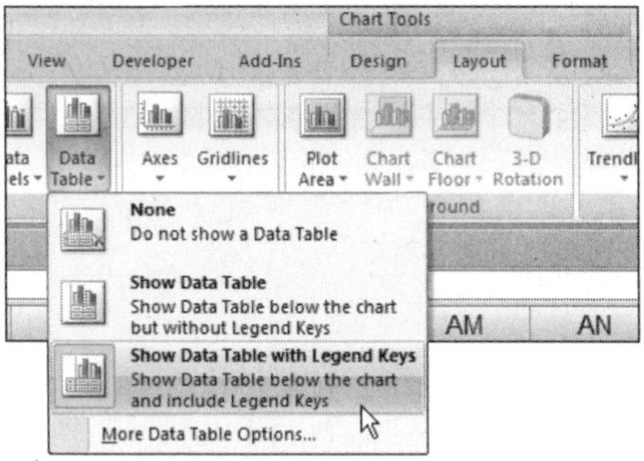

Figure 14-7:
Adding a
data table to
a chart.

3. **Right-click your newly-added data table and choose Format Data Table.**

   The Format Data Table dialog box appears. (See Figure 14-8.)

4. **Apply any additional formatting to your data table.**

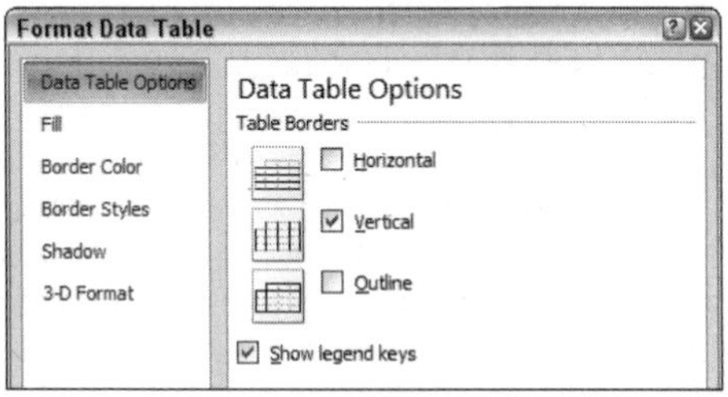

Figure 14-8:
The Format
Data Table
dialog box.

Make Effective Use of Chart Titles

Chart titles don't have to be limited to simple labeling and naming duties. You can use chart titles to add an extra layer of information, presenting analysis derived from the data presented in the chart. Figure 14-9 demonstrates this.

Figure 14-9: Use chart labels to present an extra layer of data without taking up extra space on your dashboard.

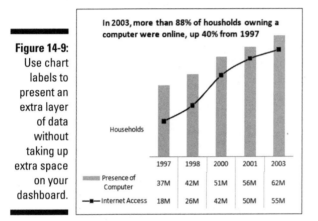

Sort Your Data before Charting

Unless there's an obvious natural order, such as age or time, it's generally good practice to sort your data when charting. By *sorting,* I mean sort the source data that feeds your chart in Ascending or Descending order by data value.

As you can see in Figure 14-10, building a chart using a dataset sorted by values enhances its readability and somehow gives the chart a professional look and feel.

Figure 14-10: Using sorted data in a chart improves readability and clarity.

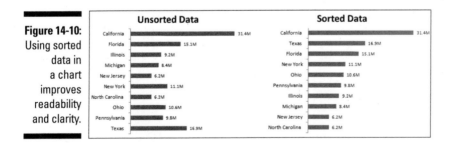

Limit the Use of Pie Charts

Although pie charts have long been considered a viable charting option for business reporting, they often aren't well suited for dashboard reporting. There are several reasons for this.

First, they typically take up more space than their cousins, the line and bar charts. Sure, you can make them small, but pixel for pixel, you get a lot less bang for your data visualization buck with a pie chart.

Second, pie charts can't clearly represent more than two or three data categories. Figure 14-11 demonstrates this fact.

Figure 14-11: Pie charts can't clearly represent more than two or three data categories.

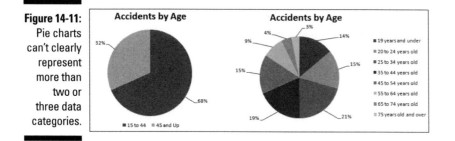

The pie chart on the left does a good job visually representing two data categories. You can easily distinguish the two categories and clearly get a sense of distribution for each category. The pie chart on the right is a different story. As you can see, when you go past two or three categories, a pie chart isn't as effective in relaying the proper sense of percent distribution. The slices are too similar in size and shape to visually compare the categories. Plus, the legend and data categories are disconnected, causing your eyes to jump back and forth from pie to legend (even in color this the legend doesn't help). Sure, you could add category labels, but that would cause the chart to take up more real estate without adding much value.

So what's the alternative? Instead of a pie chart, consider using a bar chart. With a bar chart, you can clearly represent the distribution percentages for many categories without taking the need for extra real estate. In Figure 14-12, you can see the dramatic improvement in clarity you can achieve by using bar charts.

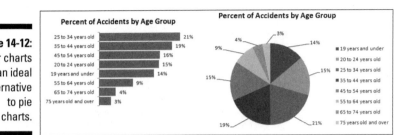

Figure 14-12: Bar charts are an ideal alternative to pie charts.

Don't Be Afraid to Parse Data into Separate Charts

Be aware that a single chart can lose its effectiveness if you try to plot too much data into it. Take Figure 14-13, for example.

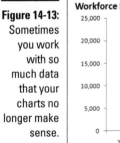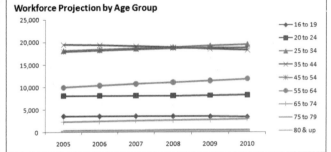

Figure 14-13: Sometimes you work with so much data that your charts no longer make sense.

You have a couple of problems here. First, the data is split into nine age groups, which forces the use of nine lines. When you start plotting more than three lines on a line chart, your chart begins to look jumbled. Second, the age groups themselves have a wide range of data values. This causes the chart's *y*-axis scale to be so spread that each line essentially looks like a straight line.

In situations like this, step back and try to boil down what exactly the chart needs to do. What is the ultimate purpose of the chart? In this case, the ultimate purpose of this chart is to show the growth or decline of the workforce numbers for each age group. Now, you obviously can't show every data point on the same chart, so you have to show each age group in its own chart. That being said, you want to make sure that you can see each age group alongside the other for comparison purposes.

Figure 14-14 shows just one of many solutions for this particular example.

Figure 14-14:
Creating
separate
individual
charts is
often better
than one
convoluted
chart.

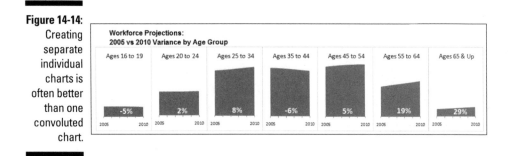

Here, I've created a separate area chart for each age group and then lined them up side by side. Each chart individually shows a general trend from 2005 to 2010. Because they're placed together, you can get an idea of the magnitude of each age group. Also, notice that I grouped the last three age groups into one group called 65 & Up. This groups the three smallest categories into one that's worthy of plotting. Finally, I used data labels to quickly show the growth or decline percentage from 2005 to 2110 for each group.

Again, this isn't the only solution to this problem, but it does do the job of displaying the analysis I chose to present.

It's not always easy to know exactly how to display your data in a chart — especially when the data is multi-layered and complex. Instead of jamming the world into one chart, step back and think about how to show the data separately, but together.

Maintain Appropriate Aspect Ratios

In terms of charts, aspect ratio refers to the ratio of height to width. That is to say, charts should maintain an approximate height to width ratio in order for the integrity of the chart remain intact. Take a look at Figure 14-15 to see what I mean.

The chart at the top of Figure 14-15 is at an appropriate aspect ratio that correctly renders the chart. The bottom two charts display the same data, but the aspect ratios of these charts are skewed. The middle chart is too tall and the bottom chart is too wide. This essentially distorts the visual representation, exaggerating the trend in the chart that's too tall, and flattening the trend in the chart that's too wide.

I've seen lots of people contort their charts just to fit them into the empty space on their dashboards. If you want to avoid distorting your charts, you must keep them at an appropriate aspect ratio. What is that ratio?

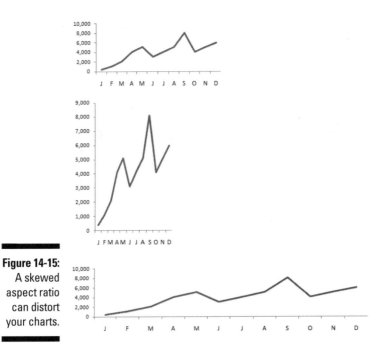

Figure 14-15: A skewed aspect ratio can distort your charts.

Generally speaking, the most appropriate aspect ratio for a chart is one where the width of the chart is about twice as long as the height is tall. For example, 1" tall by 2" wide is an appropriate ratio. 1.5" tall by 3" wide is also appropriate. The actual height and width isn't important. You can make your charts as small or as big as they need to be. What is important is the ratio of height to width.

Don't Be Afraid to Use Something Other Than a Chart

As we've already discussed in Chapter 15, some analyses just don't require a chart. Ask yourself if a simple table will present the data just fine. If the data you are reporting can be more effectively shared in a table, then that's how it should be presented. Remember, the goal of a dashboard is not to present everything in a chart. The goal of a dashboard is to present key data in the most effective way possible.

Chapter 15

Ten Questions to Ask Before Distributing Your Dashboard

*Y*ou started this book with two chapters that discuss a few design and data modeling principles that, together, make up what could be considered dashboarding's best practices. Before you send out your finished product, it's valuable to check your reporting mechanism against some of the principles covered in this book. Use the ten questions in this chapter as a kind of checklist to ensure your dashboard follows the best practices covered in this book.

Does My Dashboard Present the Right Information?

Look at the information you're presenting and determine if it meets the purpose of the dashboard you identified during the requirements-gathering stage. Don't be timid about clarifying the purpose of the dashboard with the core users. Avoid building the dashboard in a vacuum. Allow a few test users to see iterations as you develop. This way, clear communication stays open, and you won't go too far in the wrong direction.

Does Everything on My Dashboard Have a Purpose?

Take an honest look at how much information on your dashboard doesn't support its main purpose. In order to keep your dashboard as valuable as possible, you don't want to dilute it with nice-to-know data that's interesting, but not actionable. Remember, if the data doesn't support the core purpose of the dashboard, leave it out. Nothing says you have to fill every bit of white space on the page.

Does My Dashboard Prominently Display the Key Message?

Every dashboard has one or more key messages. You want to ensure that these messages are prominently displayed. To test if the key messages in a dashboard are prominent, stand back and squint your eyes while you look at the dashboard. Look away and look at the dashboard several times. What jumps out at you first? If it's not the key components you want displayed, you'll have to change something. Here are a few actions you can take to ensure your key components have prominence:

- ✔ **Place the key components of your dashboard in the upper-left or middle-left portion of the page.** Studies have shown that these areas are attracting the most attention for longer periods of time.

- ✔ **De-emphasize borders, backgrounds, and other elements that define dashboard areas.** Try to use the natural white space between your components to partition your dashboard. If borders are necessary, format them to a hue lighter than the one you've used for your data.

- ✔ **Format labels and other text to hues lighter than the ones you've used for your data.** Lightly colored labels give your users the information they need without distracting them from the information displayed.

Can I Maintain This Dashboard?

There is a big difference between refreshing a dashboard and rebuilding a dashboard. Before you excitedly send out the sweet-looking dashboard you just built, take a moment to think about the maintenance of such a dashboard. You want to think about the frequency of updates, how often data needs to be refreshed, and what processes you need to go through each time you refresh the data. If it's a one-time reporting event, set that expectation with your users. If you know it'll become a recurring report, you want to really negotiate development time, refresh intervals, and phasing before agreeing to any time table.

Does My Dashboard Clearly Display Its Scope and Shelf Life?

A dashboard should clearly specify its scope and shelf life. That is to say, anyone should be able to look at your dashboard and know the relevant time period and the scope of the information on the dashboard. This comes down to a few simple things you can do to effectively label your dashboards and reports, such as

- ✔ **Always include a timestamp on your reporting mechanisms.** This minimizes confusion when distributing the same dashboard or report on regular intervals.

- ✔ **Always include some text indicating when the data for the measures was retrieved.** In many cases, timing of the data is a critical piece of information when analyzing a measure.

- ✔ **Use descriptive titles for each component in your dashboard.** Be sure to avoid cryptic titles with lots of acronyms and symbols.

Is My Dashboard Well Documented?

It's important to document your dashboard and the data model behind it. Anyone who has ever inherited an Excel spreadsheet knows how difficult it can be to translate the various analytical gyrations that go into a report. If you're lucky, the data model will be small enough to piece together in a week or so. If you're not so lucky, you'll have to ditch the entire model and start from scratch.

By the way, the Excel model doesn't even have to be someone else's to be difficult to read. I've actually gone back to a model that I built, and after six or so months, I'd forgotten what I had done. Without documentation, it took me a few days to remember and decipher my own work.

The documentation doesn't even have to be highfalutin' fancy stuff. A few simple things can help in documenting your dashboard, such as

- ✔ **Add a *model map* tab to your data model.** The model map tab is a separate sheet you can use to summarize the key ranges in the data model, and how each range interacts with the reporting components in the final presentation layer.

- ✔ **Use comments and labels liberally.** It's amazing how a few explanatory comments and labels can help clarify your model even after you've been away from your data model for a long period of time.

- ✔ **Consider using colors to identify the ranges in your data model.** Using colors in your data model enables you to quickly look at a range of cells and get a basic indication of what that range does. Each color can represent a range type. For example, yellow could represent staging tables, grey could represent formulas, and purple could represent reference tables.

Is My Dashboard Overwhelmed with Formatting and Graphics?

By now you've probably gotten the point that, when it comes to formatting dashboards and reports, less is more. Eye candy doesn't make your data more interesting. If you're not convinced, try creating a version of your dashboard without the fancy formatting:

- ✔ **Remove distracting colors and background fills.** If you must have colors in charts, use colors that are commonly found in nature: soft grays, browns, blues, and greens.

- ✔ **De-emphasize borders by formatting them to hues lighter than the ones you've used for your data.** Light grays are typically ideal for borders. The idea is to indicate sections without distracting from the information displayed.

- ✔ **Remove all fancy graphical effects, such as gradients, pattern fills, shadows, glow, soft edges, and other formatting.**

- ✔ **Remove the clip art and other pictures.**

I think that when you compare the two versions, you'll find that the toned-down version does a better job of highlighting the actual data.

Does My Dashboard Overuse Charts When Tables Will Do?

Just because you're building a dashboard, doesn't mean everything on it has to be a chart. In some analyses, a simple table will present the data just fine. You typically use a chart when there's some benefit to visually seeing trends, relationships, or comparisons. Ask yourself if there's a benefit to seeing your data in chart form. If the data is relayed better in a table, that's how it should be presented.

Figure 15-1 illustrates a simple example. The chart on the left and the table on the right show the exact same data. The table does a fine job at presenting the key message of the analysis — revenue is at 95 percent of plan. Why use the chart that requires more real estate, not to mention more work and maintenance?

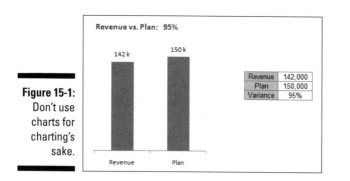

Figure 15-1: Don't use charts for charting's sake.

Is My Dashboard User-Friendly?

Before you distribute your reporting mechanism, you want to ensure that it's user-friendly. It's not difficult to guess what user-friendly means. Usually a user-friendly mechanism has the following characteristics:

- ✓ **Intuitive:** Your reporting mechanism should be intuitive to someone who has never seen it before. Test your dashboard on someone and ask him if it makes sense. If you have to start explaining what the dashboard says, something is wrong. Does the dashboard need more labels, fewer complicated charts, a better layout, more data? It's a good idea to get feedback from several users.

✔ **Easy to navigate:** If your dashboard is dynamic, allowing for interactivity with macros or pivot tables, you should make sure the navigation works well. Does the user have to click several places to get to her data? Is the number of drill-downs appropriate? Does it take too long to switch from one view to another? Again, you want to test your dashboard on several users. Be sure to test any interactive dashboard on several computers other than yours.

✔ **Prints properly:** Nothing is more annoying than printing a report only to find that the person who created the report didn't take the time to ensure it prints correctly. Be sure you set the print options on your Excel files so that your dashboards print properly.

Is My Dashboard Accurate?

Nothing kills a dashboard or report faster than the perception that its data is inaccurate. It's not within my capabilities to tell you how to determine if your data is accurate. I can, however, highlight three factors that establish the perception that a dashboard is accurate:

✔ **Consistency with authoritative sources:** It's obvious that if your data doesn't match other reporting sources, you have a data credibility issue, especially if those other sources are deemed to be the authoritative sources. Be sure you're aware of the data sources that are considered to be gospel in your organization. If your dashboard contains data associated with an authoritative source, compare your data with that source to ensure consistency.

✔ **Internal consistency:** It's never fun to explain why one part of your dashboard doesn't jive with other parts of the same dashboard. You should ensure some level of internal consistency within your dashboard. Be sure comparable components in different areas of your dashboard are consistent with each other. If there's a reason for inconsistency, be sure to clearly notate those reasons. It's amazing how well a simple notation can clear up questions about the data.

✔ **Personal experience:** Have you ever seen someone look at a report and say, "That doesn't look right"? He's using what some people call *gut feel* to evaluate the soundness of the data. None of us look at numbers in a vacuum. When you look at any analysis, you bring with you years of personal knowledge, interaction, and experience. You subconsciously use these experiences in your evaluation of information. When determining the accuracy of your dashboard, take into consideration organizational *anecdotal knowledge*. If possible, show your dashboard to a few subject-matter experts in your company.

Index

BUSINESS, CAREERS & PERSONAL FINANCE

0-7645-9847-3   0-7645-2431-3

Also available:
- Business Plans Kit For Dummies
  0-7645-9794-9
- Economics For Dummies
  0-7645-5726-2
- Grant Writing For Dummies
  0-7645-8416-2
- Home Buying For Dummies
  0-7645-5331-3
- Managing For Dummies
  0-7645-1771-6
- Marketing For Dummies
  0-7645-5600-2

- Personal Finance For Dummies
  0-7645-2590-5*
- Resumes For Dummies
  0-7645-5471-9
- Selling For Dummies
  0-7645-5363-1
- Six Sigma For Dummies
  0-7645-6798-5
- Small Business Kit For Dummies
  0-7645-5984-2
- Starting an eBay Business For Dummies
  0-7645-6924-4
- Your Dream Career For Dummies
  0-7645-9795-7

HOME & BUSINESS COMPUTER BASICS

0-470-05432-8   0-471-75421-8

Also available:
- Cleaning Windows Vista For Dummies
  0-471-78293-9
- Excel 2007 For Dummies
  0-470-03737-7
- Mac OS X Tiger For Dummies
  0-7645-7675-5
- MacBook For Dummies
  0-470-04859-X
- Macs For Dummies
  0-470-04849-2
- Office 2007 For Dummies
  0-470-00923-3

- Outlook 2007 For Dummies
  0-470-03830-6
- PCs For Dummies
  0-7645-8958-X
- Salesforce.com For Dummies
  0-470-04893-X
- Upgrading & Fixing Laptops For Dummies
  0-7645-8959-8
- Word 2007 For Dummies
  0-470-03658-3
- Quicken 2007 For Dummies
  0-470-04600-7

FOOD, HOME, GARDEN, HOBBIES, MUSIC & PETS

0-7645-8404-9   0-7645-9904-6

Also available:
- Candy Making For Dummies
  0-7645-9734-5
- Card Games For Dummies
  0-7645-9910-0
- Crocheting For Dummies
  0-7645-4151-X
- Dog Training For Dummies
  0-7645-8418-9
- Healthy Carb Cookbook For Dummies
  0-7645-8476-6
- Home Maintenance For Dummies
  0-7645-5215-5

- Horses For Dummies
  0-7645-9797-3
- Jewelry Making & Beading For Dummies
  0-7645-2571-9
- Orchids For Dummies
  0-7645-6759-4
- Puppies For Dummies
  0-7645-5255-4
- Rock Guitar For Dummies
  0-7645-5356-9
- Sewing For Dummies
  0-7645-6847-7
- Singing For Dummies
  0-7645-2475-5

INTERNET & DIGITAL MEDIA

0-470-04529-9   0-470-04894-8

Also available:
- Blogging For Dummies
  0-471-77084-1
- Digital Photography For Dummies
  0-7645-9802-3
- Digital Photography All-in-One Desk Reference For Dummies
  0-470-03743-1
- Digital SLR Cameras and Photography For Dummies
  0-7645-9803-1
- eBay Business All-in-One Desk Reference For Dummies
  0-7645-8438-3
- HDTV For Dummies
  0-470-09673-X

- Home Entertainment PCs For Dummies
  0-470-05523-5
- MySpace For Dummies
  0-470-09529-6
- Search Engine Optimization For Dummies
  0-471-97998-8
- Skype For Dummies
  0-470-04891-3
- The Internet For Dummies
  0-7645-8996-2
- Wiring Your Digital Home For Dummies
  0-471-91830-X

* Separate Canadian edition also available
† Separate U.K. edition also available

SPORTS, FITNESS, PARENTING, RELIGION & SPIRITUALITY

0-471-76871-5

0-7645-7841-3

Also available:
- Catholicism For Dummies
  0-7645-5391-7
- Exercise Balls For Dummies
  0-7645-5623-1
- Fitness For Dummies
  0-7645-7851-0
- Football For Dummies
  0-7645-3936-1
- Judaism For Dummies
  0-7645-5299-6
- Potty Training For Dummies
  0-7645-5417-4
- Buddhism For Dummies
  0-7645-5359-3
- Pregnancy For Dummies
  0-7645-4483-7 †
- Ten Minute Tone-Ups For Dummies
  0-7645-7207-5
- NASCAR For Dummies
  0-7645-7681-X
- Religion For Dummies
  0-7645-5264-3
- Soccer For Dummies
  0-7645-5229-5
- Women in the Bible For Dummies
  0-7645-8475-8

TRAVEL

0-7645-7749-2

0-7645-6945-7

Also available:
- Alaska For Dummies
  0-7645-7746-8
- Cruise Vacations For Dummies
  0-7645-6941-4
- England For Dummies
  0-7645-4276-1
- Europe For Dummies
  0-7645-7529-5
- Germany For Dummies
  0-7645-7823-5
- Hawaii For Dummies
  0-7645-7402-7
- Italy For Dummies
  0-7645-7386-1
- Las Vegas For Dummies
  0-7645-7382-9
- London For Dummies
  0-7645-4277-X
- Paris For Dummies
  0-7645-7630-5
- RV Vacations For Dummies
  0-7645-4442-X
- Walt Disney World & Orlando
  For Dummies
  0-7645-9660-8

GRAPHICS, DESIGN & WEB DEVELOPMENT

0-7645-8815-X

0-7645-9571-7

Also available:
- 3D Game Animation For Dummies
  0-7645-8789-7
- AutoCAD 2006 For Dummies
  0-7645-8925-3
- Building a Web Site For Dummies
  0-7645-7144-3
- Creating Web Pages For Dummies
  0-470-08030-2
- Creating Web Pages All-in-One Desk
  Reference For Dummies
  0-7645-4345-8
- Dreamweaver 8 For Dummies
  0-7645-9649-7
- InDesign CS2 For Dummies
  0-7645-9572-5
- Macromedia Flash 8 For Dummies
  0-7645-9691-8
- Photoshop CS2 and Digital
  Photography For Dummies
  0-7645-9580-6
- Photoshop Elements 4 For Dummies
  0-471-77483-9
- Syndicating Web Sites with RSS Feeds
  For Dummies
  0-7645-8848-6
- Yahoo! SiteBuilder For Dummies
  0-7645-9800-7

NETWORKING, SECURITY, PROGRAMMING & DATABASES

0-7645-7728-X

0-471-74940-0

Also available:
- Access 2007 For Dummies
  0-470-04612-0
- ASP.NET 2 For Dummies
  0-7645-7907-X
- C# 2005 For Dummies
  0-7645-9704-3
- Hacking For Dummies
  0-470-05235-X
- Hacking Wireless Networks
  For Dummies
  0-7645-9730-2
- Java For Dummies
  0-470-08716-1
- Microsoft SQL Server 2005 For Dummies
  0-7645-7755-7
- Networking All-in-One Desk Reference
  For Dummies
  0-7645-9939-9
- Preventing Identity Theft For Dummies
  0-7645-7336-5
- Telecom For Dummies
  0-471-77085-X
- Visual Studio 2005 All-in-One Desk
  Reference For Dummies
  0-7645-9775-2
- XML For Dummies
  0-7645-8845-1

HEALTH & SELF-HELP

0-7645-8450-2

0-7645-4149-8

Also available:
- Bipolar Disorder For Dummies
  0-7645-8451-0
- Chemotherapy and Radiation
  For Dummies
  0-7645-7832-4
- Controlling Cholesterol For Dummies
  0-7645-5440-9
- Diabetes For Dummies
  0-7645-6820-5* †
- Divorce For Dummies
  0-7645-8417-0 †

- Fibromyalgia For Dummies
  0-7645-5441-7
- Low-Calorie Dieting For Dummies
  0-7645-9905-4
- Meditation For Dummies
  0-471-77774-9
- Osteoporosis For Dummies
  0-7645-7621-6
- Overcoming Anxiety For Dummies
  0-7645-5447-6
- Reiki For Dummies
  0-7645-9907-0
- Stress Management For Dummies
  0-7645-5144-2

EDUCATION, HISTORY, REFERENCE & TEST PREPARATION

0-7645-8381-6

0-7645-9554-7

Also available:
- The ACT For Dummies
  0-7645-9652-7
- Algebra For Dummies
  0-7645-5325-9
- Algebra Workbook For Dummies
  0-7645-8467-7
- Astronomy For Dummies
  0-7645-8465-0
- Calculus For Dummies
  0-7645-2498-4
- Chemistry For Dummies
  0-7645-5430-1
- Forensics For Dummies
  0-7645-5580-4

- Freemasons For Dummies
  0-7645-9796-5
- French For Dummies
  0-7645-5193-0
- Geometry For Dummies
  0-7645-5324-0
- Organic Chemistry I For Dummies
  0-7645-6902-3
- The SAT I For Dummies
  0-7645-7193-1
- Spanish For Dummies
  0-7645-5194-9
- Statistics For Dummies
  0-7645-5423-9

Get smart @ dummies.com®

- **Find a full list of Dummies titles**
- **Look into loads of FREE on-site articles**
- **Sign up for FREE eTips e-mailed to you weekly**
- **See what other products carry the Dummies name**
- **Shop directly from the Dummies bookstore**
- **Enter to win new prizes every month!**

* Separate Canadian edition also available
† Separate U.K. edition also available

Available wherever books are sold. For more information or to order direct: U.S. customers visit www.dummies.com or call 1-877-762-2974.
U.K. customers visit www.wileyeurope.com or call 0800 243407. Canadian customers visit www.wiley.ca or call 1-800-567-4797.